Helen Rooney
2A Kelly Ridge
Carmel, N.Y. 10512

the Wilton Way of Cake Decorating

VOLUME ONE

EDITED BY EUGENE T. AND MARILYNN C. SULLIVAN

WILTON ENTERPRISES, INC., WOODRIDGE, ILLINOIS

Printed and bound in Italy by Campi Editore, Foligno.

SECOND PRINTING, 25,000

Library of Congress Catalog Card Number: 74-13330

International Standard Book Number: 0-912696-04-4

Library of Congress Cataloging in Publication Data
Sullivan, Marilynn C.

The Wilton Way of Cake Decorating

1. Cake decorating. I. Sullivan, Eugene T.,
joint author. II. Wilton Enterprises. III. Title.
TX771.S87   641.8/653   74-13330
ISBN 0-912696-04-4

ACKNOWLEDGMENTS: All decorating done by members
of the Wilton staff under the supervision of Norman Wilton.
Picture of roses on page 115 courtesy of Jackson & Perkins.
Pictures of living flowers on pages 108, 118, 119 and 123
courtesy of George J. Ball, Inc. On pages 296, 298, 301 and
304-315, freehand figure piping created by John N. McNamara,
author, teacher, decorator and artist from Southern California.

CONTENTS

Portfolios of Cake Portraits

NORMAN WILTON, since the age of fourteen, has been dedicated to the art of cake decorating and is justifiably proud of the achievements this single-minded dedication has made possible. Taught the fundamentals of this culinary art by his father, McKinley Wilton, he capitalized on the knowledge given him and—except for the years he spent as a pilot in the United States Navy in World War II—has given his entire time and energy to it. As director of The Wilton School of Cake Decorating (first conducted in a single room of the Wilton home), he developed further expertise both as a teacher and as an innovator. To broaden the horizons of decorating, Mr. Wilton then established Wilton Enterprises, Inc. and has traveled all over the world in search of new and stimulating products for decorators. As a result, Wilton has grown to be a multimillion dollar corporation, and the world's major supplier of cake decorating ideas and products. Norman Wilton is not unduly impressed with the mere growth of the company. He strongly believes, however, that opportunity for success in any area continues to exist for anyone who believes in an idea and is willing to pursue it.

THE WILTON WAY
OF CAKE DECORATING

FROM EARLY ROMAN TIMES, cake has been importantly associated with ceremonials and celebrations. But only during the relatively short span of the past three hundred years has the *decorated* cake existed as the culinary art form we enjoy today.

Both the Italians and the French experimented with richly embellished cakes before 1650, and by the end of the seventeenth century this art began to flourish. The work of these pastry chefs stimulated interest in the art of cake decorating in many countries of Western Europe, with the result that elegance in a number of expressive techniques quickly became the hallmark of both wedding and other celebration cakes.

Traditions started to develop and—as decorators in various countries expressed themselves in terms of their own cultures—a number of distinct decorating "techniques" or "methods" sprang up.

WHEN MY FATHER, MC KINLEY WILTON, founded The Wilton School of Cake Decorating nearly a half century ago, he was well-grounded in the more generally used techniques throughout the world. And, while he did not take equal pleasure and satisfaction in every "method" he respected all of them. Each probably had some influence on him.

In starting the school, my father's well-defined objective was to teach the fundamentals of decorating so thoroughly that the tools might be used for creative expression, rather than for mere copying the work of the past. Traditions, he felt, were to be built upon and added to. And, while he agreed that "rules are made to be broken," he demanded that any student of his should be thoroughly familiar with the "rules" before having the audacity to break them. Accordingly, when my sisters—Martha Wilton Ellison and Mary Jane Wilton Turner—and my brother Wesley and I joined the teaching staff of the school, we were accepted on the condition that all of us operate on these standards. Time has shown them to be correct. Once the fundamentals of decorating have been mastered, the Wilton Way can be followed with assurance that the end result will be creative and truly artistic.

WHAT IS THE WILTON WAY?

Probably the most important identifying mark of the Wilton method of decorating is its insistence on perfection of execution. The Wilton Way demands that icings be given a smooth finish; that each shell and star in a border be a perfect match for the next, that stringwork falls in graceful, even arcs; that petals of a flower curve in a lifelike, natural position. Only repeated practice can perfect the skill that makes decorating look effortless.

Equally important is the emphasis the Wilton Way puts on color—not only on the correct ways of tinting icing, but on the unlimited possibilities that color can provide. It shows you how even the simplest cake becomes a work of art when color is used freely, excitingly, and harmoniously.

Further, the Wilton Way of decorating is an evolving, ever-changing art form that permits growth and larger scope. Because it is never static, it is more challenging—and more rewarding. While the fundamentals remain constant, week by week new techniques are discovered. These may result in a quicker, gayer way to put a "picture" on a cake . . . or the creation of new flowers, never before turned out in icing . . . or a combination of stringwork and stars to give a cake a lavish frame.

Finally, the Wilton Way of decorating is economical of the decorator's time and energy. Any shortcut that does not detract from the beauty or perfection of the finished cake is permissible. Well-designed accessories such as columns, cherubs, and other novelties may be used tastefully. This does not cut down on the creativity of the decorator. On the contrary we believe the elimination of drudgery in decorating makes the art even more satisfying and fun!

IN SHORT, THE WILTON WAY IS DYNAMIC. It embraces cake decorating techniques from past and present, from all countries of the world. It encourages the freedom of self expression—the freedom that makes decorating so satisfying and creative for the decorator—but it strongly stresses the need for perfection of execution.

These qualities of perfection, freedom and efficiency have made the Wilton Way the *American way* of decorating.

VOLUME ONE, THE WILTON WAY OF CAKE DECORATING gives the fundamental techniques that allow every decorator the freedom of creative self expression.

—NORMAN WILTON

CHAPTER ONE

The Cake Decorator's Tools

This chapter provides a listing and description of the cake decorating equipment and accessories most commonly used by American decorators, both amateur and professional. Its purpose is to provide you with a handy reference that you may return to from time to time as you go through this book, and afterward. Included is a comprehensive guide on decorating tubes, together with descriptions and illustrations of a few things each one can do.

If you are a beginning decorator, you will be happy to discover what simple and inexpensive equipment is required for a start. Many of the things you need already may be in your kitchen. For example, almost everyone owns mixing bowls, a spatula and some cake pans. All you may need to add are a washable decorating cone or parchment paper to make your own, food colors and decorating tubes, and you'll be on your way to decorating fun.

As you progress to advanced or even professional decorating, you will naturally need additional tools. But even at its most involved, this pleasant craft demands far less outlay than any other of comparable enjoyment.

The most important tools you'll need as a cake decorator are your own two hands—and the skill and coordination they will certainly acquire if you practice the rules set forth in this book.

Basic Equipment for Decorators

A PAIR OF MIXING BOWLS, preferably in stainless steel, as it is durable and easy to keep clean and free of grease—essential for certain icings. If you choose bowls of plastic, be sure to clean them very thoroughly to keep grease-free. Use aluminum bowls for mixing but not storing, as they may discolor icings. Choose a 4-quart size to handle most mixing chores and a 1½-quart size with high sides for whipped cream icings.

METAL SPOONS for mixing and measuring. Wood absorbs grease and plastic is hard to keep grease-free.

A PAIR OF FLEXIBLE SPATULAS. Have one about 11 or 12 inches long to give you greater control when you are icing cake layers. And one about 8 or 10 inches long to use for filling decorating bags and marking designs into icing on top and sides of cake.

10-INCH ROUND CAKE CIRCLES of strong corrugated cardboard to keep cake layers level and make them easy to transfer from decorating table to serving plate. Also handy for trying out cake top designs.

PARCHMENT PAPER in rolls or pre-cut triangles for rolling your own decorating bags. Scissors, also.

A LARGE PRE-MADE decorating bag of plastic or acrylic-coated polyester, washable and reusable.

A COUPLER to go with pre-made bag that allows you to change tubes without refilling bag.

9 OR MORE DECORATING TUBES. Plain round tubes in two or three sizes for writing, stringwork and figure piping. Open and closed star tubes for piping stars, shells, garlands, scrolls, rosettes, swags. A petal tube for doing roses and other true-to-life flowers. A drop flower tube for turning out simple flowers and borders. Large star and petal tubes for making big dramatic flowers and borders. A good starting assortment would be tubes number 3, 4, 10, 16, 30, 103, 104, 67, 190, 199 and 124.

A FLOWER NAIL to provide a miniature, hand-held turntable upon which you'll pipe many a real-looking flower. Number 7 is a versatile size.

FOOD COLORS in at least the three basic hues—red, yellow and blue. You can mix these for many other colors such as green, purple and orange.

CAKE PANS. A set of 10-inch round pans, a square pan, a 9″x13″ sheet cake pan and a cookie sheet.

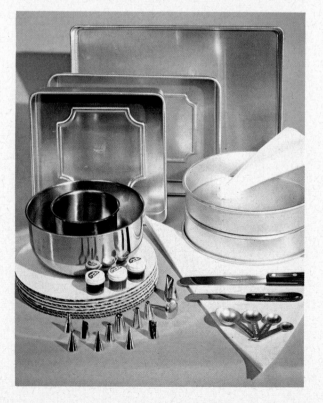

Tools for More Advanced Decorating

CAKE DUMMIES to use for display or practice cakes.

SEPARATOR SETS for tier cakes. A classic set for a large tier cake—and a shaped set for a miniature tier cake.

CARDBOARD CAKE CIRCLES in several sizes to use as bases for a variety of cakes.

PLASTIC CONTAINERS in one-pint size. Handy for holding different colors of icing. Tint icings ahead, cover tightly and store until you are ready to do your cake. Decorating goes more quickly!

ALUMINUM FOIL in gold, silver and several bright colors to cover cake circles and boards for decorative cake bases.

MORE CAKE PANS—round, square, heart-shaped—in graduated sizes for tier cakes. Shaped pans, too, for novelty cakes and cakes for children.

A HEAVY-DUTY ELECTRIC MIXER with 4-quart or larger bowl to make mixing large amounts of batter or icing quick and effortless.

A CANDY THERMOMETER for making perfect boiled icings, fondant and candy.

A DECORATING TURNTABLE in heavyweight metal that can support even large tier cakes without tipping. Choose one at least 12 inches in diameter and 4 inches high to hold many sizes of cakes at the proper height for decorating. It should turn easily to let you ice cakes smoothly, decorate quickly.

EXTRA FOOD COLORS, pre-mixed to exact tints and shades. Save time and guess-work.

ARTISTS' PAINTBRUSHES. To smooth rough spots, "paint" over seams or add fine details.

EXTRA MIXING BOWLS. Small sizes for tinting icings; large sizes to hold fillings and icings ready.

EXTRA DECORATING TUBES for unusual or advanced designs, for learning and experimenting.

EXTRA DROP FLOWER TUBES to let you pipe out an infinite variety of instant blooms.

LILY NAILS with a deep cup for flowers with a trumpet shape or long petals, in one or two-piece styles.

A LARGE KNIFE with serrated edge for doing cut-up cakes, splitting layers or levelling cake tops.

DECORATING COMBS for making quick, pretty designs in icing on top or sides of cake.

9

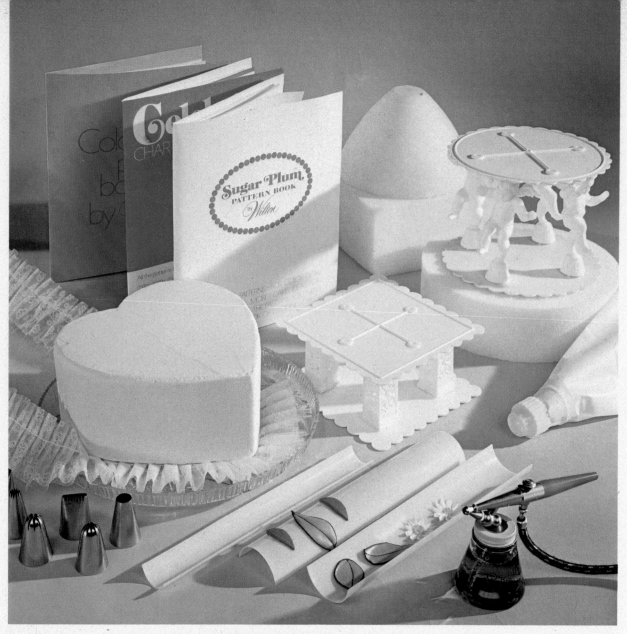

Special Extras for Dedicated Decorators

These are tools you *could* live without, but would rather not. Some you could improvise on your own, if you had to, but happily, they are now available ready-made. They're especially nice for the practiced decorator or the professional with a large quantity of cakes to turn out in a hurry. And they make special decorating effects and unusual designs easier to achieve.

PATTERNS needed to make beautiful and unusual cake designs for festive occasions the year around—many of which are shown in this book.

FANCY SEPARATOR SETS to add special flair to your tier cakes. Decorative pillars that feature angels, filigree, cupids and swans make the difference.

PRE-MADE NET RUFFLES to wind around your cake for a lovely finishing touch. Choose gold, silver and several pastels to harmonize with cakes.

SUPER-SIZE DECORATING bag to hold enough icing for a large tier cake. A valuable time-saver if you've several wedding cakes to do at once!

SUPER-SIZE COUPLER to let you change extra large tubes without refilling decorating bag. Perfect when you're decorating a tall tier cake in a single color.

CURVED PLASTIC FORMS for drying flowers and leaves into natural shapes, arching lace, filigree and other icing designs into graceful curves.

COLOR SPRAY AIRBRUSH SET for air-brushing colors on cakes, icing flowers and other decorations. Helps speed up your "get-ready" work before decorating.

LARGE SIZE DECORATING TUBES for big dramatic flowers and borders, for garnishing foods and shaping pastries and party cookies. They're the ones you use for piping cream puff dough into eclairs and cream puffs. Use them also for edging meat and vegetable platters with ripples of mashed potatoes.

10

Ways to Show Off Your Pretty Cakes

Your deftly-decorated cakes deserve a worthy setting, so it's a good idea to start your own collection of attractive cake trays and stands. For important formal cakes, select the sparkle of silver, copper or brass, the brilliance of cut glass or crystal, or the soft glow of porcelain. For gaily decorated cakes, choose cheerful china or plastic in bright colors or white, gay painted metal or natural-grain wood. Of course, for cakes sold or given as gifts, foil-covered cake boards are best.

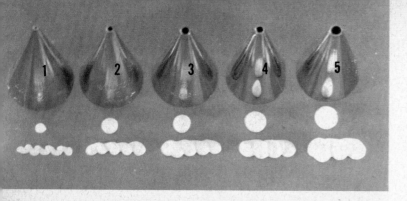

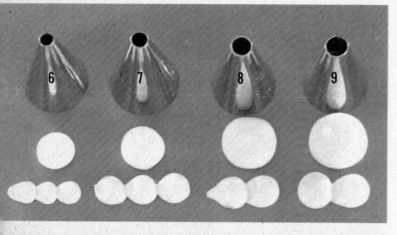

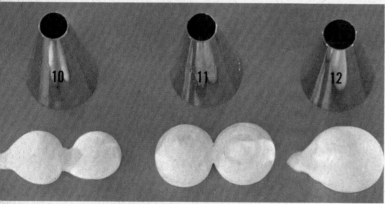

Decorating Tubes and Their Uses

Decorating tubes are little metal cones cut at the tips to produce various shapes and designs when icing is pressed through them. On the pages that follow is an assortment of the tubes used most often by American decorators, together with examples of what each can do. All are shown actual size, arranged by number and grouped according to ability—to provide you with an instant reference.

Beginning decorators will find all they need in the basic tube assortment on page 8. Within this group are tubes which do all the basic shapes and designs, plus countless flowers, leaves and borders. Once familiar with these, you will find it easier to choose other tubes to try later on.

It is best to choose tubes made of strong metal as they will resist dents and hold a true and accurate design. Metal tubes can be used with decorating bags of any material and with proper care, will last a long while. For the very largest tubes you will require an extra large size bag (18 inch) and an extra large coupler.

To keep tubes in perfect working condition, make sure they are spotlessly clean. Wash after every use in hot, soapy water, rinse in hot, clear water. If bits of icing clog up openings, don't poke in pins to clean them out. This could push the delicate designs out of shape. Rather, soak tubes in hot water until icing melts away, then air-dry and store in a safe place. If you must use them again immediately, dry thoroughly first with a towel.

THE AMAZING ROUND TUBES

TUBES 1 TO 12, pictured at left. These are the tubes with the plain, round holes. As the numbers go higher, the openings just become larger. For tubes of such simple design, it is remarkable how much they can do. In addition to the dots and lines shown, they pipe stringwork, stems, scrolls, vines and stamens for flowers. They also write script and do latticework and filigree. The slightly larger sizes pipe fruits, pastries and garnishes. Round tubes are the essential ones for figure-piping—going from small birds made with tubes 3 and 4 to fruits with tubes 4 through 7 and clowns, cookies and eclairs with tubes 8 through 12.

A GRACEFUL SWAN can be piped very quickly with a round tube. Use tube 6 or 7, depending upon the size of swan. See Chapter Twenty Two for method.

OPEN STAR TUBES FOR BEAUTIFUL BORDERS

TUBES 13 TO 18. These are the tubes with the tips shaped like a star with the points left open. Icing presses through in a pretty ribbed design, which lends itself to an almost endless number of beautiful shapes and borders—stars, shells, rosettes, puffs, garlands and ropes. So many lovely effects!

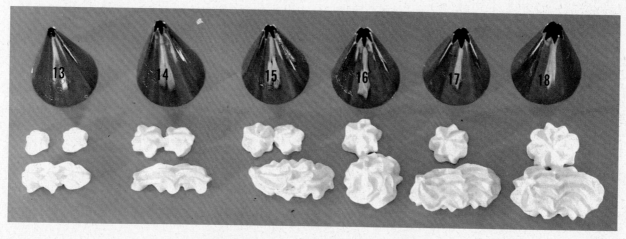

THE LARGER OPEN STAR TUBES

TUBES 19 TO 22, AND TUBE 32. For larger versions of the shapes and borders above. The big, dramatic designs they do are really breathtaking in white on a gold or mocha cake. They can also do large stylized flowers to give a cake a lovely old-world air. And large base borders on wedding cakes.

AT RIGHT: Detail of an elegant wedding cake with swirls and scrolls as lavish as baroque art designs— yet done from top to bottom with open star tubes. Use tubes 22 and 32 for base borders, tube 14 for zigzag frames, tube 19 for top shell borders, tube 14 again for stars accenting them, tube 16 for zigzag side garlands, tube 14 for "e's" framing them and for circles and fleur-de-lis at garland points.

13

CLOSED STAR TUBES FOR A LAVISH LOOK

TUBES 23 TO 35 (except 32). These are the popular star tubes with closed points. They press out designs much like open star tubes, but more sharply ribbed for a more ornate effect. Smaller tubes may be used for writing; all sizes do exquisite stars, shells, fleur-de-lis, rosettes, scrolls and more.

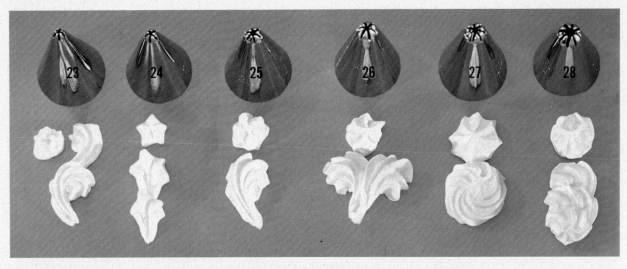

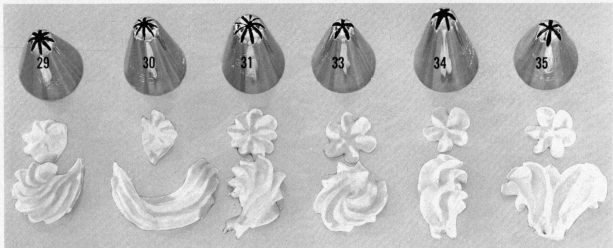

MULTIPLE LINE TUBES FOR LATTICE, SCALES

TUBES 41, 42 AND 43, each have two holes placed parallel to do twin lines, crisscross, lattice. TUBE 89 has three holes, does basketweave effect. TUBE 134 has five holes for musical scale.

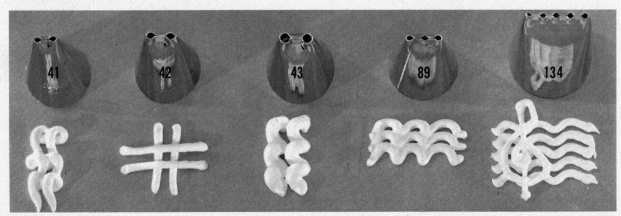

RIBBON TUBES FOR BANDS, BOWS, BASKETS

TUBES 44 AND 45 draw a smooth, broad ribbon of icing to ripple into a border or swirl into a bow.

TUBES 46, 47 AND 48 have one flat, one ridged side for piping "pleated" ribbons and weaving baskets.

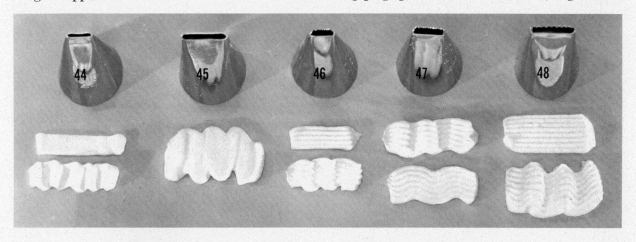

CROSS TUBES FOR FANCY BORDERS, FLOWERS

TUBES 49, 50, 51, 52, 53 AND 54 all have criss-cross cuts, little to large. Icing pipes through deeply

ridged for pretty effects—buds, ornate linework, ripply borders and a small 4-petal drop flower.

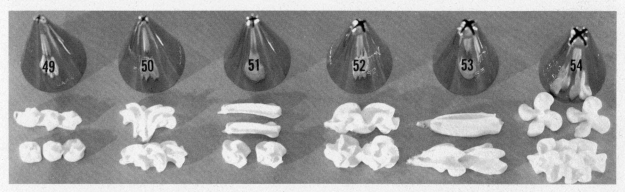

BORDER TUBES

TUBE 76 for borders that look overpiped with string.
TUBE 77, a large cross tube for rich ribbed shells.
TUBE 78, cross tube with extra cuts for fancy effects.

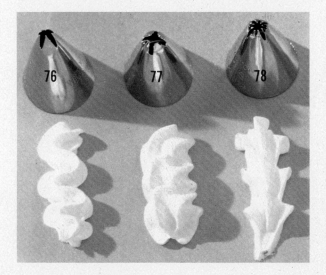

OVAL TUBES

TUBES 55 AND 57 are used for a line with a half-rounded effect. They do graceful garlands, ropes, a long shell effect, also "bamboo" basketweaving.

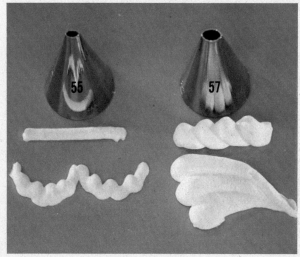

SPECIAL BORDER TUBES
FOR LAVISH EFFECTS

Tube 98 is sharply curved, with one side serrated, the other smooth. It can turn out richly-puffed shell garlands for beautiful border treatments.

Tube 105 is a round tube with six deep notches. It makes deeply-ridged shells, rosettes and garlands and stunning borders, straight or rippled.

TUBES FOR ROSES AND
MANY OTHER FLOWERS

Tubes 97, 101, 102, 103 and 104 are the petal tubes—the ones you use to pipe flowers of many kinds and sizes on a flower nail. They help you to pipe roses, carnations, petunias, narcissi, wild roses, sweet peas, daisies, dahlias, half roses and carnations, rosebuds and jonquils, as well as many, many more real-looking flowers from field and garden. All in a variety of sizes, small to large. Also, beautiful scalloped borders, deeply-draped ribbons and graceful icing bows and streamers.

DROP FLOWER TUBES—FOR QUICK, EASY BLOOMS

The tubes shown above are called "drop flower tubes" because perfectly-shaped little flowers seem virtually to "drop" out of them. Even beginners can get good results. Just squeeze, release—see Chapter Nine for exact method. Pipe ahead with royal icing, add dots of icing for stamens, or use artificial stamens. You can store them almost indefinitely. Below, the flowers tubes make, shown actual size.

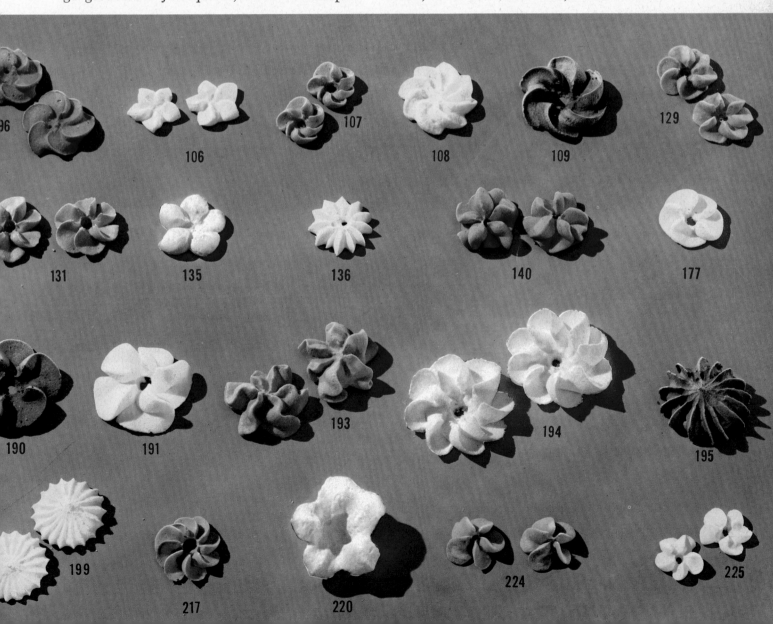

TUBES FOR LARGER DROP FLOWERS

Ideal for bigger cakes. One turn and squeeze with any of the four drop flower tubes below gives you a perfect flower from 1⅛″ to 1¼″ in diameter. Tube 2-B produces bold shells, borders, bar cookies.

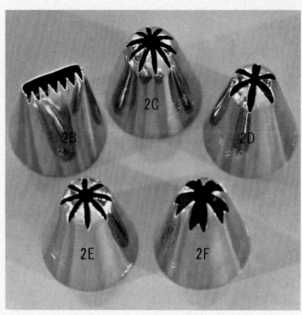

TUBES FOR LARGEST DROP FLOWERS

Biggest flowers you can pipe with a single squeeze! The flowers you press through tubes below are 1½″ to 1¾″ in diameter, depending on pressure.

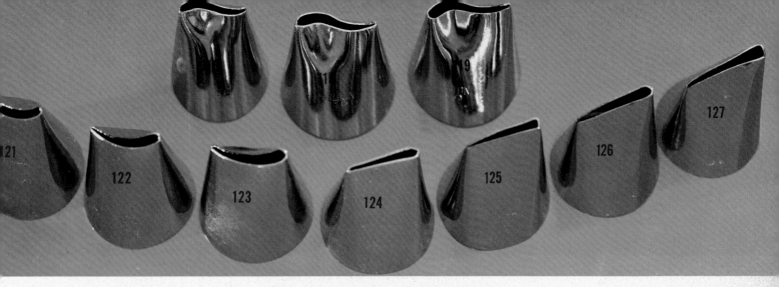

FOR FULL-BLOWN ROSES AND OTHER LARGE FLOWERS

TUBES 116, 118, 119, 121, 122, 123, 124, 125, 126 AND 127 are the ones that let you pipe huge, life-like roses. Some have curled openings to produce "instant-curled" petals. You can use the same tubes to pipe out many other large, beautiful flowers, too, as well as great ribbon swags and bows.

116   124   127

SMALL AND AVERAGE CURLED PETALS

TUBES 59, 59°, 60 AND 61 have curved openings to form curled petals for small and average-size flowers, such as narcissi, violets, pansies.

TUBES FOR FANCY BORDERS

TUBES 62, 63 AND 64 all have a curved opening that is ridged on the smallest side. These tubes do borders half smooth, half rippled for exciting effects.

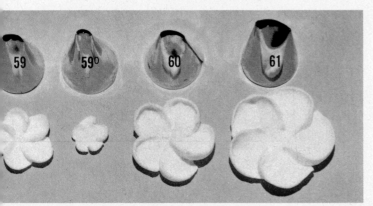

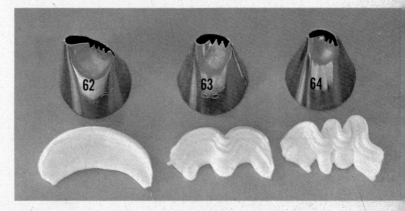

THE LEAF TUBES—TURN OUT LEAVES THAT LOOK REAL

Tubes 65, 66, 67, 68, 69 and 70 are among the most magical of all tubes. The leaves they press out look as real as if they'd just drifted off a vine. All sizes make pretty ripply borders, too.

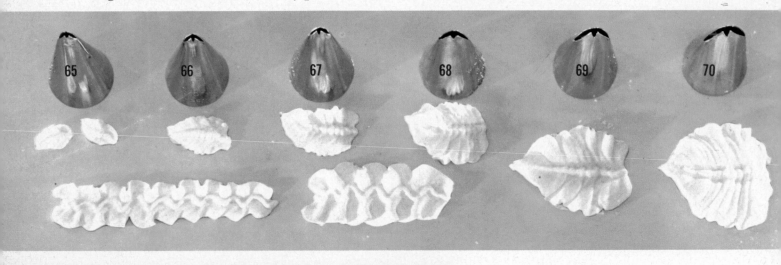

LARGE LEAF TUBES

Tubes 71, 72, 73, 74 and 75 produce larger leaves with deeply-defined center veins. They also make the special grooved petals required for poinsettias and water lilies, as well as special ferns and borders. Choose tube according to size of flowers or borders.

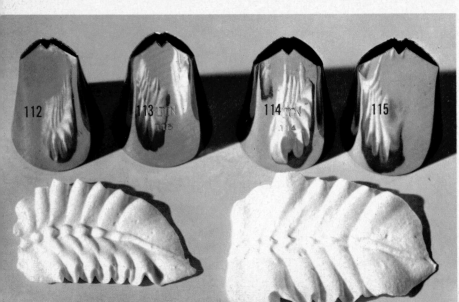

EXTRA-LARGE LEAF TUBES

Tubes 112, 113, 114 and 115 make extra-large leaves and other large designs that require a leaf tube. Tube 112 makes leaves from ¾ to one inch wide. Tube 113 makes leaves from 1¼ to 1½ inch wide. Tube 114 makes leaves from 1⅛ to 1½ inch wide. Tube 115 makes leaves 1½ inch and more wide.

FLUTED TUBES

Tubes 79, 80 and 81 have fluted tips, which can produce concave or convex lines. They also pipe lily of the valley blossoms in various sizes.

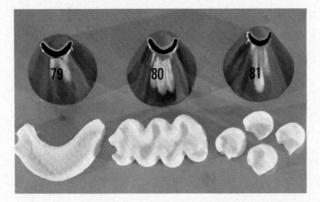

SQUARE & TRIANGLE TUBES

Tube 83 makes squared-off lines and tiny square beads for unusual borders. Tube 85 gives lines and beads a triangular look. Try them for new effects!

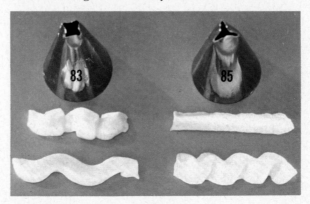

RUFFLE BORDER TUBES

Tubes 87 and 88 have one end star-shaped, the other straight for ripply borders that lie flat against cake.

Tube 95 is French leaf tube for deeply-grooved designs. Tubes 99 and 100 do double-fluted ruffles.

RIPPLE RIBBON TUBES

Tubes 401, 402 and 403 make extra-wide ribbon borders with a single squeeze and zigzag movement (once made only by rolling and shaping gum paste). The three tubes make ribbons ½″ to 1½″ wide.

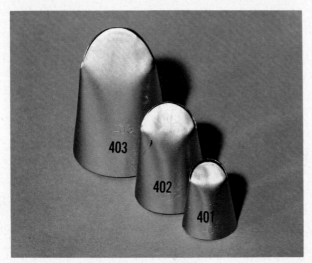

21

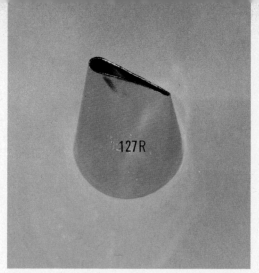

A TUBE FOR A GIANT ROSE

TUBE 127-R is double-size, so you can pipe double-size flowers with it. In fact, you can pipe a rose 5½″ in diameter—large enough to decorate an entire cake top! To work with a tube this large, use a super-size flower nail, 2 or 3 inches in diameter, or attach a 3″ cardboard square to a number 7 nail. Then proceed, referring to rose directions in Chapter Nine. Use a stiffened boiled icing, soft enough to press out of the tube easily, yet stiff enough to keep the petals on your extra-large rose from "wilting".

TUBES TO DO TINY TRIMS

TUBES 1-S, 65-S AND 101-S pipe out tiny flowers and leaves of just the right size to decorate mints, miniature sugar cubes and petits fours. Tube 1-S is the writing tube, tube 65-S the leaf tube, and tube 101-S the flower tube.

TUBES FOR EXTRA-LARGE BORDERS

TUBE 2-A makes bulb borders with bulbs of ½″ to 1″ in diameter. Fine for very large cakes.

TUBE 2-B makes shells and ripple borders in heroic proportions of ¾″ to 1¼″ wide.

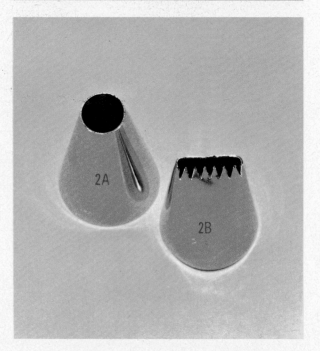

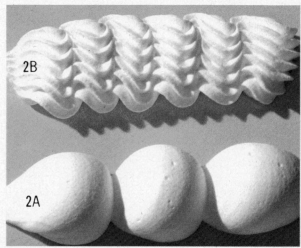

TUBES FOR GIANT BORDERS

TUBE 1-A makes giant bulb borders with bulbs from ¾″ to 1¼″ in diameter, depending on pressure.

TUBE 1-D makes shells and ripple borders from 1″ to 1¼″ wide. It is also useful for making bar cookies. Both tubes shape pastry such as eclairs, cream puffs and lady fingers and garnish foods as well.

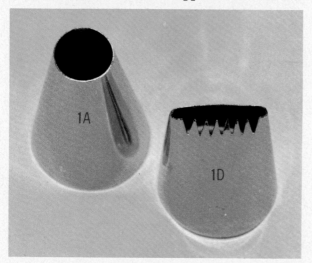

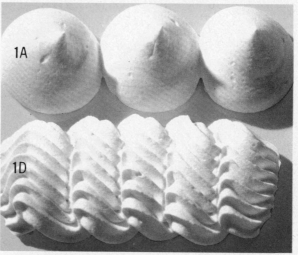

TUBES FOR THE PASTRY MAKER

TUBES 1-A, 4-B, 6-B AND 8-B are essential for forming luscious cream puffs, lady fingers, eclairs, press cookies and French crullers.

TUBE 1-D does big bar cookies. All can garnish foods with mashed potatoes, meringue and whipped cream. Also pipe shells, borders 1″ to 2¼″ wide.

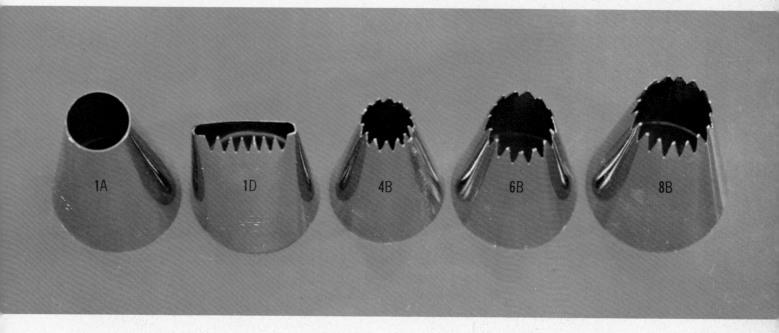

A Portfolio of Party Cakes

Here's a festive array of decorative cakes for any type of party—birthday, anniversary, shower, Valentine's Day, even engagement celebrations! All gay and colorful, these first two flowery cakes will brighten any occasion.

PRIMROSE, a 12″ x 4″ cake square covered with clusters of vibrant blossoms is truly fresh and delightful. To decorate, make lots of brilliant blue primroses using a flower nail and tube 102. Refer to Chapter Nine for detailed flower-making directions. After piping all your flowers, use the same decorating tube and nail to make four-petalled leaves, following the leaf-making instructions given in Chapter Ten.

When flowers and leaves are dry, ice the cake. Make curved guidelines above and below each of the cake's top edges. Then using a zigzag motion and tube 17, overpipe these guides along with the cake's top borders and side corners. Frame the cake base with tube 18 zigzag; then pipe sprays of tube 3 beading on cake top and side corners. Position flowers and leaves with icing and the cake's complete. Serves 30.

BLUE PETUNIA, a 10″ x 4″ round cake framed with brilliant petalled blossoms. Refer to Chapters Nine and Ten for flower-making instructions, then pipe about a dozen petunias and the same number of wild roses. Next, ice the entire cake white and, with a toothpick, trace a curving outline of a design on top of the cake. Now referring to the detailed directions in Chapter Twelve, fill in this toothpick tracing with tube 2 strings of latticework. Frame the latticework design with tube 16 scrolls, hiding any uneven latticework edges, and drape these icing scrolls down over onto the cake's sides. Attach the petunias and wild roses with icing, then trim with tube 65 leaves, referring to the leaf-making instructions in Chapter Ten. The cake complete is a proud presentation to make on any special day! Serves 14.

Decorative flowers can be made and displayed in an endless variety of ways to give beauty and freshness to cakes of all types. Here three cakes—a round, a heart and a mini-tiered trio—are all fancied with flowers and yet each one is distinctively different in shape and trim!

FLOWERS AND LACE. Make the exquisite net flowers referring to instructions found in Chapter Eleven, and substituting tube 1 fleur-de-lis for petal "veins". Follow the same procedure to make net leaves. Set all aside to dry, placing net petals on a gently curved surface. To assemble flowers pipe tube 14 centers on wax paper, push in petals and add artificial stamens.

With net trims complete, ice a 12″ x 3″ cake. Mark a circular guideline on the cake top about 2½″ from the outer edge with a toothpick. Then, pipe tube 2 icing lines from this guideline to the cake's edge. Pipe tube 15 shells around the inner circle. Using the same tube, pipe shells around the top border, then frame both sides with more shells. Pipe tube 15 shells around the base of the cake. Curve a tube 16 garland over this border, overpiping each garland four times. Now attach the net leaves and assembled flowers with icing and the cake's complete to serve at any special party. Serves 22.

RUFFLED HEART. A party cake in the pink of romance! To start, make several tube 103 wild roses following the directions given in Chapter Nine. Also in advance, make lots of tube 225 drop flowers with tube 1 centers. Set aside to dry.

To decorate the 9″ x 4″ heart, first place the layered cake on a ruffle-trimmed board cut into a heart shape. Edge the base with tube 19 rosettes and attach the drop flowers with icing. Next pipe tube 16 white ruffled garlands around the cake side, frame with tube 103 deep pink ruffles and pipe a double row of tube 2 stringwork. Then attach drop flowers with dots of icing around the top border. Pipe tube 3 stems on top of the cake and add swirls of tube 1 beading. Attach wild roses to the stems with icing and trim with tube 65 leaves. This frilly heart is not only a lavish Valentine, but an affectionate way to say Happy Anniversary, Happy Mother's Day or Happy Sweetest Day. Serves 12.

FLOWER-DECKED MINI-TIER. Three round cake tiers— a 5″, a 6½″ and an 8″—the perfect party size for family get togethers. The tiers, all made from a single cake mix, are decorated with lots of tiny tube 225 drop flowers. Make these blossoms in advance referring to directions found in Chapter Nine.

When the flowers are dry, ice and position the middle and top tiers on 5½″ and 7″ separator plates; the lower tier on a foil-covered board. Edge the

bases of the lower two tiers with tube 16 shells. Drop curved string guidelines around the sides of these same tiers and attach drop flowers with dots of icing to cover them. Next, heap a mound of icing on the topmost tier and position a full cluster of drop flowers. Make a border of additional drop flowers around this tier's base, keeping the flowers side by side. Now assemble the tiers with 4½″ long plastic twist legs and ring each leg of the separator plates with flowers. Trim the floral arrangements with tube 65 leaves. With the decorated tiers assembled, you now have a mini-masterpiece to convey best wishes for a happy birthday, happy anniversary or any special occasion! Serves 12.

LOVEGLOW, a star-studded cake to shine at a bridal shower or engagement party. To decorate, make tube 14 bachelor buttons and tube 103 daisies, drying daisies on a curved former. Refer to Chapter Nine for flower-making directions. Next, ice a 9″ x 3″ heart and a 12″ x 4″ round cake, positioning as shown. Edge both cake bases with an inverted single Star-Bright border referring to Chapter Six, page 92 for directions. Use tube 22 for white rosettes, tube 16 for white stars, tube 3 for stringwork, tube 14 for yellow stars atop stringwork and tube 16 for yellow zigzag. For cake top borders pipe tube 22 white rosettes, tube 16 yellow star centers and tube 16 yellow rosettes above. Ornament cake with bride and groom, attaching flowers with icing and trimming with tube 67 leaves. Serves 34.

MORNINGSTAR. A magnificent wedding cake that sets the theme for Loveglow in color and trim. Make tube 14 bachelor buttons and tube 103 daisies, drying daisies on a curved former. Refer to Chapter Nine for flower-making directions. When dry, at-tach some flowers to florist wires with icing and push into gathered net nosegay, tying with ribbon. Ice the 18″ x 4″, 14″ x 4″, 10″ x 4″ and 6″ x 3″ tiers. Assemble with 3″ grecian and cupid pillars. Use 8″ round separator plates for top tier, a 12″ round plate on top of 14″ tier, and an 11″ square plate below 10″ tier. Mound icing on separator plates and posi-tion flowers trimming with tube 67 leaves. Refer to directions on page 92 to pipe the fans on 18″ and 14″ tiers. Edge top plates with tube 16 zigzag. Refer again to page 92 and pipe double Star-Bright bor-ders around bottom square and middle round tier bases. Use upright and inverted single Star-Bright trims for all other tier borders, with the exception of the 6″ tier top. For all single and double Star-Bright borders pipe tube 22 white rosettes, tube 16 white stars, tube 3 stringwork, tube 14 yellow and blue stars, tube 16 yellow rosettes and tube 14 zig-zag edgings. Frame top tier with tube 22 white rosettes and tube 16 yellow rosettes and stars. Posi-tion nosegay for the finishing touch. Serves 320.

28

MORNINGSTAR
Decorating directions
on opposite page

29

FLOWER BASKET. Make tube 59° violets, tube 101 daffodils and tube 102 leaves, (like the pansy's petals), referring to directions in Chapter Nine. Use tube 46 and directions in Chapter Twelve to pipe the icing basket on a lightly oiled inverted custard cup. When dry, turn right side up, insert an iced styrofoam ball and an entwined pipe cleaner handle, and attach flowers with icing.

The basket complete, ice a 12″ x 4″ round cake. Edge the cake base with a tube 17 circular swirled border, then overpipe with tube 2. With tube 17, frame the cake top with an "e" motion border. Fill each "e" loop with a tube 17 rosette. Mark two rings on the cake top with a toothpick and pipe with tube 16 zigzags. Position the basket, pipe tube 2 stems and leaves and attach flowers with icing. Serves 22.

VASES OF VIOLETS. Make tube 59° violets, referring to instructions in Chapter Nine. Next, pipe filigree icing vases and parasol following directions in

30

Chapter Twelve. When dry, trim the parasol with violets, tube 2 bead flowers and ribbon.

The cake is a 10″ x 4″ round on a 14″ bevel. To decorate, edge the bevel with tube 14 shells, piping tube 2 beading above them. Add scrolled trim using a zigzag motion and tube 14. Overpipe these scrolls twice, once with a tube 14 straight line, then with a tube 2 string. Next, use directions given in Chapter Seven to make a scalloped pattern for the top of the cake. Trace pattern, then overpipe with tube 2. Now mark off six spaces around the top edge of the cake. Press a filigree vase over each of these marks to indicate an outline and attach violets. Place a filigree vase over each cluster of violets attaching with icing and adding additional flowers. Pipe tube 14 zigzag garlands between vases. Above them pipe tube 14 scrolls, overpiping with tube 2. Add tube 2 beading and violets, trim with tube 65 leaves. Serves 14.

HEART'S FANCY. A pretty cake ruffled with icing garlands and pink petalled roses. Ice a 9″, 2-layer heart cake. Use tube 101s to make the tiny roses and tube 104 for the large deep pink rose. To make the flowers refer to the detailed directions given in Chapter Nine. When flowers are dry, start trimming the cake by first marking off the top and bottom edges into 2½-inch spaces with a toothpick. When you have the cake completely marked, refer to the step-by-step directions in Chapter Eight for making the frilly Ruffles-and-Roses border. You'll need your ready-made tube 101s roses along with tube 14 for the ruffled garlands, tube 65s for the tiny leaves, and tube 1 for the strings and hearts.

The lavish border complete, pipe several tube 2 long green stems on the cake top and decorate them with tiny roses, attaching them with icing. Position the large tube 104 rose with a dot of icing. Trim the petite roses with tube 65s leaves and the large petalled rose with tube 68 leaves. Finished, this pink ruffled heart is a perfect party cake for any romantic occasion! A most thoughtful way to wish someone happy Valentine's Day or happy Sweetest Day! Serves 12.

GARDEN GAZEBO. Fresh as its name, a variety of icing flowers make this 10″ x 4″ cake a summer favorite! Shape flowers first using tube 103 for the wild flowers and daisies, tube 104 for the roses and sweet peas and tube 225 for the tiny drop flowers. Pipe fern leaves onto iced florist wires with tube 4. Set in styrofoam to dry. (Refer to Chapters Eight, Nine and Eleven for detailed instructions.)

When flowers are dry, decorate cake by first framing the base with a tube 104 curved ribbon border. Then edge the top side with a triple row of tube 4 stringwork and do the top border with tube 4

beading. Next, at four points around the base of the cake pipe mounds of icing and attach floral bouquets. Then with more icing, attach drop flowers to the ribbon and string border points.

Top the cake with a gazebo housing two sugar bells glued back to back for a "vase". Fill "vase" with icing and arrange ready-made ferns. Then, with icing, attach more garden bouquets to the cake top at several points around the gazebo base. Trim tiny blossoms with tube 65 leaves, larger blooms with tube 66 leaves. Circle the cake top with a delicately chained plastic fence. Serves 14.

SHOWER THE BRIDE with good wishes and a cake that previews her wedding! First make the intricate filigree and icing laces using tube 2 and the directions from Chapter Twelve. Cover a ball-shaped pan and two small plastic parasols with wedge-shaped pieces of net to pipe the filigree parasols. Then on a flat surface pipe tiny icing laces for the bride's parasol and dress. When dry, position lace on bride's parasol with icing; then with more icing attach top to an iced dowel rod "handle". Attach the bridesmaid's parasol tops to plastic "picks" with icing.

The wishing well is a 3″ x 3″ styrofoam piece that's iced and then traced with toothpick "brick"

lines. A rim is piped around the well top with tube 10, then blue piping gel "water" is added. To make the well "roof", use tubes 4 and 46 and the basket weaving instructions from Chapter Twelve and pipe icing onto 4½″ x 2″ cardboard pieces. When dry, attach to plastic picks with icing and push into wishing well top.

Next, pipe two filigree baskets on Australian net nails, again referring to directions in Chapter Twelve. Then make flowers using tubes 101, 101s, 2 and 1 for daffodils and tube 65 for stephanotis, referring to Chapter Nine. When dry, attach some of the flowers to wires with icing; then place styrofoam

in basket bottoms and insert wired flowers.

To make the wedding party, ice small dome-shaped cakes and push in doll picks. Pipe tube 101s ruffles on bridesmaids and tube 102 ruffle on bride. Add beading with tube 3. Make veil and bouquet ruffle of fine net. Then attach made-ahead lace to bride's hem with icing.

A 12″ x 18″ x 3″ rectangle and 10″ and 12″ x 2″ round cakes are stacked, trimming the curves to resemble steps. Ice the cakes green using wax paper to cover the pathway. Pat cakes with sponge to effect "grass," then ice pathway white using corn syrup in icing for glazed look. Edge base borders with shells using tube 20 for rectangle, tube 16 for 12″ tier and tube 14 for 10″ tier. Use tube 74 for tier tops; then position wedding party, baskets, parasols, well and unwired flowers with icing. Serves 60.

A LOVE CAKE colorfully expresses the feeling of the heart. Start by making sugar hearts using molding methods described in Chapter Eighteen. Then ice a 9″ x 4″ petal-shaped cake in assorted colors. Frame the top with tube 9 bead borders, adding a vertical row of beads in between each petal curve. Next position the sugar hearts with icing and, with an appropriate decoration, spell out your loving wishes. Serves 12.

ROSE RHAPSODY is a versatile cake suited to so many different occasions—from a formal party for a newly-engaged couple to a birthday get-together with family and friends.

Before decorating the cake refer to the spatula-striping techniques explained in Chapter Three. Then stripe a decorating bag pink, fill with white icing and pipe the flowers using tube 124 for the large roses and tube 104 for the rosebuds. Follow directions in Chapter Nine for making flowers. Then, after you've made and dried a number of each size blossom, carefully turn the rosebuds upside down

and pipe five tube 3 sepals on each one.

Now ice a 10″ x 4″ round cake white and place on a silver foil-covered board. Then put two green stripes in a decorating bag fitted with tube 4B, fill with white icing and pipe scrolled curves of icing across the cake top, continuing the scrolls on opposite sides of the cake. Edge the cake base with tube 199 puffs, piping tube 14 stars above and between each. Next, green stripe a decorating bag fitted with tube 14 and pipe zigzag curves around the base of each puff. To finish, attach flowers with icing and trim with tube 68 leaves. Serves 14.

Rehearsal dinner complete with cake makes the evening before the wedding a special one to be remembered. Before decorating the cake, make white roses in advance with tube 102 following the directions from Chapter Nine. When dry, attach the roses and about a dozen or more silk decorator leaves to iced florist wire. Dry again and assemble into a nosegay as directed in Chapter Eleven.

Then assemble the three cake tiers—a 12″ x 4″, 6″ x 4″ and tiny 2⅛″ x 1″ round. Edge all bases with shells using tube 32 for the large tier, tube 16 for the middle tier and tube 14 for the top tier. For the top border of the bottom tier, first pipe tube 104 ruffles around the cake, then fill in above ribbon with tube 16 zigzag. Finish this border with a double row of tube 4 stringwork and tube 102 icing bows.

For the two smaller tiers, pipe standing shell top borders using tube 22 for the middle tier and tube 16 for the top tier. Drop a row of tube 4 stringwork around the middle tier's top border.

Push plastic stair-step candle holders into the side of the cake and position a miniature bridal party. Place the nosegay on the bottom tier. Serves 28.

CHAPTER TWO

Icing...Basic Material of the Decorator

A sculptor cannot create his masterpieces from just any bit of clay. He must find the right sort and use it in just the right way. So it is with the sculptor of cakes. Your "clay" is icing. Made properly, it will allow you to create beautiful scrolls, ripples, shells, stars and all the colorful flowers of nature. It will cover your cake with a smooth decorating surface or with glamorous swirls and designs. Together with the filling, it will keep your cake moist and delicious and hold the layers smoothly in place. But if your icing is not made exactly right for the role you want it to play, the result will be a sad waste of time, skill and ingredients. For this reason, it is vitally important to make icings correctly.

You can use a single icing for coating, filling and decorating your cake, or a combination of several. In this chapter, are recipes for a variety of icings and coatings. All have been tested carefully and will give consistently good results.

Icings for Decorating

All these recipes are fine-tasting and handle well in the decorating cone or bag. Each has its own special look and purpose.

Whichever icing you choose, it must be of exactly the right consistency for the designs you wish to make. Too soft and you'll produce a "blob" instead of a shell, star or petal. Too stiff and your leaves won't point or your stringwork "drop". The recipes given will produce icings of medium consistency, ideal for borders and most flowers. They should peak at least ¾-inch on the spatula.

Thin the icing to pipe leaves and stringwork by adding white corn syrup. Here is an approximation of the amounts needed—only experience and practice will enable you to judge when the icing has just the right consistency. Add one teaspoon of corn syrup per cup of icing for string work. Add two teaspoons per cup for leaves. The syrup will give the icing more elasticity and a handsome gloss.

Stiffen the icing for some flowers by adding a little sifted confectioners sugar. Again, experiment until you achieve the right consistency.

A *regular electric mixer* can be used for all of these recipes. (Do not attempt to use a hand mixer.) If you double the recipes you must use a heavy-duty mixer, such as the KitchenAid K5A, or a model with similar power. The dedicated decorator will find a heavy-duty mixer an invaluable aid.

BUTTERCREAM ICINGS

One of the most popular and delicious of all icings, buttercream can be used for many purposes. It is simple to make, easy to manage, pipes perfect borders and spreads smoothly to fill and frost cakes. Refrigerate if kept longer than a day. Freeze or air-dry buttercream flowers, place on cake just before serving.

WILTON BUTTERCREAM

Sweet, rich, creamy-textured. Makes 3 cups.
  ⅓ cup butter
  ⅓ cup solid, white vegetable shortening
  1 teaspoon clear vanilla
  ⅛ teaspoon salt
  1 pound confectioners sugar, sifted
  5 tablespoons cool milk or cream

Cream butter and shortening together with an electric mixer. Beat in sugar, 1 cup at a time, blending well after each addition and scraping sides and bottom of bowl with a spatula frequently. Add milk and beat at high speed until it becomes light and fluffy. Keep icing covered with lid or damp cloth and store in refrigerator. Bring to room temperature and rebeat to use again.

WILTON SNOW-WHITE BUTTERCREAM

This will be your choice for wedding cakes, or any cake where a pure white appearance is important.

⅔ cup water

4 tablespoons meringue powder

1¼ cups solid white shortening, room temperature

¾ teaspoon salt

¼ teaspoon butter flavoring

½ teaspoon almond flavoring

½ teaspoon clear vanilla flavoring

11½ cups sifted confectioners sugar

Combine water and meringue powder and whip at high speed until peaks form. Add four cups sugar, one cup at a time, beating after each addition at low speed. Alternately add shortening and remainder of sugar. Add salt and flavorings and beat at low speed until smooth. Thin with two teaspoons of white corn syrup for leaves and strings. Yield 8 cups. Recipe may be cut in half or doubled.

BOILED ICINGS

Satiny boiled icings are light and fluffy and flow smoothly out of the tube.

You can make boiled icing with meringue powder or egg whites. You can rebeat meringue boiled icing and it will rise to its original consistency. It may be stored for a week or more. Egg white boiled icing will not return to original consistency when rebeaten and spoils rather quickly. It has a better flavor than meringue boiled icing.

All boiled icings tend to crust, especially in dry weather. This can be prevented by adding a softener—either nulomoline (available at baker's supply houses) or glycerine. In cool weather, add about 2 teaspoons to a quart. In warmer, more humid weather, use less.

Important: be sure no grease or oil ever touches boiled icing. Keep pans, spoons and decorating tools grease-free or icing will break down. Do not add flavorings, as most are oil-based.

WILTON BOILED ICING—MERINGUE

Fine for borders and trim. Dries too crisp for covering cakes.

4 level tablespoons meringue powder

1 cup warm water

2 cups granulated sugar

¼ teaspoon cream of tartar

3½ cups sifted confections sugar

Boil granulated sugar, ½ cup water, cream of tartar to temperature of 240° F. Brush sides of pan with warm water to keep crystals from forming. Meanwhile, mix meringue powder with ½ cup water, beat 7 minutes at high speed. Turn to low speed, add confectioners sugar, beat 4 minutes at high speed. Slowly add boiled sugar mixture, beat 5 minutes at high speed. Keeps a week in refrigerator, covered with damp cloth. Rebeat before using. Yields 6 cups.

WILTON BOILED ICING—EGG WHITE

A snow-white, good-flavored icing suitable for covering and filling the cake. Borders are not quite as clear-cut as if piped with meringue boiled icing.

2 cups granulated sugar

½ cup water

¼ teaspoon cream of tartar

4 egg whites (room temperature)

1½ cups confectioners sugar, sifted

Boil granulated sugar, water, cream of tartar to 240° F. When boiling starts, brush sides of pan with warm water to prevent crystals forming. Brush again halfway through, but do not stir. Meanwhile, whip egg whites 7 minutes at high speed. Add boiled sugar mixture slowly and beat 3 minutes at high speed. Turn to second speed, gradually add confectioners sugar and beat 7 minutes more at high speed. Cover with damp cloth while using. Rebeating will not restore. Yields 3½ cups.

ROYAL ICINGS

These are the smooth, hard-drying, near-permanent icings used by professionals for display cakes and decorations that last indefinitely. Ideal for making flowers and other trims in advance. Once hardened, they never soften or crumble. The perfect "cement" for attaching flowers to cake separators or ornaments, or putting sugar molds together.

Royal icings also can be made with either powdered meringue or fresh egg whites. The egg white royal has more strength, so it is the better choice for latticework, icing net or other delicate work that needs an extra-strong icing.

As with boiled icings, any touch of grease will break royal icings down. Not good for icing "real" cakes, but perfect for icing display dummies.

ROYAL ICING—MERINGUE

3 level tablespoons meringue powder

1 pound confectioners sugar

3½ ounces warm water—slightly less than ½ cup

½ teaspoon cream of tartar

Combine ingredients and beat slowly until blended together, then beat at high speed for 7 to 10 minutes. Keep covered at all times with a damp cloth. To restore texture later, simply rebeat. For lighter icing, add one tablespoon water, continue rebeating. (This makes a more brittle flower.) Yields 3½ cups.

Silver White Cake (4 Egg Whites)

High, fluffy, showy. Delicately flavored. Reminiscent of White Mountain Cake, the rage of the Gay Nineties and the first popular "white" cake to be created. See color picture, p. 128.

2¼ cups SOFTASILK Flour	½ cup soft shortening
1½ cups sugar	1 cup milk
3½ tsp. baking powder	1 tsp. flavoring
1 tsp. salt	4 egg whites (½ to ⅔ cup), unbeaten

[handwritten: Double 4½ C / 3 C / 2 C / 2 tsp] *[handwritten: Double 1 C / 2 C / 2 tsp / 8]*

Heat oven to 350° (mod.). Grease and flour two layer pans, 8 or 9x1½" or an oblong pan, 13x9½x2". Measure flour by dip-level-pour method or by sifting (*see p. 6*). Blend flour, sugar, baking powder and salt. Add shortening, ⅔ cup of milk and flavoring. Beat 2 min., medium speed on mixer or 300 vigorous strokes by hand. Scrape sides and bottom of bowl constantly. Add rest of milk and egg whites. Beat 2 more min., scraping bowl frequently. Pour into pan(s). Bake *layers 30 to 35 min., oblong 35 to 40 min.* Cool. Elegant with lemon filling (*p. 177*), a fluffy icing (*p. 174*) and flaked coconut.

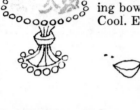

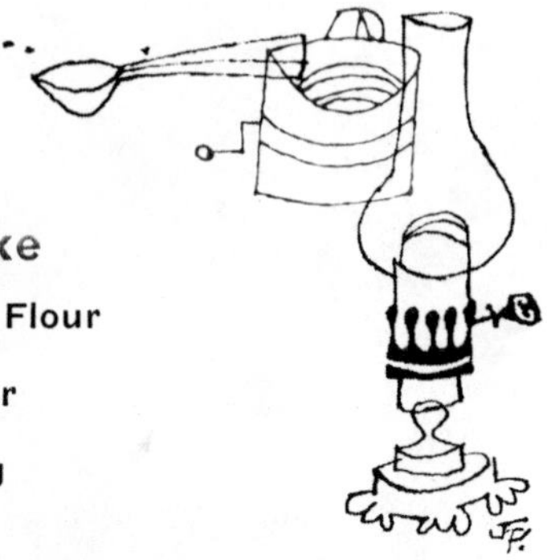

3-Egg White Cake

2¼ cups SOFTASILK Flour
1¼ cups sugar
2½ tsp. baking powder
½ tsp. salt
½ cup soft shortening
1 cup milk
1½ tsp. vanilla
3 egg whites (⅜ cup), unbeaten

Mix and bake as for Silver White Cake (*above*)— except bake *oblong cake 35 min.*

Maraschino Cherry Cake

2¼ cups SOFTASILK Flour or 2 cups
 plus 2 tbsp. GOLD MEDAL Flour
1⅓ cups sugar
3 tsp. baking powder
1 tsp. salt
½ cup soft shortening
¼ cup maraschino cherry juice (5-oz. bottle)
16 maraschino cherries, cut in eighths
½ cup milk
4 egg whites (½ to ⅔ cup), unbeaten
½ cup chopped nuts

Heat oven to 350° (mod.). Grease and flour two layer pans, 8 or 9x1½" or an oblong pan, 13x9½x2". Measure flour by dip-level-pour method or by sifting (*see p. 6*). Stir dry ingredients together. Add shortening, cherry juice, cherries and milk. Beat 2 min., medium speed on mixer. Add egg whites. Beat 2 more min. Fold in nuts. Pour into pans. Bake *layers 30 to 35 min., oblong 35 to 40 min.*

132

Orange Satin Ribbon Cake

Bake Silver White Cake (*above*) in layers. Cool. Split each layer crosswise. Spread Orange Satin Filling (*below*) between layers and on top. Sprinkle ¼ cup chopped toasted almonds on top.

Orange Satin Filling

1 cup sugar
4½ tbsp. cornstarch
½ tsp. salt
1½ cups orange juice
½ cup water
4 egg yolks, beaten
¼ cup butter
3 tbsp. grated orange rind

Mix sugar, cornstarch and salt in saucepan. Gradually stir in orange juice and water. Bring to boil over low heat, stirring constantly. Remove from heat. Stir at least half of hot mixture into beaten egg yolks. Blend into remaining hot mixture. Bring to boil again; boil 1 min., stirring constantly. Remove from heat and blend in butter and orange rind. Cool.

Miracle Marble Cake

Rich chocolate and dainty white . . in intriguing marbled effect. "Guests at my home exclaim over it especially when I serve fingers of it with pink strawberry ice cream on white milk glass plates," says N. Faye Woodward of Lawrence, Kansas.

Make batter for Silver White Cake (*above*). Pour ⅔ of batter into pans. To remaining batter add 1 sq. unsweetened chocolate (1 oz.), melted, mixed with ¼ tsp. soda and 2 tbsp. warm water. Pour here and there over white batter. Cut through batter with knife several times for marbled effect. Bake. Cool. Frost with chocolate icing.

puddings and other desserts. (Don't thaw before arranging on desserts. They will soften in just a few minutes.) If decorating, use immediately after whipping. If filling or topping cakes, you can let it stand for several hours first in the refrigerator.

STABILIZED WHIPPED CREAM

1 teaspoon plain gelatin mixed
   into 4 teaspoons cold water
1 cup heavy whipping cream (at least
   24 hours old and very cold)
¼ cup confectioners sugar
¼ teaspoon vanilla

Add gelatin to cold water in a small metal or pyrex cup. Set in small pan of boiling water and heat until gelatin dissolves and looks clear (do not stir). You must now cool gelatin to room temperature and since this happens very quickly, begin at once to whip cream. (Make certain bowl and beaters are also very cold, especially in summer.) When cream is whipped to a medium consistency, pour dissolved gelatin into center all at once and continue beating. Add confectioners sugar and vanilla also at this time. Beat only until cream stands in stiff peaks and clings to side of bowl. (This will happen just a few seconds after you add all ingredients.) For best decorating results, do not overwhip. 2 cups.

TO VARY WHIPPED CREAM

Use recipe above and vary flavor by folding in 2 tablespoons sifted, unsweetened cocoa, or 2 tablespoons shredded toasted almonds, or ¼ cup sieved ripe fruit—peaches, apricots or fresh berries.

Icings for Coating Cakes

You can use any of these decorating icings for coating cakes, except royal icing. Soften with a little white corn syrup, if necessary for spreading consistency. Or try this delicious basic icing.

SEVEN MINUTE ICING

Very fluffy, snow white and it never fails. Gives cakes a coating that is crisp on the surface, yet remains soft and creamy inside. Delicious flavor!

2 egg whites
1½ cups sugar
5 tablespoons cold water
¼ teaspoon cream of tartar
1 teaspoon vanilla

Put all but flavoring in top of double boiler and beat with electric hand mixer at medium speed until well blended. Then place over rapidly boiling water and continue to beat at high speed for 7 minutes. Remove from heat, add flavoring, and beat again at high speed until icing is spreading consistency. 2 cups.

ROYAL ICING—EGG WHITE

3 egg whites (room temperature)
1 pound confectioners sugar
½ teaspoon cream of tartar

Combine ingredients, beat at high speed for 7 to 10 minutes. (Any good-quality home mixer can handle it.) Very quick-drying, so keep covered with damp cloth. Yields less volume than royal icing made with meringue powder and rebeating will not restore. An excellent consistency for borders and flowers. Yield, 3 cups.

PACKAGED ICING MIXES

We do not recommend using a packaged icing mix for decorating as brands vary greatly. They may be used to fill and cover the cake—then add trim with the buttercream or boiled icing recipes given above.

WHIPPED CREAM ICING

A light and luscious touch for any cake, especially the delicate variety such as angel food or sponge. If you "stabilize" whipped cream as described here, the cake you decorate with it will keep nicely for a day or two in the refrigerator. Or you can pipe out rosettes and flowers and freeze them on a cookie sheet, then keep them frozen in a plastic bag for weeks, to be used for decorating cakes,

WILTON MULTI-PURPOSE FONDANT

Fondant is the elegant coating for cakes and petits fours with the fine, shiny finish. It is the only ingredient in mints and the rich, creamy center for chocolates and bon-bons. Fondant takes a bit of doing, but is well worth the effort because it has so many uses, and because, tightly covered, it will keep at room temperature for weeks. This recipe yields 10 pounds, but it can be cut in half.

FONDANT RECIPE

7 pounds of granulated sugar
4 cups water
1 pound glucose

Combine all ingredients in a large, heavy saucepan. Heat until all the sugar is dissolved. When syrup looks clear, wash down sides of pan with a brush dipped in warm water to remove any clinging sugar crystals. Repeat this procedure several times. Increase heat and boil until it reaches 240° F. on a candy thermometer. Now it is ready to be worked.

1. At once, pour mixture onto a marble slab or marproof plastic table top and let it cool to lukewarm. (You can make a "frame" with dowel rods to contain it on a small table.) When mixture begins to set and you can touch it comfortably at edge, start to "work it" with a candy scraper.

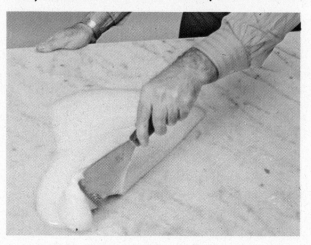

2. With your hand holding the scraper palm up and blade of scraper lying almost flat, push under edge of mass and move toward center. Lift as much as possible and fold over onto rest with a circular motion. Repeat under, up and over movement again and again. Approach mixture from all sides, keeping it in motion.

3. Soon fondant will begin to thicken and whiten as you work. Keep pushing, lifting and folding over. When it becomes so stiff and thick you can stand the scraper straight up in it (this takes about 4 minutes), pile in a mound, cover with damp cloth, let rest a few minutes.

4. Then knead stiff, chalky mound of fondant and it will soften quickly, becoming smooth and creamy. This formula does not have to be ripened, but can be used immediately. (Keep covered with a damp cloth while using to prevent drying.) Store at room temperature in air-tight container.

HOW TO ICE WITH FONDANT

Seal cake first, preferably with a thin coat of buttercream icing. This gives the fondant a white undercoat to help mask the cake and provide a crumb-free surface. (See next page for a step-by-step illustration of how to ice a cake.) Let buttercream icing set a bit while you prepare fondant for pouring and coating.

Put two cups of fondant into a double boiler and add desired flavoring and food color. Warm over heat, stirring constantly until fondant is of a pourable consistency. (Do not overheat or it will become too thin and may lose its characteristic shine.) Fondant should be thick enough to cover cake, soft enough to pour and spread by itself.

Set cake or petits fours on a wire rack and pour fondant over, touching up bare spots with a spatula. Place cookie sheet under rack to catch fondant that drains off to use again.

You can easily double your batch of fondant without having to start from scratch again. Simply combine it with a second recipe of ingredients cooked to 240°. Put finished fondant into mixture at that point and stir for about 3 minutes. Magically, you will have double the amount of fondant, ready for pouring over a cake or into mints. For candy centers, let cool and thicken, then knead until creamy. For just a few extra pounds, mix part of finished fondant into equal amount of ingredients.

Ways of Sealing Cake

To prevent crumbs and to provide your cake with a smooth, perfect surface for icing, it is wise to "seal" it first. You can simply thin buttercream icing for this purpose, spreading it on cake, then letting it crust before applying final coat of icing. Or, use the apricot glaze favored by many pastry chefs. Chill cake first, then brush all over with hot glaze.

Dry before proceeding with final coat of icing.

APRICOT GLAZE. Put one cup of apricot jam through a sieve and heat to boiling. Remove from heat and stir in two to four tablespoons of cognac, kirsch or other liqueur. (This is optional, but adds greatly to the flavor.) Use hot.

Ways of Glazing Fruits

When fresh fruit is used as a topping or trim for cakes and tarts, bring out its beauty with a shining coat of glaze. For "white" fruits (grapes, pears, peaches, pineapple), brush on the apricot glaze given above. For red fruits, brush on currant glaze —made same as apricot, but with currant jelly. Use while hot, serve same day.

Cake Fillings

All but the royal icings given are suitable for filling cakes as well. Here we give one more to vary many ways. For a quick and easy filling, you can also use any flavor of jam or fruit preserves. When choosing a filling for your cake, keep in mind what a cake filling should accomplish. It should not only hold the layers together and keep the cake moist, but also add texture, contrast, color and flavor.

PASTRY CREAM FILLING

Rich, yet delicate, ideal for any cake, for pies and tarts, too. Easy to vary. Fills a 9" cake.

  3 tablespoons flour
  ⅛ teaspoon salt
  ⅜ cup sugar
  1 cup half cream/half milk
  4 egg yolks
  1 teaspoon vanilla

Mix the flour, salt and sugar in a saucepan and blend in a little of the cream. Place on medium heat and stir constantly. Add the rest of the cream and the vanilla and continue stirring until the mixture reaches the consistency of medium cream sauce. Stir a little of the sauce into the egg yolks, then pour egg yolks into the sauce in pan. Cook for a few minutes on low heat until thickened. Remove from heat, add vanilla and cool quickly. To prevent a skin forming, brush with melted butter. Stir a little before using.

CHOCOLATE FILLING

Make basic cream filling and after removing from heat, add two ounces of melted, unsweetened chocolate to the mixture along with the vanilla.

MOCHA FILLING

Follow recipe for basic cream filling, but reduce amount of milk/cream by two tablespoons, substituting two tablespoons extra-strong fresh coffee.

How to Prepare Cake for Icing

Nothing sets off skillfully piped flowers and borders like a flawlessly iced cake. To achieve this, you must first give cake layers a smooth surface that will not crack or crumb when you spread on the icing. Here are two ways: a favorite "home" method and a quick way used by professionals.

PROFESSIONAL METHOD

REMOVE CAKE from oven, turn over on piece of parchment paper to cool. No rack necessary—idea is for cake top to steam and stick to the paper.

COOL UPSIDE-DOWN in pan for 5 minutes only and pan will lift off easily. (No longer, or grease in pan will cool and stick.) Let cake cool upside-down.

PLACE CARDBOARD CAKE CIRCLE on bottom, slip spatula under paper. Turn cake upright, peel off paper. Crust will also peel off, leaving smooth flat top.

IF RING OF CRUST is left at edges, roll off gently, using a feather touch. Cake may be assembled with both layers right side up. No glaze needed.

CLASSIC METHOD

REMOVE CAKE from oven, place upright in pan on cooling rack. Let cool in pan 5 to 10 minutes. Run knife around edges before turning out of pan.

TURN CAKE OUT of pan on towel-covered rack (to prevent marks). Quickly, turn upright on first rack again to cool. If too dome-shaped, chill, trim top.

PLACE BOTTOM LAYER right-side up on cardboard base. Fill to ⅛ inch from edge to prevent oozing out. For flat surface, add top layer upside-down.

TO SEAL IN CRUMBS and provide a smooth surface brush assembled cake with hot apricot glaze. Or spread on thin coat of buttercream. Dry, then ice.

1

2

BEGIN ICING SIDES FIRST, working from bottom toward top with long, even strokes, building up edges a tiny bit higher than top of cake. Icing on a turntable is strongly recommended, but if you are decorating on a serving plate, here's how to keep it neat. Put four 3″ wide strips of wax paper under cake edges before you begin to catch drips. After cake sets, pull strips out gently.

NEXT HEAP ICING ON TOP and spread it out to blend with built-up edges. Now your cake is completely covered with icing, but must be smoothed to a glossy finish and excess icing removed. The next three pictures show just how to do this.

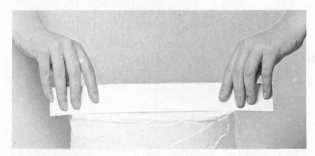

3

4

SMOOTH TOP TWO WAYS. Place long stiff cardboard strip across top, holding both ends at slight angle as in upper picture. Pull straight across cake top, bringing the surplus icing toward you. Or place your spatula flat on cake top, halfway across as in lower picture. Press down lightly, holding spatula still and revolve turntable. For even smoother look, dip spatulas in hot water first.

SMOOTH SIDES LAST. Hold spatula to side of cake with one hand and slowly spin turntable with other hand. Or turn cake plate slowly around with your other hand if not using turntable. Again, for a super-smooth finish, dip spatula in hot water. For two quick, professional ways to ice display dummies, see the following page.

How to Ice a Display Dummy

This requires a slightly different technique, as cake display dummies are made of styrofoam and are very lightweight. There are two basic methods you can use, both equally effective.

ICING ON A TURNTABLE

To ANCHOR DUMMY, first pipe three dots of icing directly on turntable and press a square of waxed paper on dots to secure it. Then pipe three more dots of icing on top of waxed paper to hold dummy.

IMMEDIATELY, press cake dummy down onto icing dots, making sure it is well-centered on turntable. Let icing set, then test. Be certain dummy is securely fastened to turntable before you begin to ice it.

ICE SIDES FIRST. Spread icing on cake sides, then, holding spatula motionless against side with one hand, revolve the turntable with other hand. Dip spatula in hot water for a sleek, smooth finish.

ICE TOP LAST. Swirl icing on top, then draw cardboard strip across top, holding with both hands as shown on page 45. Or lay spatula flat halfway across top and hold motionless while you revolve turntable.

ICING DUMMY HELD ON FORK

INSERT STURDY FORK into bottom of dummy as shown and use it as a kind of handle. You can then ice the dummy holding it up in the air.

ICE TOP FIRST. Swirl icing on top, place spatula flat halfway across top and hold motionless, pressing down slightly, while you revolve dummy on fork. Dip spatula in hot water first for smoother look.

ICE SIDES LAST. Spread icing on sides, turning dummy as you do. Then hold spatula flat against side while you revolve dummy on fork. Do just a portion at a time if necessary, but finish all before icing dries.

To REMOVE FORK. Brace half of dummy on edge of table. Steady other half with one hand, pull out fork with your other hand.

PINK ROSE WEDDING CAKE

Shining fondant icing gives this cake its rosy glow! Serves 150. To make it, first pipe 75 roses in 3 sizes with tubes 101, 102 and 104. Then bake 3 tiers, 14″ x 4″, 10″ x 3½″ and 6″ x 3″ round, coat with fondant as shown on page 43. Assemble, edge base of tiers with shells, using tubes 16, 14 and 13 from bottom to top. Circle separator plate with tube 14 reverse shells. Position roses, add tube 65 leaves.

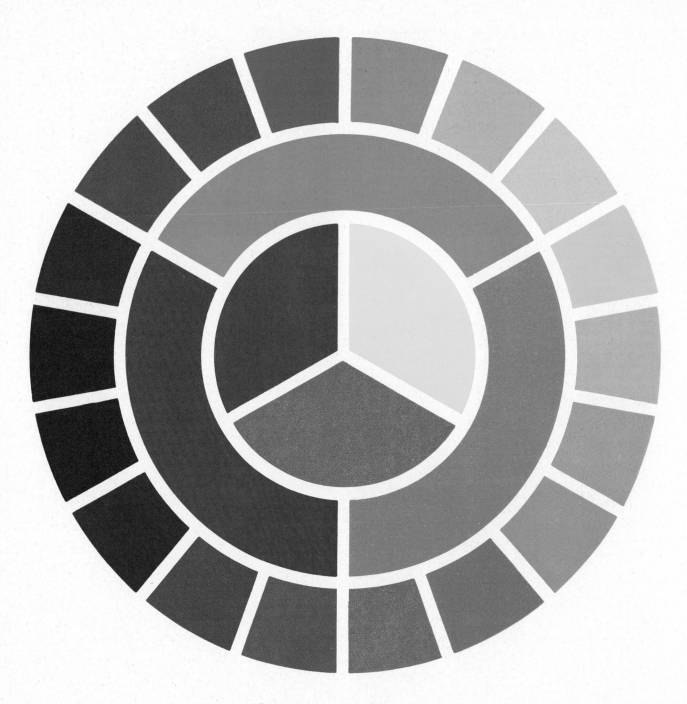

The Decorator's Color Wheel

In the center are the 3 primary colors—red, yellow and blue. From these, all others can be made.

In the inner ring are secondary colors—orange, green and violet, made by mixing equal amounts of primary colors. Mix red and yellow for orange, yellow and blue for green, red and blue for violet.

In the outer ring are tertiary colors—achieved by mixing varying amounts of one primary color with the adjacent primary. Mix a large amount of red with a small amount of blue and you will get a red-violet. Do the opposite for a blue-violet. Increase or decrease amounts for many hues in between.

All colors on the wheel are shown at their fullest intensity or brightness. And notice that some are naturally deeper, or have more value, than others. Yellow has the least value, or is the lightest of the primary colors. The addition of white to a color produces a tint, decreasing both its intensity and value.

A primary and a secondary color directly opposite each other on the wheel are called "complementary". Examples: red and green, blue and orange, yellow and violet.

CHAPTER THREE

The Techniques of Color

Color is the magic touch that makes all the difference in everything we see. The eye actually sees *only* color. The glory of a garden, the appeal of a painting, the attractiveness of a costume depends to a large extent upon its colors. This is especially true of the edible art works of decorators.

The most important thing a decorator should remember about color is not to be afraid of it. A few simple rules and a little experimenting will help you achieve harmonious color schemes for your cakes.

MONOCHROMATIC CAKES

The simplest color scheme is monochromatic—that is, decoration in all white or a single, pale color.

The classic all-white wedding cake is a beautiful example. Just as attractive are cakes in a single pastel—pink, yellow, green. Monochromatic cakes should be decorated with borders and trim quite heavy and sculptural, so the play of light and shadow will give interest.

If you are in a hurry to decorate a cake, or are in doubt as to the correct color scheme to use, the monochromatic approach is a beautiful time-saver.

LEARN BY OBSERVATION

The best way to understand color is by close observation. Look carefully at all the objects around you. Observe colors pleasing to you, and those less pleasing. A pink package with scarlet lettering. Brilliant zinnias in a yellow bowl. A pale blue dress belted in kelly green. A lime green chair holding a turquoise cushion. The subtle colors of a worn oriental rug. These observations will expand your awareness.

AN EASY WAY TO EXPERIMENT

All of this observation can be used to determine color schemes for cakes. Since the material for decorating is icing, make a batch of boiled icing and prepare for an hour or two of pure pleasure. The short time you spend will be enormously useful to you at other times when you must decorate quickly and wish to be assured of a beautiful color scheme.

Get out some white cake circles, or white cardboard, and jars of paste colors. You will need only three: the primaries . . . lemon yellow, sky blue and red. Tint small amounts of the icing in these three colors, using as much color as possible. With a spatula, place a dab of each next to each other on the white board. The effect is gay, joyful, childlike.

Add white to each color and place on another side of the board. Now you are combining pastels. The effect is much daintier and very pretty.

Make secondary colors by mixing red with yellow, yellow with blue and blue with red, achieving orange, green and violet. Observe their effect on the white background. Add white to make new tints, and play them one against the other. You will find some combinations very pleasing to you—and others not as attractive.

Now match up complementary colors—red with green, yellow with violet, blue with orange. These are strong and exciting combinations.

Mix close, or analogous, tints. Add light blue to pink and make lavender. Add yellow to pink and make peach. Put all three tints next to each other— lavender, pink and peach. A soft, feminine scheme, very closely related, very pretty.

Save the color combinations you like best. They will be very helpful to you in future decorating.

Easy One-Color, or Color-Plus-White Schemes

A beautiful, tried and true, color plan for cakes is to use one color in varied intensities. It's like running up a scale on a piano from low to high. Just as lovely, just as successful, is to use one color in contrast with white. Here are some pretty examples.

The heart cake (1) presents pinks, from palest to deepest, for a look that's dramatic, yet feminine and appealing. The stylized flower cake (2) is in just one color, golden yellow, beautifully set off by dramatic designs in bright white. The green cake (3) shows how effective subtle tints of the same pastel can be. And the daisy cake (4) displays a cheerful mix of pale and bright yellow, accented by white. The green leaves are such a natural part of the flowers that here they become, in terms of color, almost a neutral.

HOW COLOR CHANGES THE MOOD

These "Hearts and Flowers" cakes illustrate what a difference color can make, by showing a single Color Flow design in three brilliant color schemes. At top, bright pink, gold and lime give it a sweet, feminine look. At center, primary colors, yellow, deep pink and blue, make it seem young and exciting. And at lower right, lime with touches of lavender and apricot give it a very delicate, "art nouveau" air. All three designs are set off by pastel cakes. Displaying colors on a pale, neutral background is one of the most effective ways to use them. To decorate the cake, use a pattern and Color Flow directions in Chapter Fourteen. Use tube 16 rosettes, tube 2 dots and string. Attach the heart part of design first, on dots of icing, then attach the flower frame above heart with more icing.

Analogous or Closely Related Colors

Some of the subtlest, prettiest cakes are decorated in analogous, or closely related colors. These are very easy schemes to plan, and almost always successful. Analogous colors are close to each other on the color wheel—either side by side or going from the center of the wheel to its outer bands.

This garlanded tier cake is a perfect example of an analogous color scheme. Its plan is red to yellow, each color being mixed with white to a dainty tint. The three tiers are iced in tints of pink, peach (achieved by mixing pink with a little yellow) and yellow. The drop flower garlands on each tier reiterate and strengthen the closely related color scheme.

The pink base tier has garlands of lavender (pink mixed with blue), pink (red mixed with white), and peach-pink (pink mixed with a little yellow) drop flowers. The peach middle tier is trimmed with peach, pink and yellow flowers. The flowers on the yellow top tier are peach, yellow and yellow-green. All the flowers are of varying intensity, having been mixed with varying amounts of white. Each tier can stand alone as an example of a related color scheme —with the three together covering nearly half of the entire color wheel.

THE TWO CAKES BELOW show other variations of closely related color schemes. The "love" cake combines red-orange, pink (a tint of red) and red-violet (red combined with blue). The "good luck" cake is decorated in varied blue-to-green hues. The aqua (green-blue) ribbon twines through green letters on a paler green. Both cakes are iced in white

Decorating in Complementary Colors

The color directly opposite a primary color on the color wheel is its complement. Thus the complement of red is green; the complement of blue, orange; and of yellow, violet. Complementary colors are direct opposites and produce strong and exciting effects when used together. A subtle variation of a complementary color results from the use of the secondary color with the two adjacent tertiary colors opposite it—green combined with red-orange and red-violet; orange with blue-green and blue-violet; and yellow with red- and blue-violet.

FULL INTENSITY COMPLEMENTS

Since these colors are so strong and exciting, they present a challenge to the decorator. The holly cake (1) shows red and green at their fullest intensities played against a white background. Each color makes the other look brighter. The white background makes each appear at its most vivid state and provides a neutral background.

A workable rule for using strong complementary colors is: use both at equal, or near-equal, intensity. Pastel green appears weak against brilliant red. A second workable guideline is: pose the complements only against white or a neutral pale tint.

COMPLEMENTARY TINTS

When complementary colors are reduced in intensity by the addition of white their quality becomes pretty, rather than exciting.

In CAKE 2, pink (a tint of red) is combined with pastel green (a tint of full green). The effect is sweetly feminine. Here the pink and green are used in almost equal amounts or areas; but a pale green cake with just a touch of pink, or a pink cake trimmed with just green borders at top, side and base would be equally effective

In CAKE 3, orange and blue are used, again each color is reduced to a tint by adding white. The effect is very pleasing. If orange and blue were used at full intensity, the effect might be garish and much less appetizing. White borders give definition to the tiers.

From these two examples we can observe that tints of complementary colors are easy to use and are very effective. A white or neutral background is not needed to set off the tints. And, most important, colors that might appear overly bright and unappetizing become very acceptable when each is reduced to a tint.

53

Color Schemes Inspired by Nature

Many decorators turn first to nature in planning their color schemes—and certainly there is no better guide to follow.

In CAKE 1, the dainty, realistic tints of the flowers are as close as possible to those of the real flowers. Each is pastel, none is stronger than another.

In CAKE 2, the colors of the grapes and apples are again true to nature. Here the hues are richer and more subtle. A pale gold background sets them off.

CAKE 3 poses fruits in the most intense, yet natural, hues imaginable, against a snow-white background.

In each cake, the colors are varied, but in each they are at equal, or near-equal, intensity. None overwhelms another. We may gain still another guideline from them: when following nature's colors, keep them at equal or near-equal intensity. Pastels with pastels, brights with brights, rich colors with those equally rich. And observe that a neutral or pale background displays bright or rich colors at their best.

Three or More Colors Give Interest

There are times when every decorator likes to use colors with abandon—and certainly a variety of colors can produce a very exciting cake. Combining many colors on a cake takes a little more planning and experimenting, but it is a happy challenge to a decorator. The four cakes on the facing page are examples of the successful use of many colors.

CAKE 1 on page 55 displays the coat-of-arms of Canada in vivid hues of red, green, gold and blue.

CAKE 2 is a bright pink Noah's Ark with a deck-load of turquoise, yellow and orange animals—some outlined in green. These colors are never seen in nature, but here they combine for a happy, young effect.

ON CAKE 3, a yellow cub clings to a gold-and-scarlet mother bear, against a pink-and-orange cake. Turquoise and red-violet fishes swim in a lime-green sea on Cake 4. Colors in both cakes are bright and very intense.

Cakes 2, 3 and 4 make a point to remember: never be afraid to be original. Dream up your own interesting color effects. Put bright blue petunias on lime-green lattice. Try violet roses tied with bright aqua ribbons. Decorating is fun, and color makes it much more fun.

To assure harmony, however, use the guideline previously given: keep all color trim on a cake at equal, or near-equal, intensity. And when in doubt as to color combinations, experiment first with dabs of tinted icing on cardboard.

Some Colors are not Appropriate

Color is the most important and immediate component in the appearance of a beautiful cake, but one fact should be always remembered. Cakes are made to be eaten. Make them look as delicious as they taste. A few colors do not appear edible, so they should be used on cakes with great care and discretion. Bright blue or deep violet are not appetizing, so consider using their tints—pastel blue or lavender—when coloring icing for a large area. Black and grey do not appeal to the appetite either, so use them seldom if at all. Even Color Flow outlines look cleaner and more attractive when done in a deep color rather than black.

ANOTHER GUIDELINE

It's important to keep all colors used in decorating fresh and clean-looking. Do not mix a color with another color opposite, or far away from it, on the color wheel. Examples: green icing mixed with even a little red will become muddy. If you add yellow to violet icing the resulting color will be murky and unattractive.

However, you can mix colors close to each other on the color wheel very successfully. Add a little yellow to a bowl of pink icing and you will obtain a very pretty apricot color, as you will see on the next page. Mix a drop of blue color into green icing for an interesting aqua color.

But the last word on color is—enjoy it! Experiment, observe, form your own tastes, and use color lavishly for happy effects.

While theoretically all colors can be mixed from the three basic primaries, decorators prefer to have an assortment of paste or liquid colors for convenience and speed in tinting icings. The next pages give you detailed methods for tinting icing and for special coloring techniques.

55

How to Tint the Icing

To MIX IN A SINGLE COLOR. Begin with a single drop of liquid food coloring and mix in thoroughly before adding more. And have icing a tiny bit stiffer than you need it, as liquid color may thin it slightly.

To MIX IN MORE THAN ONE COLOR. Add one of the colors to icing first, blend in, then add the other. If you want peach, for example, add red until icing is pink, then add yellow until you reach peach.

Special Coloring Techniques

SPATULA METHOD

FOR A TWO-TONED EFFECT. First put a one-inch strip of tinted icing down to the "point" of your decorating cone with spatula. Fill cone with white icing.

Flower pipes out with tinted petal tips, scroll emerges with tinted edges, as in beautiful "Rose Rhapsody" cake from Party Cake Portfolio, page 36.

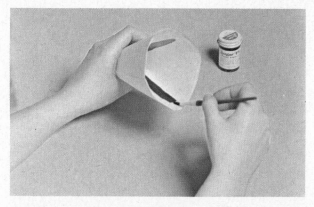

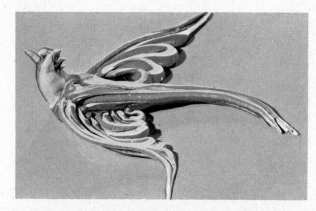

BRUSH STRIPING. For deep multi-colors! This original Wilton method is simple to do. Just brush two or three ⅛" wide vertical stripes of paste color into cone right out of the jar. Fill rest of cone with white or tinted icing. For the brilliant bird in flight above, the decorating cone was striped red and green, and the cone filled with yellow icing. The bird piped out of the tube brightly striped.

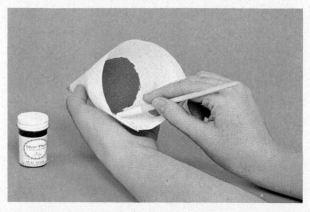

DEEP COLOR. To achieve a deep, rich color—the kind decorators once tried for in vain—use Wilton's special technique. Brush paste color right out of the jar all around entire inside surface of decorating cone. Fill cone with icing in deepest possible tone of same color. The result—deep, deep color such as the red of the poinsettias and the green of the leaves in this pretty Christmas cake.

SPRAY METHODS

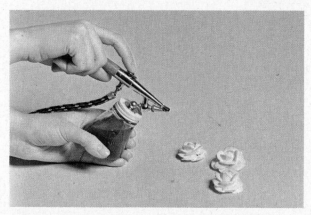

SPRAYING FLOWERS and other decorations. Put water tinted with liquid food color, pale or deep, into atomizer. Spray completely dry icing flower or decoration, then dry thoroughly again before placing.

FOR STENCIL SPRAYING. Place stencil on cake top. Color water as deeply as possible, then spray a fine mist for just an instant. Lift stencil off carefully. Design will appear on cake top.

CHAPTER 4

The Decorating Cone
and How to Make It

To hold your decorating icing and tubes, two basic kinds of decorating cones are recommended: parchment paper cones you roll yourself, or ready-made bags of plastic or acrylic-coated polyester.

The greatest advantage of ready-made bags is that, with them, you can use a coupler that permits you to change tubes without refilling bag. A coupler is a little plastic nozzle that drops into the bag at the point where the tube usually goes. Decorating tubes fit right on it and a nut that comes with it twists on to keep tubes securely in place. Also, since you can obtain ready-made bags in extra-large sizes, a coupler could permit you to decorate most of a one-color cake with a single bag of icing!

For most decorating purposes however, the most versatile cones are those you make yourself of parchment paper. They are sanitary and disposable and of course you never need to wash them. You can make as many as you want at very little cost and in small or large sizes. You can also prepare separate ones for every color of icing and have them all filled and ready before you start on your cake.

Beginners sometimes fear that parchment cones will be difficult to make. Not so! You can learn to twirl a perfect one in a few minutes. Parchment paper is available in pre-cut triangles or 9-inch wide rolls. The following pages will show you how to fashion decorating cones from both.

HOW TO MAKE A DECORATING CONE
FROM A PARCHMENT TRIANGLE

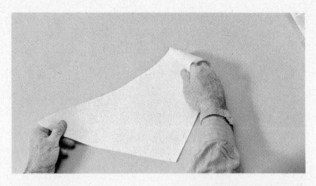

1. Lay flat with longest side at top.

2. With right hand palm up, grasp right-hand corner between thumb and forefingers and then turn corner inward.

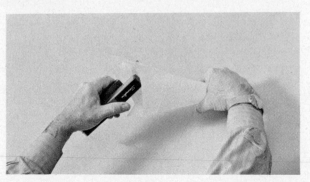

3. Roll right hand toward center, *drawing right hand corner toward you as you roll* and a cone shape will form.

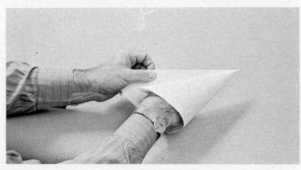

4. Then twirl left hand corner all the way around cone and move it back and forth until point of cone is needle sharp. (Bringing all three corners of the triangle together at top of cone is a good way to assure a sharper point.)

5. Fold top in or staple to secure if you wish.

HOW TO MAKE A DECORATING CONE
FROM A PARCHMENT RECTANGLE

A decorating cone may also be constructed from a 9″ x 17″ inch rectangle of parchment paper, cut from a standard 9-inch wide roll. This is just as easy to roll as the triangle once you get the knack of it. And to make smaller size decorating cones (for tube writing or tiny trims), cut a 9″ x 17″ rectangle in half. (See facing page for smaller decorating cone construction.)

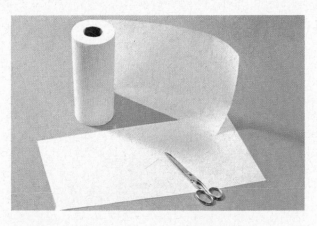

1. Take a 9-inch roll of parchment paper, cut off sheet about 17 inches long. Lay flat on work surface as shown in corresponding picture.

2. With right hand palm up, grasp right top corner of paper between thumb and forefinger and turn inward as shown (thumb must touch back of paper). At same time, hold left top corner of paper with left thumb and forefinger (thumb must touch front of paper).

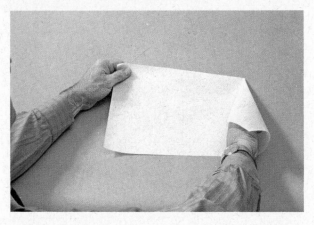

3. Now, with your hands in the correct position, roll your right hand inward, drawing right corner toward you until you reach the center of the parchment rectangle. This will initiate the cone shape that you will complete in the next step.

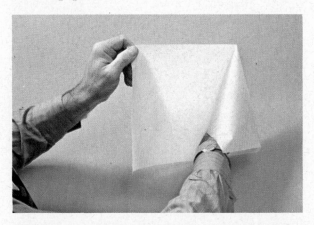

4. Keeping your right hand touching the center of the rectangle, twirl your left hand (still holding left edge of paper) around cone, and move it back and forth until point is needle-sharp.

5. Make sure left thumb and forefinger end up at top of cone, grasping top edges to secure cone shape. Fold in top or staple to secure.

HOW TO MAKE A SMALLER CONE FROM A HALF-RECTANGLE

1. A small cone for tube writing or adding tiny trims can be made from half a parchment rectangle. Cut a 9 x 17 inch length from a parchment paper roll, then cut in half diagonally as shown.

2. Use technique similar to that given for triangle on page 59, but start with top right corner on short side of this triangle.

3. Tuck long "tail" that extends from top inside cone before filling and folding down.

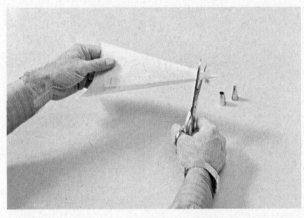 

HOW TO FILL YOUR DECORATING CONE WITH ICING

1. Hold completed cone at top with fingers inside, thumb outside. Cut off tip about ½ to ¾ inch from end, depending on size of tube. (Be cautious—start small and trim more if needed.) Drop tube into the decorating cone and you're ready to add icing.

2. Take some icing on a small, flexible spatula and fill cone. (Not over ¾ full or icing may back out top when cone is squeezed.) To remove icing from spatula inside cone, press against fingers holding cone on outside.

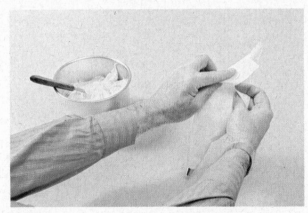 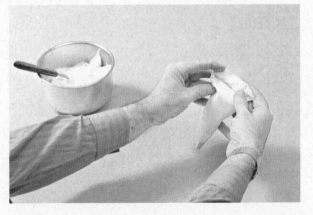

3. After cone is filled, use "diaper fold" shown to close top. It's important that you leave no openings through which icing can back out as you squeeze the decorating cone to pipe beautiful trims.

4. Continue folding cone down as you use up icing. If you are using several colors of buttercream (not royal or boiled icing), fill all cones for cake before you decorate.

CHAPTER FIVE
The ABC's of Decorating

Every art or craft, no matter how much creativity it allows, has certain cardinal rules that must be observed. So it is with cake decorating. Use the ABC's that follow as your guide, practice patiently, and you will have no trouble learning to decorate. Make a batch of practice icing and do the exercises in this chapter on the back of a cake pan or cookie sheet. Then do them again, and again.

The Decorator's Alphabet

A. HAVE ICING AT PROPER CONSISTENCY. Not too stiff or you will have trouble squeezing it through the decorating tube. Not too soft, or your designs will turn into blobs. The recipes given in Chapter Two will produce icings of medium consistency, perfect for these first practice exercises. Directions will be given on how to adjust icings for other designs as they come up.

B. HOLD CONE AT THE CORRECT ANGLE. So important, the proper angle is designated with every design in this chapter. For example, when you are asked to hold the cone at a 45 degree angle, this means 45 degrees to the decorating surface, whether that is on top or at the sides of the cake. For side and base of cake, it is vital to keep borders at *eye level*, even if you must raise the cake or (in the case of a tier cake), stand on a stool yourself in order that you may accomplish this.

C. LEARN TO CONTROL YOUR PRESSURE. First, hold the cone correctly. Place it in your right hand with thumb at top, fingers at top side. (See pictures below.) Use your *right hand only* to press out icing, and first two fingers of your left hand to guide or steady the cone. Now, press the cone gently until the icing flows out at a speed you feel you can control. The idea is to maintain a steady, even flow of icing while you move the cone in a free and easy glide across the surface. And to be able to stop pressure completely and break off cleanly, when necessary, so you can finish a design without pulling up points or curling ends. Practice will soon give you the correct feel of it.

Basic positions of the cone

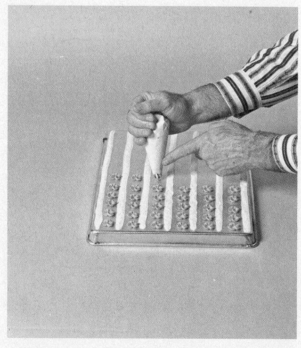

1. PERPENDICULAR. For drop flowers, dots, stars or rosettes, you should hold the cone straight up and perpendicular to your work surface. (This allows the icing to mound up as you press it into instant flowers or designs.)

2. FLAT AS POSSIBLE. For drawing lines or writing script, turn your hand almost palm up so that cone lies nearly parallel with surface. Touch surface lightly, pressing icing out evenly as you go.

3. MOST TOP BORDERS. A 45 degree angle lets you hold the cone at a comfortable slant while you press out shells, scrolls and other designs on the top or at top edge of the cake. It also puts the border on at a slight angle to cover cake edges more evenly.

4. BOTTOM BORDERS. The cone is held at a 45 degree angle for bottom borders, also. This causes the border to lie at a slight slant and helps to give the cake a more finished appearance.

5. SIDE BORDERS. You'll get better control when piping side borders and also you'll be able to obtain a clearer view of what you're doing, if you angle the cone slightly to the right as you move it along.

6. STRINGWORK. Hold the cone perpendicular to the surface. Point it straight at the cake and pull toward you to let the string drop. This is the correct hold also for piping stars, dots, rosettes and drop flowers on the side of your cake.

Practicing Pressure Control

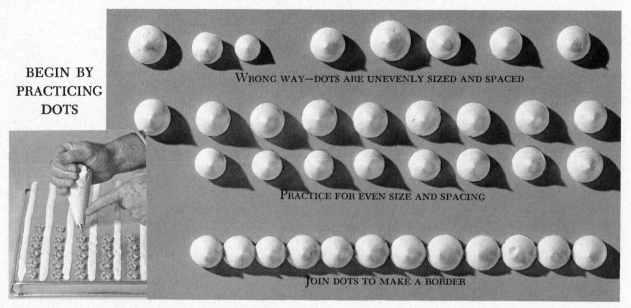

BEGIN BY PRACTICING DOTS

WRONG WAY—DOTS ARE UNEVENLY SIZED AND SPACED

PRACTICE FOR EVEN SIZE AND SPACING

JOIN DOTS TO MAKE A BORDER

Make a cone, drop in tube 6 and fill with practice icing (stiffened just a tiny bit with confectioners sugar). Hold cone straight up, touch tube lightly to surface and hold it there. Squeeze with a steady, even pressure and icing will begin to mound. Now—very important—raise tube with icing as it mounds, keeping tip buried in icing. Then stop pressure completely and take away tube, level with top of dot, breaking away to the right. If dots still have points or tails, smooth back to roundness with a damp finger and a *very* light touch.

CIRCULAR MOTION MAKES ROSETTES

YOUR FIRST ATTEMPTS MAY BE UNEVEN

TRY TO SHAPE SMOOTHLY, SPACE EVENLY

JOIN FOR A NEAT BORDER

Drop tube 19 into your cone and fill with medium consistency icing. Hold cone straight up, just above the surface. Apply gentle pressure, let icing build up, make a short swirly movement, then stop pressure and move away, breaking off cleanly.

As you can see, the size of the rosette depends as much upon the amount of pressure you apply, as upon the tube you use. When joining rosettes in a border, be sure to make them all of uniform size to give the border a neat even appearance.

The rosette is another basic shape worth perfecting, as it makes an effective border.

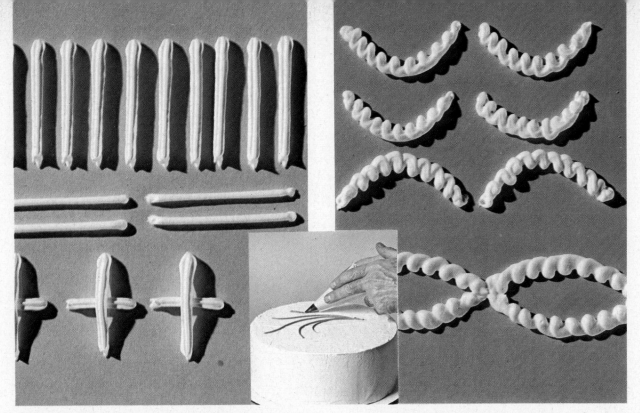

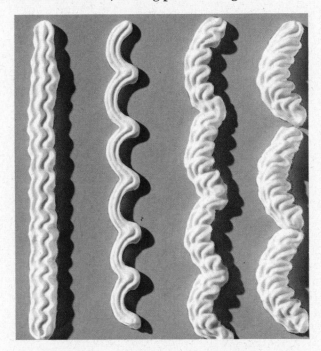

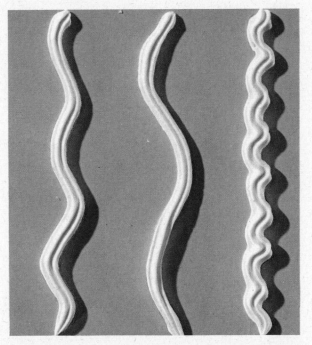

STRAIGHT LINES. Use tube 14, medium consistency icing and hand position shown above. Touch tube lightly to surface and draw it along, pressing out icing evenly as you go. Try to make all lines same size and thickness, with ends cut off neatly. Do all from side to side, turning pan to change directions.

CURVED LINES. Using tube 3, medium consistency icing and the hand position shown above, try some curves. Touch surface and move hand slowly down, then up (adding a circular motion for a pretty effect). Practice, then turn curve over by moving hand up, then down. Join curves for a border.

ZIGZAG EFFECTS. With tube 14 and hand position above, touch tube to surface and draw along as for straight line. But instead, make very short back-and-forth motions to create a straight line of tiny zigzags. Then do wider zigzags, joined and separated scallops, using an "e" motion for the last two.

LONG SWEEPING CURVES. Again use tube 14 and hand position above. Touch tube to surface and draw it along, moving your hand up and down for long, sweeping curves. Strive for uniform thickness and even spacing of curves as you go. Try some shorter curves, too, to improve your control.

65

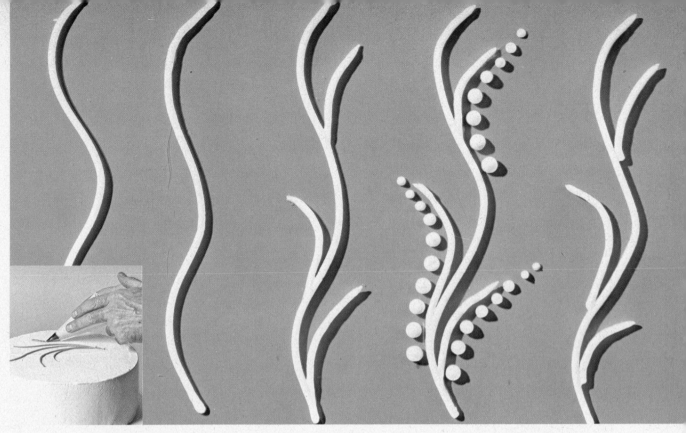

TURN CURVES INTO VINES. Continue with tube 3, hand position shown above. Move along, making low, sweeping, but uniform curves to effect the graceful appearance of branches. Then, with a much lighter pressure, pipe small curves to simulate branches as shown. To blend branches into vines smoothly, begin branches *at* vines and draw *away* from them. Add a few dots with tube 3 at tips of branches and you've an effective and decorative side border accent for a cake of any size. (Vine pictured at above right shows how *not* to join branches.)

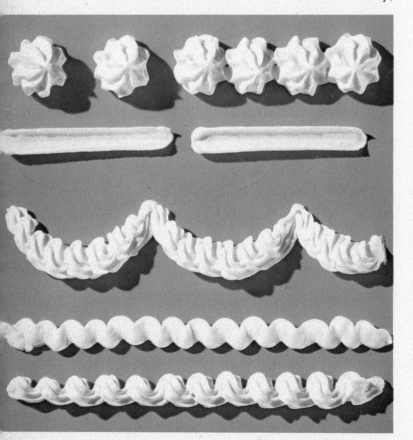

EXPERIMENT WITH OTHER TUBES

Now that you have the feel of your decorating cone, try a few of your other tubes. Using the control you've learned, press out some stars with tube 21, a concave line with tube 79, graceful scallops with tube 14. And see the change that occurs when you do a zigzag motion first with tube 101s, then with tube 14. We think you'll be pleased with the control you've already gained. And you will also see how the control you acquire using one kind of tube carries over to every other tube you try. A lighter pressure will continually produce a finer icing design, a heavier pressure a more pronounced icing trim. And regardless of the tube size a smooth, even pressure, whether light or heavy, is the most important step in producing beautiful decorating effects. With this in mind, you can attempt any design you desire.

CONTROLLING THE SHELL

Now, try that most essential of all cake decorations —the shell. This simple, pure and beautiful design borders more cakes than any other. To pipe it perfectly, first fit your cone with tube 22 and use position 3 or 4 on page 63. Touch surface lightly and press heavily, hesitating long enough to let shell build up and fan out. As it does, lift tube just enough to go along with icing. Then relax pressure as you pull hand down sharply and draw across surface to bring shell to a point. Finally, stop pressure and pull away. Pipe the next shell on tail of first and so on. Once you can pipe a shell, try some curved in different directions, starting as before, then circling left or right before bringing to a point. An alternating row becomes the reverse shell border. Three together become the lovely fleur-de-lis.

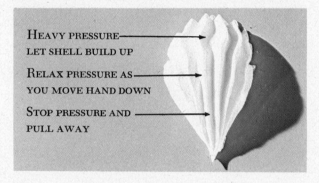

HEAVY PRESSURE—LET SHELL BUILD UP

RELAX PRESSURE AS YOU MOVE HAND DOWN

STOP PRESSURE AND PULL AWAY

SHAPING THE GARLAND

Use tube 14 and the same position for the shell. Touch tube lightly to surface and press gently at first, moving tube up and down in very close zigzag fashion to describe garland shape. Build up pressure as you move toward center and relax pressure as you move out to end. Then stop pressure and move away. For the scalloped garland shown, use a tight zigzag motion and a steady, even pressure, moving down, then up to form a shallow curve. For half garland, drop a string guideline first, then "fill in" keeping top straight as shown.

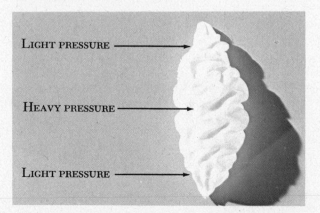

LIGHT PRESSURE

HEAVY PRESSURE

LIGHT PRESSURE

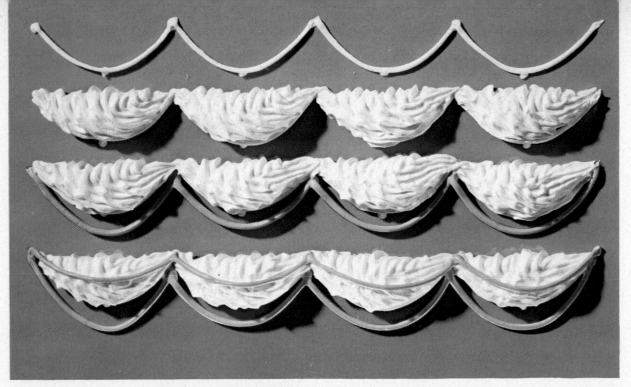

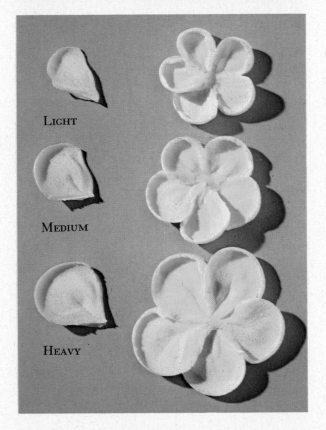

Light

Medium

Heavy

THE SWING OF STRINGWORK

Graceful stringwork adds a dramatic touch to so many borders. It looks difficult, but it is quite easy to do, once you know the secret. To begin with, your icing must be exactly right. Use royal or boiled, slightly thinned so it will flow easily out of the tube, but firm enough, so it will hold together. Prop your practice pan upright, use tube 3 and hand position shown at left.

Touch tube to surface to attach icing, then pull straight away from surface. Let icing drop down easily, move on about 1½ inches and touch surface to attach icing again. *Important:* do not move tube *down* with string. Hold tube *up* and let string *drop by itself.* For second row, touch tube under first row to attach icing and begin again. For an attractive border, do a row of garlands, then drape contrast stringwork under and over.

WHAT PRESSURE CAN DO

The same tube can produce its design in several different sizes, depending entirely upon how much pressure you apply on your decorating cone. For example, the same 104 petal tube produced all three of the flowers at left—the first with light pressure, the second with medium pressure, the third with heavy pressure. The deciding factor is not only the size of the tube, but how well you can control your pressure on the decorating cone.

SHELLS AROUND THE "ROSES". A cake top design you should now be able to do. Use tube 19 to pipe circle of shells and row of rosettes, 3 for stems. Center contrast dots in rosettes for "stamens".

LOTS OF DOTS. Another cake top design to practice. Happy young border can be done with a single tube 9. Tint icing in three contrasting colors and pipe alternating color of dots all around as shown.

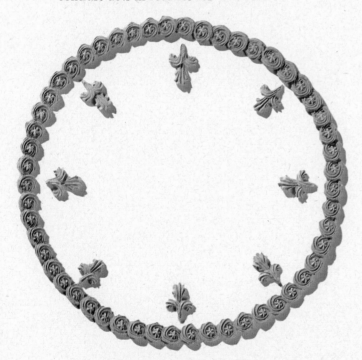

RING OF ROSETTES. Very elegant border, yet it couldn't be easier to do. Just use tube 16 to pipe rosettes all around edge of cake top and to crown each rosette with a star. Do eight fleur-de-lis inside circle with tube 14.

RIBBON-GO-ROUND. Graceful topping for any cake—takes just two tubes. Do ribbon swags all around edge with petal tube 104. Do dots at each point inside with tube 4 and your border is complete!

A Happy Portfolio of Cakes for Children

Cakes are fun to make for anyone, but a special pleasure comes from decorating cakes for children! From tots to teens, every youngster loves cake, but when a cake is especially decorated just for him, it's an exciting event!

In this portfolio you'll find a collection of cakes designed to appeal to children of all ages—from babies to young boys and girls to teenagers. And each cake is sure to be a treat for you as well as the youngsters!

ABC CAKE all sweetened with cookies cut from your favorite cookie dough recipe. Use alphabet and heart cutters and ice in pastel Color Flow, outlining and trimming the letters with tube 2.

To decorate the 6″ x 3″ and 10″ x 4″ cakes, first pipe base bulb borders using tube 5 for the small tier and tube 12 for the larger tier. Then frame the bulb border on 10″ tier with tube 2 strings, first piping pink icing under one bulb and curving up over the next and so on around the cake. In the same manner pipe blue strings under and over the opposite edges of all the the bulbs thus completing the border's frame. Next pipe all the string side borders with tube 3 and edge both tier tops with shells using tube 14 for the 6″ tier and tube 16 for the base tier. Prop ABC cookies with toothpicks

and attach heart cookies to cake sides with icing. For adorable finishing touches, trim bassinet with tube 1 flowers and wheel accents, fill with candy.

SMOOTH SHINY FONDANT frosts this lovable cake for baby! To make fondant icing refer to Chapter Two; then place 6″ x 4″ and 10″ x 4″ cakes on a wire rack, heat pastel pink fondant to pouring consistency and cover cakes. When icing has set, position cakes and edge bases with bulb borders using tube 9 for 10″ and tube 7 for the 6″ cake. Next figure-pipe rattles with tube 9 and maximum pressure for the large balls, minimum pressure for the small balls. Pipe tube 2 rattle handles, tube 1 bows and you've a cake as sweet as baby himself!

Both cakes serve 20.

DECORATE A GAY PONY CAKE!

A party pony turns a cake into an enchanting treat for children. The cake trims are all made with star tubes which makes the decorating fun and very easy to do!

Make the pony and all of the side "pony tail" decorations first. Just tape wax paper over the appropriate patterns, outline "tail" designs with tube 3 and fill in with tube 15 royal icing stars. Remember to pipe all the stars tightly together so that when the icing is dry you can easily peel the designs off the wax paper and place them on the cake.

The cake, an 8″ x 3″ square, is iced white. When the pony design is dry, it's attached to the cake top with icing. The pony tail decorations are then attached to the sides of the cake at all four corners. When side decorations are "glued" into position with icing, fill in the corners where designs meet with more icing stars. This will make each corner cake trim appear to be one piece. Frame the top of the cake with tube 18 yellow stars and the base with tube 16 green stars and the proud party pony is ready for serving! Serves 12.

COLOR FLOW CIRCUS CLOWNS JUMP FOR JOY!

Truly eye-catching decorations, Color Flow trims are especially nice for busy decorators because they can be made in advance to save time on cake decorating day. Here a quartet of Color Flow clowns dance around a cake as gay as a circus!

To decorate, make circus clowns using appropriate Color Flow pattern and instructions found in Chapter Fourteen. (Note: after flowing in clown figures, allow to dry very thoroughly. Then turn over and flow in other sides, so clowns appear complete on both sides.) In addition to clowns, make

Color Flow disks for side trims and candle bases.

When Color Flow trims are dry, ice and position a 10″ x 4″ square cake on a foil-covered board and edge base with tube 19 rosettes, top with tube 16 rosettes. To position clowns, first pipe a tube 9 icing ball over the base border, then attach Color Flow clown to cake side with icing. Position Color Flow circles on cake sides with icing, then pipe tube 16 rosettes on cake top circles, push in candles while rosettes are wet and set them aglow! Cake serves 20.

CAKES THAT MAKE THE PARTY

THE RAG DOLL. A little girl's favorite toy turns into a cake with a pan and one cake mix. To decorate, first outline the different color parts of the doll with tube 3 and white icing. Then pipe tube 16 icing stars between the outlines. Start with the flesh-color face and hands, then the green dress and booties, next the apron and stockings. Pipe the doll's golden locks and red "c" motion apron print with tube 3. Edge the stockings and sleeves with tube 16 red icing stars. Pipe ruffled pantaloons, collar and cuffs with tube 104.

For the doll face, pipe tube 9 eyes, tube 12 cheeks and flatten with a damp finger. Pipe a tube 3 smile and collar and bootie bows. Serves 12.

THE COWBOY, a young boy's favorite hero right out of the wild west! To start make cookies and cactus. Roll out your favorite cookie dough and shape ponies with cookie cutters. Outline "spots" with white softened Color Flow icing, then flow white Color Flow icing around spots to cover cookie. Dry, fill in spots with brown Color Flow icing; then outline ponies and add manes and eyes with tube 3. For cactus, insert a soda straw, (cut to the length you wish the cactus to be), about ¾ of the way up through tube 1E and a decorating bag of green icing. Squeeze bag as you pull out iced "cactus" straw. Repeat procedure using thin wires and tubes 32 and 17 for cactus sprouts. Stick all cactus pieces in styrofoam to dry, then attach sprouts to main cactus with icing. Pipe tube 2 cactus "needles" and once again set to dry.

Ice the 10″ x 4″ cake tan and edge top with tube 16 rope borders and base with tube 18 rope borders. Attach pony cookies and cowboy with icing, stick cactus in cake top and pipe tube 2 "grass" and birthday wishes. Cake serves 14.

NOAH'S ARK. Cut out a cargo of animals from cookie dough and bake. Frost with Color Flow icing, adding tubes 2 and 3 features. Next, shape a sugar mold house and assemble with royal icing, referring to Chapter Eighteen for directions. Decorate with tube 103 roof "shingles", edging roof ends with tube 16 zigzags.

For the cake, chill two 11″ x 15″ sheet cakes, fill and place one atop the other for a depth of about five inches. With a sharp knife and gentle sawing motion, cut cake into boat shape starting wide at the top and tapering in at the bottom. Frost, pulling spatula across cake sides to simulate "boards". Pipe a tube 7 border around cake top and overpipe with tube 16 zigzags. Secure cabin and cookies with icing and sail off to party fun. Cake serves 35.

WALT DISNEY* CHARACTER CAKES

Decorate the children's favorites and invite them to a party! Just one cake mix and a little time will produce any of these colorful cakes.

DECORATE GOOFY. Grease and flour pan and bake cake, using one cake mix. Unmold and chill. Outline all areas with tube 4. Fill in with tube 16 stars except for eye and tooth areas. When outlines have set, flow in these areas with thinned icing. Pipe nose and eye pupils with tube 10 and flatten with fingertip. Dry, then glaze with corn syrup. Cut Goofy's ear from black construction paper, about 8″ long and 2″ at widest point. Attach with icing.

OTHER FRIENDS ARE JUST AS EASY TO DECORATE! Use the same techniques as for Goofy. Each takes one cake mix, each serves 12.

Walt Disney's Goofy, Donald Duck, Pluto,
Minnie Mouse and Mickey Mouse
° © Walt Disney Productions

77

A QUARTET OF FUN-FILLED PARTY CAKES

A BEAUTIFUL BELLE is fun to make with a dome-shaped pan and one cake mix. Just bake, unmold, cool, insert a doll pick and decorate!

Pipe tube 225 drop flowers in advance and dry, referring to Chapter Nine for directions. Position cake on a ruffle-trimmed board and insert doll pick. Divide the cake skirt into sixth's and at each point pipe nine tube 104 white ruffles. Pipe another row of eight ruffles above these, then another with five, forming six ruffled triangles.

Next, use same tube to pipe pink ruffled garlands from triangle to triangle continuing up to the doll's waist. Then cover dress bodice and sleeves with tube 16 icing stars, and attach drop flowers to skirt and dress neckline with icing. Trim the flowers

with tube 65 leaves for a true party doll! Serves 12.

A BOUQUET OF ROSES. To start this flowery cake, make lots of tube 103 and 104 buttercream roses and buds and freeze until decorating time. Refer to Chapter Nine for detailed flower making directions. Next, bake a dome-shaped cake, chill and cut off about two inches of the peaked top. Place the cake on a ruffle-trimmed base cut slightly larger than cake size and frost. Now cover the cake with the pink roses and buds, attaching them with dabs of icing. Trim the flowers with tube 67 leaves, place a ribbon bow with streamers at the cake's base and celebrate! Serves 12.

A TEEPEE TREAT. Bake a dome-shaped cake and ice.

Then about 2″ from the cake top pipe tube 3 orange dots, alternating tube 3 zigzag rows of brown and orange icing above them. Again with tube 3 drop a curved string drape around the cake's top and add tube 2 dots. Sketch triangles at the cake's base with a toothpick. Outline with tube 16 red stars, fill with brown stars. Decorate door with tube 3 and more tube 16 stars. Place toothpicks (dyed with food color) in the cake's top. Serves 12.

TELEPHONE A BIRTHDAY MESSAGE. Start by making tube 102 daisies following directions in Chapter Nine. Dry thoroughly. Then bake two 9″ x 13″ cakes and cut one into 6½″ x 9″ halves and stack. Chill, then slice off front of top layer for "desk phone" shape.

Next, cut the other 9″ x 13″ cake into two 4½″ x 13″ pieces. Cut one half into a 4½″ x 9″ "receiver" and ice the other half for extra party guests. Ice phone and receiver and place on tray. Then with a toothpick, trace three circles for a dial and overpipe with tube 7. Edge both cake tops and

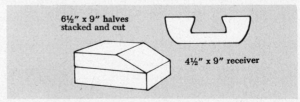

6½″ x 9″ halves stacked and cut

4½″ x 9″ receiver

bases with tube 19 shells, adding an extra string of shells on the cake tray for a phone "cord". To finish, attach flowers with icing, trim with tube 67 leaves and add plastic teen figures. Write message with tube 4. Serves 15.

CHAPTER SIX

How to do the Basic Border

Borders are the beginning of all cake artistry. If you know but a few basic designs, you can turn out cakes with a very professional look. And when you know a number of them, you can create many original effects. But borders have yet another purpose. They smooth cake edges, cover flaws and give your cake a more perfect, uniform appearance.

In this chapter, the most frequently used borders are shown, arranged from those that are easy to do, to those that require the greatest care and skill.

However, it is important to remember that any border design, no matter how complex, is just the sum of simple borders or designs. In all of the ones that follow, you will recognize the familiar shell, bulb, string and other basic designs that you have already mastered. Just practice, be patient with yourself and soon you will be able to do them all. The Classique cake below is decorated only with perfectly executed borders. (See page 248 for complete decorating directions).

Drop flower border. Very pretty, very simple to do. Just press out a row of any drop flower design—the lovely star flowers above, or any of the many-petaled varieties. (There are 21 different drop flower tubes together with examples of the flowers they produce, shown on page 17.) For this border, use tube 19 and drop flower method on page 110. Strive for a neat, uniform row.

Zigzag border. A simple design, easy to do, yet very handsome at top or base of a cake. Use tube 19, position two on page 62 and method at bottom of page 65. This tube will give you a wide, richly-ribbed border, but you can also use many other tubes for attractive zigzag effects—round tubes 1 to 12 and the open or closed star tubes. The choice is yours, the effect always lovely.

Small zigzag border. A dainty version of the larger zigzag border above. Ideal for smaller cakes, perhaps the top tier of a two-to-four tier wedding or anniversary cake. Use tube 13 for the small zigzag border shown and the same position and technique used in the large zigzag border above. Remember to keep your pressure smooth and even and side-to-side movements uniform as you go along.

Rope border. An attractive casual border, perfect for a child's western party cake. You can make the rope border in any size, but for this one, use star tube 20 and position one or two on page 63. To begin, make a shallow turned-down curve. Then tuck tube under arch of curve and do a shallow "S" curve over the first as shown. Continue this way, striving for even, uniform curves.

Flute or ruffle border. A pretty, dainty border made by using hand position two on page 62 and tube 103. Hold decorating bag, so wide end of tube touches surface, narrow end stands up and points out slightly. Use a smooth even pressure and a slight back-and-forth motion. Jiggle hand gently as you go for ruffled ribbon effect.

Standard Wilton School Borders

BASE OR TOP EDGE BORDERS

SHELL BORDER—a string of shapely shells, as perfectly turned out as any you'd see at the seashore, makes a beautiful border for any cake. You can use any of the star tubes to make the shell border, depending on the size you want it to be. The border above, intended for a larger cake requires tube 22. Follow the directions for shells on page 67. Start second shell on tail of first, continuing this way all around.

SHELL WITH FLUTE—a large and showy border, most effective at the base of a wedding cake tier. Pipe a row of shells with tube 30, then edge with a fluted flounce. To make flute, hold tube 104 with wide end touching center of one shell's tail, narrow end turned out slightly. Press out icing, maintaining an even flow and using a back-and-forth motion as you go. End at point of next shell. Repeat on each shell.

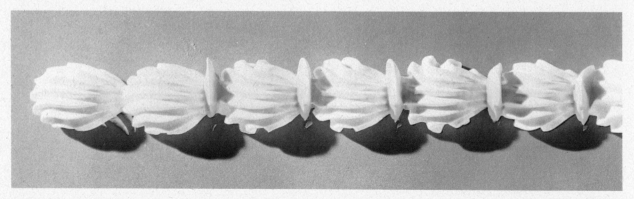

SHELL-AND-RUFFLE—a rich variation on the classic shell border. Begin with tube 30 and press out a row of regular shells. Then with tube 104 and hand position 3 on page 63, press lightly and place little ruffles between shells as shown. Very fast, yet very impressive on the cake.

REVERSE SHELL BORDER. One of the loveliest of all! Appropriate on nearly every cake, and a special favorite for wedding cakes. Follow directions on page 67, and, as with the classic shell, use the tube that best suits the size of your cake. For this puffy, deeply-ribbed reverse shell border, tube 30 was used. Shells were turned quite sharply to each side and kept close together for a richer effect.

SIDE OR TOP SURFACE BORDERS

COLONIAL SCROLL BORDER. Lavish effect for side of cake. First pipe outline of scroll around cake (first step above). Use tube 4, position three on page 63 and glide along with a light, even motion. Then go back over outline with same tube, moving out and back to form stems and creating feather effect with small circular movements.

REVERSE COLONIAL BORDER—for even more lavish side effects! Use tube 3 and the same technique as for the regular Colonial border above, except to turn every other scroll up instead of down. And there is one other difference. When you do the upturned scroll, make the circular feathering movement in a clockwise direction. Another example of the versatility of the plain round tube.

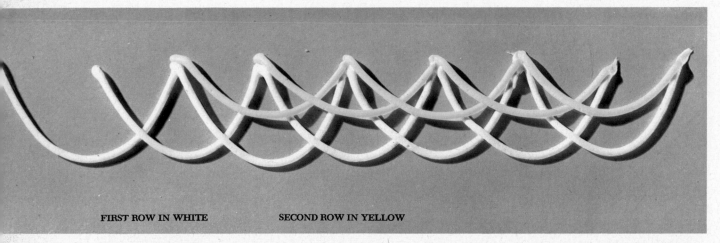

FIRST ROW IN WHITE   **SECOND ROW IN YELLOW**

DOUBLE DROP BORDER—a beautiful accent for any basic design. Adds a lavish touch to shells, ruffles, crescents, zigzags, garlands, stars. And very easy to do. Just use the basic technique explained on page 68 for stringwork. (Note: more than one color was used for the stringwork on this page, so you could follow the successive rows more clearly.) Mark off every inch all around cake edge. Then use tube 3 and touch one mark to attach icing, let string drop, skip next mark and attach to the mark that follows it. Go back to missed mark, attach string, drop, skip a mark, attach, and repeat all around the cake. Then drop a second row directly above first (shown in yellow) and go around the cake as before.

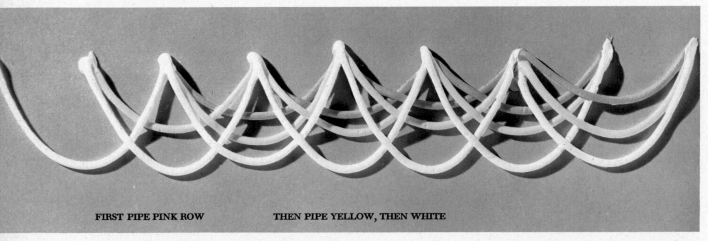

FIRST PIPE PINK ROW   **THEN PIPE YELLOW, THEN WHITE**

TRIPLE DROP BORDER—even more dramatic! Adds old world elegance to any cake design. Use the same tube and general technique as for double drop border above, but this time, start with shortest string first (shown in red). Drop second row a little longer than first (shown in yellow). And third row a little longer than second (shown in white). The fascinating thing about both these borders is the interwoven effect that results. It looks as though a most complex procedure is required to achieve it, but it is simply a charming optical illusion.

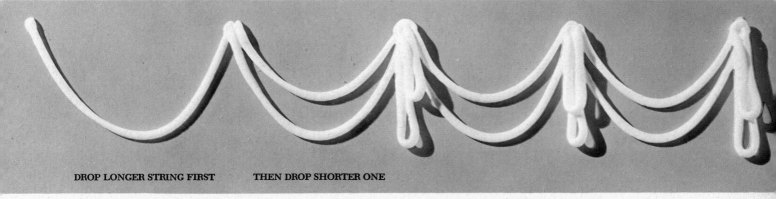

DROP LONGER STRING FIRST　　　**THEN DROP SHORTER ONE**

LOOP-DRAPED STRING BORDER. A pair of loops add a finishing touch to a graceful string border. To do, simply attach string, drop, attach again with tube 3 all the way around cake, about an inch or two apart. Then do a second row just above the first. Finally at each point, drop a long loop, then a short one on top of it. (Attach string, drop, then attach again at same point.)

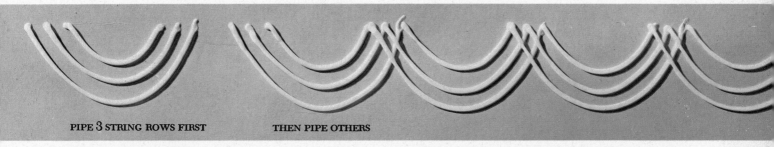

PIPE 3 STRING ROWS FIRST　　　**THEN PIPE OTHERS**

THREE BEARS BORDER—a delicate border of great charm for a petite cake. (Or use a large tube for a cake of greater dimensions.) Pipe it with a clever "cross-over" technique. Use tube 1 and drop three strings, the two shortest ones first. Make the shortest string about an inch wide, start second about ¼ inch outside first, and third about ¼ inch outside second. Then attach icing to end of longest string and drop for shortest string of next set. Attach icing to end of middle string and drop for next middle string. Attach to end of shortest string and drop for longest string of next set. Repeat all the way around.

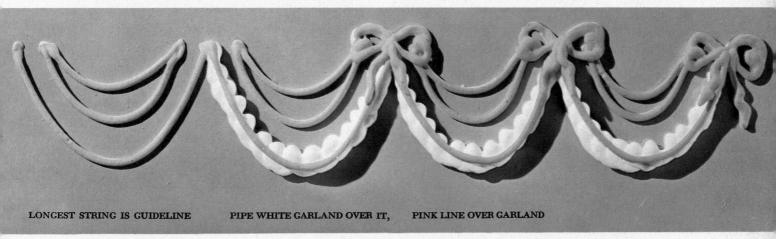

LONGEST STRING IS GUIDELINE　　　**PIPE WHITE GARLAND OVER IT,**　　　**PINK LINE OVER GARLAND**

ITALIAN BOW BORDER. A very pretty, very feminine border, perfect for a little or big girl's special cake. To make it, mark cake 2 inches apart all the way around, and drop a string about 1½ inches deep from mark to mark with tube 3 and pastel icing. About ¼ inch in from each mark, drop two shorter strings as shown. Now pipe over the longest string all the way around with white icing and same tube, doing short up and down motions for a rippled effect. Drop one more pastel string over this and finish with string bow-and-streamer at each point. Vary the color scheme for a different effect.

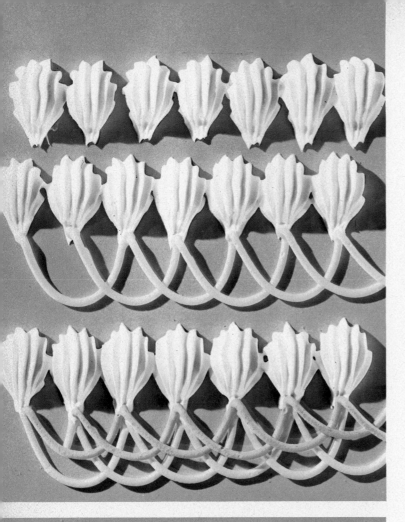

CROWN BORDER

A very dramatic, very elegant side border for the top tier of a wedding cake. Or for a tier cake or tall cake of any kind. And, best of all, you can do it in just three easy steps. (Note: three colors are used here just to illustrate the method. This border can also be done entirely in one color or white.)

First make a row of upright shells with tube 30 all the way around the cake, as shown in first row of illustrations at left. Next, as shown in yellow in second row of illustrations, attach icing to the point of one shell with tube 3. Let string drop, skip a shell and attach string to the shell following it. Go back to missed shell, attach string, drop, skip a shell, attach again. Third, as shown in pink in third row of illustrations, attach a shorter row of string the same way—attach to one shell, skip a shell, attach to next, go back to skipped shell and repeat around cake.

CHANDELIER BORDER

Deck your cake with richly-ribbed shells, hung like jewels from rows of gracefully-draped stringwork. They're delightfully simple to do, despite their elegant appearance. It takes just three steps as shown in the illustrations at left. Again, three colors are used to show the three steps as clearly as possible for you.

First, pipe upside down shells as shown in the first row of illustrations at lower left, using tube 32 and keeping them about 1½" apart to provide room for the stringwork that will go between. Follow tips on making shells, page 67. Next, as shown in second illustration in pink, attach shortest string first, using tube 2. Attach string to point of one shell, drop and attach to point of next shell. Then pipe longer string shown in yellow, in same way. Final effect is shown in third illustration. A beautiful border for the top edge of a cake tier!

PLUME BORDER

Ready to parade around your cake sides, saluting any great occasion. Make it with comparative speed of wide-ribbed shells, draped with row-on-row of graceful stringwork.

Begin, as shown in the first illustration at right, by pressing out a row of upright shells, according to directions on page 67, and using tube 105. Build up a good full base, then draw to as thin a point as possible, spacing them about ¼″ apart all around the cake. Next, as shown in the second illustration, pipe a dot with tube 2 about midway between shells at the point where they begin narrowing. Using this dot as a guideline and same tube, drop a drape of stringwork from one dot to the next, swinging just below point of shell as you go. Then, as in third illustration, drop two shorter strings above first, draping them over the point of shell.

DRAPED LATTICE BORDER

One of the most impressive borders of all! A worthy adornment for cakes little or large, it is used at top edge of a tier or cake. A flat lattice border, as shown on page 153, goes on the surface of cake top or side.

To make this draped version, first pipe string-work guideline about 3″ wide and 1″ deep around cake with tube 3, as in first row of illustrations at right. Next pipe scallop garland over the guideline with tube 16 as in next row. Now, as in third row, pipe string guideline over garland and, starting directly above center, drop tiny tube 2 lines of icing, working diagonally from top to guideline. Then go to opposite side of garland and drop lines in opposite direction. Finally as in last row, conceal garland guidelines with tube 2 dots, and cover dots with another string. Hide tops of lattice with tube 14 reverse shells. Drop tube 3 string under all.

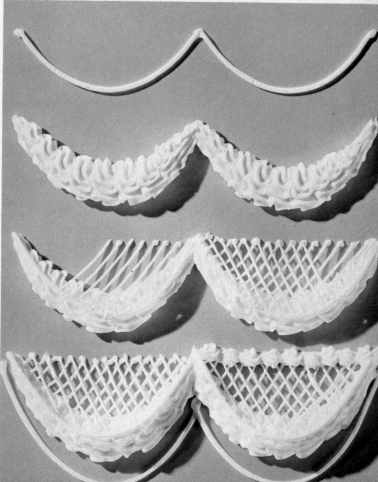

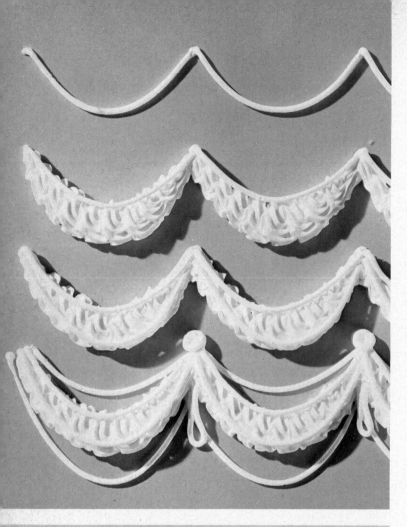

SCALLOPED GARLAND BORDER

A graceful side effect for any cake, from wedding centerpieces that soar several tiers, to two-layer birthday treats. Four easy steps and it's done, a graceful combination of two basic designs that you have already mastered.

At left, first row of illustrations shows the guideline you pipe to begin with tube 4—about 2½″ wide and 1″ deep all the way around top edge of cake or tier. Next, as shown in the second row of illustrations, you pipe a scalloped garland with tube 16 directly over guideline. (Page 67 gives step-by-step method for piping a scalloped garland.) Then drop a string with tube 3 from top edge. And, as in third row, drop another string at bottom edge. Add the final flourishes as illustrated in the fourth row. Drop tube 3 strings above and below garlands, twirl a knot at each point and drape a loop below it.

SCALLOPED GARLAND WITH FLUTE

A frilly, feminine border that adds charm to a cake meant to please a lady, or little lady. You can use it at top edge of cake or halfway down side (Be sure to mark halfway point with tiny dots of icing all around cake first, if that is your choice.)

Begin, as shown in first row of illustrations at left, with a stringwork guideline about 2½″ wide and 1″ deep, using tube 4. Then, as in second row, pipe a ruffle of fluted ribbon scallops over the guideline with tube 103. To pipe ribbon, hold tube with wide end touching guideline, small end pointed out and down. Then move along with an up-and-down motion to ripple icing as you press it out. The third row illustrates next step—filling in ribbon with a scalloped garland, using tube 14. Drop a tube 3 string (shown in yellow) between ribbon and garland. Finish with more string, as in fourth row— at top edge of garland, below ribbon.

HALF GARLAND BORDER

Puffy and pretty and just the thing for so many, many cake designs. One of the most popular for wedding cakes. And not very complicated, as it is the combination of just two basic designs. This version is for a smaller cake, substitute larger tubes of same type for a larger cake.

First, pipe a guideline with tube 3 as shown in first row of illustrations at right, about 1¼" wide, ½" deep. Then, press out half garlands with tube 16 as shown in second row (see page 67 for half garland instructions). Third row illustrates how to drape a very shallow string (shown in yellow) across top of garland, with tube 4. And fourth row shows how to complete this handsome border, with 2 rows of string draped below it.

If you want a striking touch for top tier of a tall cake that is supported by pillars, try this. *After* cake is delivered—pipe border at bottom of tier so stringwork hangs suspended!

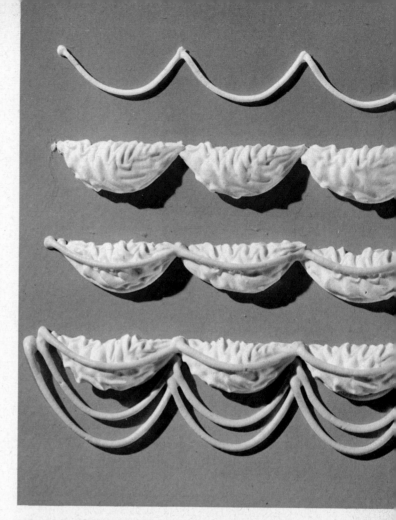

FANCY FENCE BORDER

Very charming look for the side of your cake. And such a simple variation of the classic full garland you can do it with ease.

Measure down from top edge of cake about 1¼" and mark with tiny icing dots all the way around. Then pipe full garlands over the dots as shown in the first illustration at right, using tube 14 and following method for piping full garland shown on page 67. Next, as illustrated in second row, pipe straight lines for "fence posts" between each garland up to top edge of cake with same tube. Then drape a string between posts with tube 3. Third row shows the finishing touches to add, still using tube 3—a second drape of string between posts, plus one atop the garlands and one draped beneath them. Finally, twirl little love knots at each post top. This border is also very effective at the base of a tier or cake.

89

STRING-ALONG. Bold top edging for a large cake tier. Three tubes make quick work of it. Pipe a row of large white bulbs with tube 9. Then add color accents. Curve a fluted string under each bulb with tube 13. Drape tube 3 stringwork beneath as follows. Attach string to right of one bulb, let it drop, skip next bulb and attach string to bulb that follows. Go back to skipped bulb, attach string, repeat all around. Also effective in all white.

DIMENSIONAL SHELLS. Rows of small shells are combined for an effect both dainty and dramatic. A ridge of icing underneath lifts color-tinted center row for an exciting three-dimensional look. Use shell tube 18 to pipe ridge first, next side shells, and finally tinted shells at top.

BOLD SHELLS-AND-SWIRLS. A fine demonstration of the way color can set off a border and give it a rich, raised look. Start with a row of bold shells, piped with tube 105. Edge beneath, using tube 3, bright contrast icing and a quick "e" motion.

STARSHINE. Lively touch for a little cake, pretty touch for any cake. Pipe a row of stars with tube 22, letting each remain separated slightly from the others. Then top each star with a down curved "C" scroll, using tube 13. Finish with tinted leaves between stars, using tube 65.

STAR CIRCLES. A quick, easy way to glamorize a simple star border. Colorful accent for any cake, especially a child's cake or novelty design. Pipe large separated stars with open star tube 21. Add overlapping curves of color at top and bottom of stars with tube 14, to join into a single border.

90

SHELL SWIRL. Very showy, yet it takes just two tubes, little effort. Pipe a row of puffy shells, swirled to one side, using tube 32. Then with petal tube 104, pipe tinted half ruffle beneath each shell.

SHELL TURNABOUT. A lovely rhythmic design with swirl of the reverse shells set off by alternating curves of color. Pipe big dramatic reverse shells with tube 32. Then add "e" motion edging with tube 14, curving over one shell, under next, repeating all around cake.

SHELL BALLET. A border of graceful beauty for larger cakes. Do it easily with three tubes. Begin with a row of puffy shells done with tube 32. Arch fluted curves around them, first at top, then at bottom, using tube 74. Then tuck tube 65 down to point of each shell and pull out a tinted, ruffled leaf.

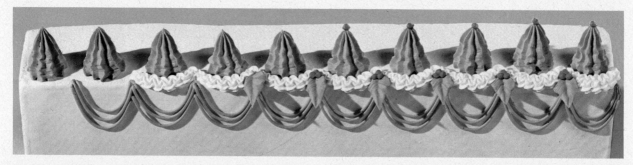

MERRY CHRISTMAS. Pretty mix of designs makes a charming display around a happy holiday cake. Do it one-two-three in the following manner. Pipe a row of standing green shells on edge of cake top to look like tiny Christmas trees. Use tube 30 and leave ¼" between them. Next pipe three rows of green stringwork between shells, using basic technique on page 68 and tube 3. Then with tube 14 and white icing, add tiny zigzag scallops around base of shells. Deck at points with tube 65 leaves and use tube 3 again to add a trio of tiny red "berries" to top of each leaf. Add single red dot to top of each "tree" with same tube. The final effect—little Christmas trees in the snow!

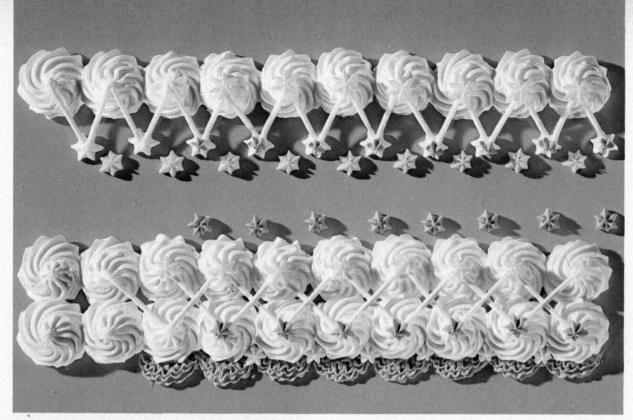

STAR-BRIGHT. The border that circles round the beautiful Morning Star cake on page 29.

FOR SINGLE STAR-BRIGHT BORDER at top, pipe a single row of tube 22 rosettes at top edge of cake. Make all same size, about ¾″ across. Then mark cake ¼″ below and exactly between rosettes and pipe a tube 16 white star. Then, working diagonally from centers of rosettes to centers of stars, drop 1″ lengths of tube 3 white string to achieve the "laced" effect. Trim with tinted stars, using tube 14.

FOR DOUBLE STAR-BRIGHT BORDER above. Pipe two rows of tube 22 rosettes at base of cake, centering one above the other. Then pipe a tube 3 string from center of one top rosette diagonally to center of next bottom rosette. Repeat around cake, then pipe crossed-over string same way in opposite direction, repeating all around again. Then add color touches with tube 14. Curve a zigzag scallop around bottom rosettes directly on cake plate. Pipe accent stars above top row of rosettes.

FOR HALF-CIRCLE FANS, make a pattern, using the tips given in Chapter Seven. Cut a 4″ diameter circle in half, fold in half 3 times fan style. Then fold in half lengthwise to mark place for center rosettes. Open, pin to cake and use to indicate points where rosettes will be piped. Then use tube 14 to pipe rosettes at point and center of fan and tube 16 for rosettes at end of fan. Next drop tube 3 strings from rosettes at point of fan to center rosettes and from center to end. Accent with tube 14 stars.

FOR QUARTER-CIRCLE FANS, use half the pattern you made for half circles and the same method.

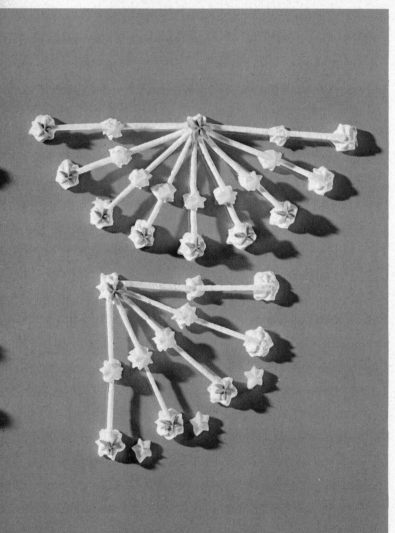

CHAPTER SEVEN

Measuring and Making Patterns

As you progress from simple to complex borders, you will begin to find it advantageous to measure and use patterns. Careful measuring gives even the most elementary borders great grace and beauty. And patterns allow you to add elegant designs to cake tops and sides. This chapter shows quick, easy ways to measure cakes and create your own patterns.

This lovely "Lover's Circle" cake shows the magic patterns and measuring can work! 12½" round, 3½" high cake with an 8" round, 1" high layer atop it, is placed on a 16" cardboard circle. Filigree bevels are formed of 12 individual sections piped on a pattern. Side border is similar to one on page 103. To make filigree and flower hearts, see Chapter Twelve.

MEASURING ROUND CAKE TOPS

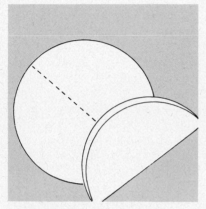 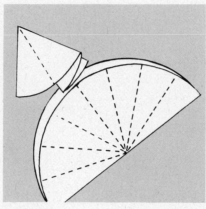 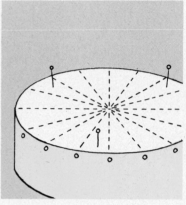

Use round parchment pan liners the same size as your cake top. Or, lacking these, place your cake pan on parchment cone paper or wax paper, trace around bottom with a pencil and cut out. Then simply fold circle in half, then into quarters, eighths and even sixteenths if you wish. (Be sure to fold it fan-style for more accurate results.) Unfold and you will have a perfectly divided cake top measure. Secure to frosted cake top with straight pins and mark divisions at cake edge with tiny dots of icing.

MEASURING ROUND CAKE SIDES

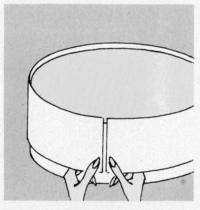 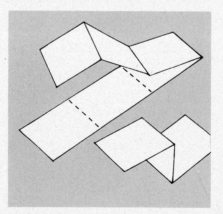 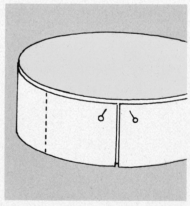

Use top dots as guides to measure sides of cake and put tiny dots halfway down all the way around. If you wish to measure sides only, cut a strip of paper long enough to reach around cake with ends just meeting. Then fold in half, in fourths, eighths, or whatever divisions you wish. Pin on cake and mark divisions again with tiny dots. You can then pipe curves, scallops, puffs, stringwork, shells or whatever you wish from dot to dot. All will be exactly the same length. To keep uniform depth, measure halfway down for stringwork, a little more than half for garlands and mark lightly all the way around to guide you as you decorate.

MEASURING TOP AND SIDES OF A SQUARE CAKE

You can measure these quite easily with a ruler. Or cut a strip of paper the length of one side, fold as for round cake sides and use to measure both sides and top edges all around. You can use the same piece of paper to make a pattern, as we'll explain a little farther on in this chapter.

The Easy Way to Make Patterns

When you were quite young, you may have spent occasional rainy afternoons making paper "snowflakes". You cut notches, circles and curves into a piece of folded paper to produce a pretty openwork design. We will show you how to make beautiful patterns for your cake tops and sides, using something very like that simple technique.

ROUND TOP-OF-CAKE PATTERNS

 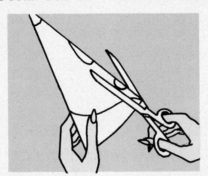 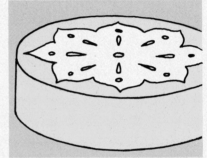

First decide the kind of design you want—perhaps a lovely circle of petals or graceful scallops. Curved designs are easier and generally prettier than straight geometric designs. If you plan an eight-petal design, fold a circle of paper the size of cake top into sixteenths. (Always make twice as many folds as designs so you can cut both sides at the same time and thus achieve a perfect match.)

Then, starting at the outer (open) edge, draw a half petal or other design as shown. With paper still folded, cut out pattern, making sure to start design ½ to one inch in from edge of cake, depending on size of border to be used. Then unfold pattern, pin to cake top and trace around with another pin to transfer to cake. Remove pattern, then trace with icing stars, tiny shells or contrast icing.

ROUND SIDE-OF-CAKE PATTERNS

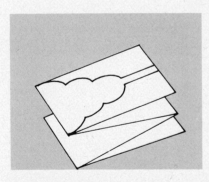  

As you did when measuring round cake sides, cut a strip of paper that reaches around cake, with ends just meeting. Then fold it fan-style, first in half, then in fourths, eighths, or as many divisions as you want. Draw pattern in center, measuring off equal margins at all sides. To cut center of design out, staple first to keep folds from slipping apart, then cut as shown in first step above. If cutting around design, be sure to leave a joining strip of paper between each design as in second step, then cut.

Unfold, pin to cake and transfer design with another pin. Remove pattern and trace design in icing. Be sure to line patterns up with top patterns. For example, the third step above illustrates how to place side designs so that they lie directly below petal points on cake top.

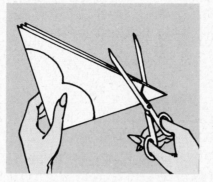
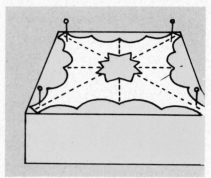

SQUARE CAKE TOP PATTERNS

These can be done in a similar fashion to round cake pattern. First fold a square of paper exact size of cake top in half, then fold in half again and finally into a triangle. (Be sure to fold so all open ends are at one side of triangle.) Draw a half scallop or other design, starting from open end and stopping short of top point, which is center of cake. Cut out, unfold, pin and trace onto cake.

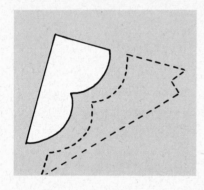
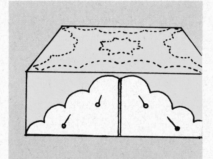

SQUARE CAKE SIDE PATTERNS

You can use the scallops you just cut out of the top pattern, pin them to top or base of side. This gives you a pattern that matches top perfectly! Or if you wish a different design, take a strip of paper exact size of side, fold into divisions desired. Draw in design as you did for side of round cake pattern and cut from center or around outline. Pin to cake and trace as usual.

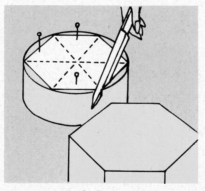

HEXAGONAL CAKE PATTERNS

If you have not baked the cake in a hexagonal pan, you can still achieve a six-sided cake. First fold cake circle the size of cake top into sixths, draw a line from point to point and cut off curve. Unfold, pin to cake which has been chilled firm first, and cut it to match. Then refold hexagon into sixths, then twelfths and cut half a design—petal, scallop or whatever you wish. Unfold again, pin to cake, outline with a toothpick. For octagonal cakes, follow same procedure, except fold circle into eighths for cutting cake, sixteenths for pattern.

Measuring and Making Patterns
for a Tier Cake

A pretty tier cake begins with tiers that are sized to achieve a pleasing symmetrical shape and perfect balance. A good way to decide which tier sizes to use is to subtract four inches, for a fairly large cake, from each tier going upward. For example, if your base tier is 16 inches round, you should choose a center tier 12 inches round and a top tier 8 inches round. The depth of your tiers can also influence the total look of the cake. If top tier is not a bit shorter it will look too tall for its diameter. So if base tier is 4 inches deep, top tier should be 3 inches deep. This is a workable, general rule—of course there will be exceptions.

EASY WAY TO MEASURE—by pillars! When you assemble a tier cake, using separator plates and pillars, you have built-in measuring help. Just mark cake with a toothpick or icing dot below each pillar and your cake is divided exactly into fourths. Mark halfway between pillars and your cake is divided

into eighths. A dot halfway between these marks, of course, divides cake neatly into sixteenths.

WHEN DESIGN IS ON TIER TOPS. It is best to make pattern, trace and even complete decorating *before* cake is assembled, as design may have to be worked inside or around pillars. We'll use the "Heritage" cake on page 105 to illustrate this technique.

FIRST PREPARE CAKE TIERS. Place a 16″ two-layer tier on a 22″ board, a 12″ tier on a 16″ separator plate and an 8″ tier on a 12″ plate. Next, build bevel edges, if tiers are not baked in bevel-edged pans. Mark base of each tier one inch up all around and mound icing from that mark down to edge of base and separator plates. Use spatula to spread into a smooth, even slope. Ice tiers, make patterns.

DESIGN LARGEST TIER FIRST. Fold a paper circle size of tier into sixteenths. Unfold and mark tier off into sixteenths at top and bevel edges. Refold circle and draw pattern, using the method shown on page 95. Then repeat for center and top tiers. Cut out all three patterns and check how well they match by placing one on top of the other, starting with largest. Finally, pin to tier tops and transfer designs to cake with a pin or toothpick.

NEXT DESIGN SIDE OF CENTER TIER. Cut a strip of paper exact depth and circumference of center tier and fold into sixteenths. Then unfold and mark center tier into eighths at top edge and sixteenths at bevel edge. Refold strip and draw pattern, using method on page 95. Cut out, pin to cake. To make certain side and top pattern line up evenly, position side pattern so topmost point of side scallops lie directly under point of top scallops. Use toothpick to transfer design to cake. Begin decorating!

Using Ready-Made Patterns and Dividers

If you would like a quick way to measure cakes or design patterns, there are a number of aids.

FOR MEASURING—a pair of plastic wedges exactly $\frac{1}{16}$ of a 10″ cake top that hook together to measure $\frac{1}{8}$th, $\frac{1}{10}$th and $\frac{1}{12}$th. There are dial dividers with swing-around arms, and a gate-style divider that expands to measure cake top.

FOR PATTERNS—there are ready-made patterns, pattern-presses made like oversized cooky cutters and a plastic template that lets you dial designs.

CHAPTER EIGHT

How to do Advanced Borders

For experts only! These beautiful and involved icing designs are best not attempted unless you truly have mastered all that has gone before. They require painstaking, patient planning, accurate measuring and marking and just about perfect control. Here, design is added to design, and in some cases, layer upon layer of overpiping is needed. And because one design or color is continually played against another, inaccuracies and errors show up more clearly than ever. However, these borders do offer a challenge to the ambitious decorator and it is vital to master them if you are interested in entering cake decorating competitions. At the very least they are a worthy test of skill for any decorator who wants to try a hand at them.

In this chapter, we start out with the simpler variety, then go on to borders so dazzlingly complex, they look almost impossible to do. Of course, they're not. And if practice and determination brings you to the point (as it certainly must) where you can do such things, we promise you it will be vastly satisfying.

Nosegay wedding cake, shown at left, has graceful borders, composed of simple dots and stringwork, yet see how exquisitely they are placed and what a beautiful effect they make. The secret is the very accurate measuring and precise, careful and even piping of dots and strings. To do the pretty side borders, divide tiers into fourths, using cake pillars as a guide. At each fourth, drop a large tear shape of string, using tube 2 (pipe two strings in an upside-down "v" from top edge of cake tier, then touch tube to left string, drop a string drape and attach it to right string). Do longest tear shape first, then a second shorter one draped over first, finally a third one, shorter still. For large base tier, do four tear shapes. Add little dots as shown. See entire Nosegay Wedding Cake with directions for decorating on page 135.

RUFFLES AND PUFFS. First pipe a row of standing puffs on cake top along edge with tube 199 (use a figure-piping technique, holding tube in place as you press cone so icing builds up into a round puff before you break it off). Then, with small petal tube 101s, pipe a tiny slanted pastel ruffle across puffs from back to front. Next, use tube 2 to drop a triple stringwork border, with method on page 68. Then pipe a white zigzag scallop around front of puffs with tube 14 and with same tube, overpipe scallops with a grooved pink line. Overpipe five rows of straight lines on this in alternating colors for a high curve of icing that stands at a slant. Use tubes 5, 4, 3, 2 and 1 in that order.

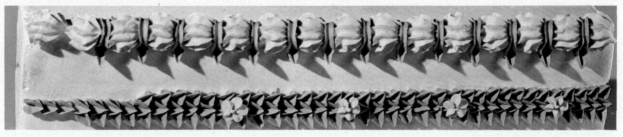

A PRETTY PAIR of leaf and shell borders are designed especially to use together for a cake with a feminine flair. Exquisite as a trim for a frilly shower or party cake. Begin with a row of puffy tinted shells, piped directly along top edge of cake with tube 30. Between each shell, pipe an arched fluted line with tube 76, bringing it to a stand-out, leaf-like point. For side border, use tube 76 again to pipe three rows of tiny leaves—middle row pointing straight ahead, upper row turned up, lower row turned down. Top every two inches with a tinted drop flower piped ahead with tube 224 and centered with a contrast dot.

MIRROR BORDERS for cake top and base should be within the capabilities of most practiced decorators. Mark top and base of cake every one and one-quarter inches all the way around. Pipe tinted zigzag scallops with tube 14 from mark to mark, above and below top edge of cake and at base of cake as shown. Add fleur-de-lis with same tube between scallops, under top border and above base border. Fill in scallops with white garlands, using tube 16, doing half at a time as shown at top of cake for great, full puffs. For base border, do white garland under scallop, then edge around base with tinted scallop piped flat on cake plate. Finish with rosettes between scallops and top each with a white star, using tube 14.

CROWNING GLORY. A rich, lavishly-scrolled crown border that's so impressive, it can turn a simple round cake into a masterpiece! Yet it is easier to put together than it might appear at first glance. As with all complex borders, it requires very careful execution as flaws and uneven piping are more evident when designs are played against each other. First, pipe a row of standing puffy shells with tube 199, starting them at top edge of cake and letting them build up a bit at the start so they rise slightly above edge. Drop a single string drape from points of shells all the way around with tube 2 and pipe tiny white stars with tube 14 to hide where strings and points join. Use tube 14 again to pipe white "C" scrolls back-to-back on top of stars and curve zigzag around tops of shells.

CREAM PUFF. A lush look that's really a mix of simple designs. Again, it requires great care. First, pipe a row of large pastel puffs on top of cake along edge with tube 199. Then do arrow shapes at cake edge, directly under puffs. Pipe narrow vertical zigzag lines with tube 13 in one continuous motion, starting very short and going longer and longer until you have done about five. Then pipe lines shorter and shorter until you are back to edge of cake again. Continue around cake. With same tube, do white zigzag "S" that begins under one puff and curves up over next one. Repeat all around. Next, frame curves under puffs with second curve of zigzag. Finish with tube 3, draping pastel stringwork over zigzag curves and framing arrow border with pastel dots.

HEARTS AND FLOWERS, for all the occasions that love inspires! These borders are as quaint and charming as an old-fashioned valentine. Mark cake edge first in this manner—2½" apart, then 1½" apart. Alternate same way all around. Use tube 14 and in the longer space, pipe a zigzag garland. In the shorter space, pipe a zigzag heart with top curves done flat on top of cake. Next overpipe hearts once and scallops twice. Pipe tiny green leaves within the hearts and scallops with tube 65 and attach tiny red roses as shown, made in advance on toothpicks with tube 101s (see page 115 for directions). Drop tiny latticework strings over scallop roses with tube 1, from edge of scallop to edge of cake, as shown on page 87. Use tube 14 again to hide ends of latticework with tiny shells at cake edge. Add tube 2 red beading.

GIRLISH RUFFLES, so right for sentimental tributes of every kind. Mark cake every two inches all the way around and use star tube 16 to do the extravagant puffy ruffles. First pipe zigzag scallops from mark to mark to about an inch below cake edge. Then fill scallops with zigzag half crescents. Complete puffs with zigzag scallop done flat on cake top over crescent. Drop three rows of pastel stringwork over lower half of puff and drape a loop between each. Now with tube 16 again, draw a curved line at outer edge of top scallop, being careful to hold tube steady as you go, so star grooves do not twist or turn. Next, use tube 5 to pipe a white line in top groove of tube 16 line. Then pipe a pastel line over white one with tube 2, keeping it a bit forward so finished high curve of icing slants out.

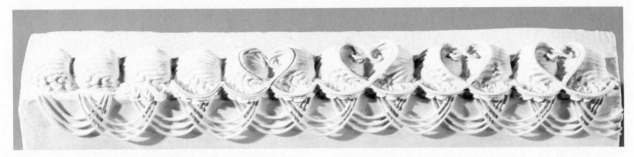

SWEET HEARTS. A most romantic look for cakes that celebrate love—with hearts raised high and lush draped stringwork. First pipe a row of puffs with tube 199 on top of cake about ⅛" in from edge. Drop three rows of pastel stringwork under puffs with tube 2, starting at left of one puff and attaching to right of next puff. Go all around cake this way. Then overlap string drapes, beginning them at left of original second puff. Do a white zigzag scallop with tube 14 around base of puffs. Use same tube to pipe a grooved pastel line on scallops and to center a grooved heart shape on each pair of puffs. (Do hearts one half at a time, starting with a curlicue at top and finishing at point.) Again, take care to hold cone steady. Overpipe with tube 2, laying string in top grooves.

LA PLUME. A large, dramatic border with grace of motion and a feeling of grandeur. Meant for banquet and wedding cakes. Begin by marking cake every three inches at top edge, then pipe a white zigzag scallop from mark to mark on side, using tube 16 and letting it swing down about 1½ inches below cake edge. Next, fill each scallop with a crescent puff, using same tube. Pipe a trio of stringwork drapes over each puff with tube 2, then do a triple zigzag scroll directly over crescent and swinging onto cake top for a "feather plume" effect. Overpipe outer edge of scroll with pastel grooved line using tube 16 again, trying to keep grooves from twisting or turning as you go. Then overpipe white lines into top grooves with tube 2. Finish with a white leaf between scrolls, using tube 67.

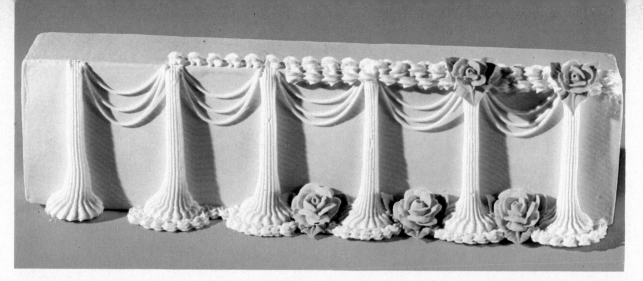

GRECIAN GLORY. For pillars, press out a tube 199 standing shell directly on cake plate at base of cake. Let build up slightly, so bottom of shell flattens out a bit. Then, keeping an even pressure, pull smoothly upward so shell flows into pillar shape. Cut off at cake edge. Pipe pillars all around cake sides, an inch apart at base, two inches apart at top. Then drop three rows of stringwork between pillars, using tube 2. Next, add three rows of shells with tube 14—first on top of cake along edge, second on side along top edge, with third centered atop first two. Pipe trios of leaves at tops of pillars and between bases of pillars with tube 67. Attach pastel icing roses, made ahead with tube 101.

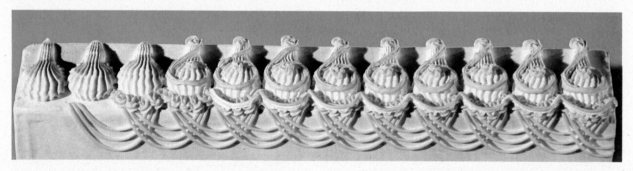

L'ESPRIT. A border with lots of swing and movement and a very Continental look. Adds great elegance to any cake. Begin with row of elongated white puffs, piped on cake top about ¼" from edge, using tube 199. Then, starting between two of the puffs, pipe a pastel triple stringwork border, overlapping the rows as shown. Next, with tube 16 curve a pastel frame of zigzag around puffs. Use same color and tube to pipe "question mark" scrolls on top of puffs. Then with tube 14 again, but white icing, overpipe zigzag frame with a grooved line, keeping grooves straight. Finally, with tube 2, pipe a pastel string into top groove.

COUNTERPOINT. A pretty medley of designs to swing rhythmically around a cake. Ripply strings on a slant are easy to pipe with two-hole parallel line tube 41. Just mark cake at edge every two inches, then with a back-and-forth movement, zigzag lines from one mark at top to directly below next mark at base. Then, between each set of lines at top edge, pipe a pair of puffy shells with tube 19, positioning one on top of cake, the other on side of cake, alternating same way all around. Next, use tube 14 to curve a zigzag line over and under shells and to add a rosette at point of each shell. Finally, with tube 2, top zigzag curve with a string of pastel icing and center rosettes with a dot.

LA MER. Like bold ocean waves, these classic curlicues of icing crest high and handsome! Begin by piping a row of white puffs on top of cake about ¼" away from edge with tube 199. Next add the triple stringwork border using tube 2 and overlapping rows as shown. Then with tube 16, curve a frame of white zigzag around puffs. With same tube, but pastel icing, overpipe zigzag scallops with a grooved line, keeping grooves straight up as you go. Also use this tube and icing to pipe grooved scrolls on top of puff. (Do each "C" separately, but bring tail of one clear to top of next one before breaking off and starting the following "C".) Then, into top groove of "C's", overpipe a white line with tube 5. Pipe a pastel line over the white with tube 3, then a white line over the pastel with tube 2. Do same kind of overpiping on grooved line over scallops—but use tubes 3, 2 and 1.

ROSE BALLET. Lively lilting look for cake sides, with tiny wild roses that dance along between two rippling rows of dots. It also requires a pattern (see page 95 or 96) for curves that dip into each other as shown. Make it about 1¼" wide, cut out, attach to cake sides with toothpicks and outline. Remove pattern and follow curves to do inner white beading with tube 2. Add pastel beading along white with tube 3, then finish with outer white beading, with tube 2 again. Do tiny flowers free-hand, piping green stems with tube 1 from point of top curve to point of bottom curve, then from point of bottom curve to point of top curve and so on. Pipe tiny branches with same tube, mini-leaves with tube 65. Use tube 1 to do "dot" roses, center with contrast.

FORGET-ME-NOT. Cut pattern for side of cake as directed on page 95 or 96, making it about 2½" wide. Attach to cake sides with toothpicks and outline. Remove pattern and follow scallops with tiny blue beads, using tube 1. Use same tube to do a green vine that curves between scallops. (You can draw a light guideline first if you wish.) Add tiny stems, then pipe mini-leaves at tips with tube 65s. Attach forget-me-nots made ahead with tube 101s and centered with tiny yellow dots. Position a cluster of three blossoms on one curve of vine and let a single blossom "grow" from the next curve.

RUFFLES AND ROSES. The romantic border used for the pretty "Heart Fancy" cake on page 32. For rose fans, make tiny tube 101s roses first. For ruffles that hold roses, measure cake top and sides carefully.

Place cake on foil-covered base and mark off top and bottom edges into 2½" spaces with a toothpick. Then do ruffle part of borders first, using tube 14. For top border ruffles, pipe zigzag scallops at edge of cake top. Fill scallops with zigzag garlands and do zigzag scallops over them to form deep curves on cake top. Overpipe top garland twice, first with pastel, then white. Add pastel "frame" by piping zigzag down left side of each puff and curving it under. Repeat all around cake. Do bottom ruffles with same tube. Pipe wide white scallops directly on cake base, then overpipe twice, first with pastel, then white.

Now do rose fans. Pipe a pair of tiny tube 65s leaves into each curve on cake top and at bottom edge of cake within scallops. Carefully attach tiny roses with icing. Finish with tube 1. Pipe fan strings from edge of curves and scallops to a point on cake 1½" above bottom curves and in from edge of top curves. Add tiny pastel hearts at string points (join two teardrops), overpipe all with pastel string.

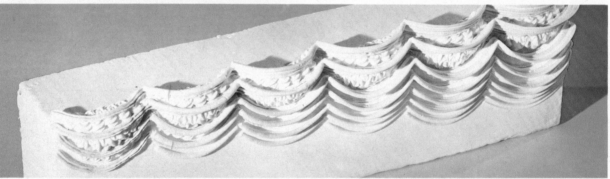

DIMENSIONS. An elegant border design that makes the most of light and shadow to crown your cake with row upon row of richly rippling scallops. A challenging exercise in the technique of overpiping! Begin by marking cake every two inches at top edge, then pipe a white zigzag scallop from mark to mark on side, using tube 16 and letting it drop about 1¼" below cake top. Next, with same tube, fill scallop with zigzag crescent, and over it, pipe a zigzag scallop that moves onto cake top. Do a tube 16 grooved pastel line on top scallop, on crescent, below crescent and on cake below first scallop.

Now the overpiping begins in earnest! Remember to let each line dry before you add another atop it. Pipe a white tube 5 line into the top groove of each tube 16 line, and one on cake beneath lowest one. Pipe a pastel tube 4 line on each tube 5 line, plus one on cake below. Pipe a white tube 3 line on each tube 4 line, plus one on cake below. Then do a pastel tube 2 line on each tube 3 line, plus one on cake below. Pipe a tube 1 line on each tube 2 line, finishing with one on the cake. As you overpipe, try to lay line of icing close to outer edge of the line it tops, for curves of icing that slant out gracefully.

PRETTY PICOT LACE. The borders with the quaint, crocheted appearance that give a charming, old-fashioned air to the "Heritage" wedding cake on page 251. (Complete decorating directions are given with the cake.) An exquisite touch for any cake, picot lace borders take great care and patience. But the airy effect they add is well worth it.

First, divide top edge of cake tiers or bevel base layers into eighths if small or average size, and into sixteenths if large size. To do this the easy way, see page 94. Or, if you are decorating the Heritage cake, see page 97, which has complete directions for making the tier-top patterns for this cake. Once you've made these patterns, you can use them as a guide for measuring tier sides, too.

With sides measured, you're ready to pipe the picot trim. Divide each 8th or 16th section into 6ths by eye. (Or, if you find this difficult, cut a strip of paper exact length of one section and fold into sixths. Pin to cake and mark sections.) Next, using tube 1 for entire border, drop 6 tiny string-work garlands, each about ½″ deep, across top of section. Then, working from within center of each little garland, drop a second row of 5 garlands beneath them. In next row, do 4 garlands, then do a row of 3, then 2, then 1 until you achieve "v" shaped lace design shown. Add picot trim to outer edge of "v" by making a triangle of tiny dots, piping 3, then 2, then 1. Do double picot triangles for diamond-shaped trim at top edge of "v". If you are decorating the Heritage cake, you will also use the little picot triangles to edge tier top scallops and to join top lace borders to those on base bevel layer. And to trim side border on center tier.

Be sure to pipe picot lace in pastel on a white cake. Then the pretty picot pattern will stand out with almost 3-dimensional clarity to look almost like real lace.

105

LOVER'S CIRCLE. A cake with a quaint, romantic air that celebrates love with rings and wild roses.

PREPARE RINGS AND ROSES FIRST. Make ring pattern by drawing around a half dollar. Do 32 and extras in case of breakage. Cover with wax paper, trace with egg white royal icing and tube 4. Begin and end circles with curlicues for extra strength. Pipe tube 101 wild roses ahead as shown in Chapter Nine.

THEN PREPARE CAKE. Place a 12″ round, 4″ high cake on 16″ board. For bevel edge, mark 1″ up from base and mound icing from mark to board edge. Spread into slope with spatula. (Or bake layer in bevel pan.) Place on larger, foil-covered board.

MAKE PATTERN FOR CAKE TOP. Fold 12″ cake circle into sixteenths, as shown on page 94. Cut off one inch at wide end for border. Open, mark divisions on cake top, then divide sixteenths in half (by eye) and mark. Refold circle, cut out heart shapes and octagonal center, then trace.

MAKE BEVEL PATTERN. Measure down from top of cake to divide bevel into eighths. Cut a curved piece of greaseproof paper to fit ⅛th of bevel. Invert on cake top, trace pair of hearts. Outline on bevel.

THEN DECORATE CAKE. Outline cake top design and the heart shapes with tube 14 white zigzag, then overpipe with tube 2. Write "Love" in white with tube 2, overpipe in red. Attach flowers, pipe tube 67 leaves. Press tube 199 puff in each 32nd space at cake edge. Tuck in rings between puffs as you pipe them. Do frame of tube 144 zigzag inside puffs, add tube 3 side strings. Edge bevel with tiny tube 14 shells. Last of all, carefully attach flowers under rings. Pipe two tiny leaves, then pipe another leaf under flower and use toothpick to slip it into place.

CHAPTER NINE

The Beautiful Art of Flowers

Making flowers of icing is a truly satisfying experience. They turn out looking almost as real as if you'd just picked them out of a garden. Because the results are so spectacular, flower-making may look difficult. But once you know and practice each easy step, you'll be able to turn out beautiful blossoms by the basketful!

It is important to make each flower as true to nature as possible. A flower must have petals of just the right shape and number or it won't look at all like what it's supposed to be. This isn't difficult. It just takes care and planning. Once you learn to make the petals and leaves for all the flowers in this book, you'll have all the basic shapes and techniques at hand. Then, by carefully observing the bloom itself, or by using a good color illustration as a guide, you'll literally be able to make any flower in the world!

HOW TO START

There are several ways to make icing flowers. Press them out instantly with a drop flower tube. Pipe them on the surface of a pan or cake. Or form them on a flower nail (flat or cup-shaped). It all depends upon the effect you want to achieve and whether the flower you wish to make has petals that lie flat or curve upward. Some of the flower designs in this book are made in sections to be assembled later. You can quickly learn to do all with equal ease and success for your cakes.

ICINGS TO USE

Flowers last best when they are piped of royal icing. It dries hard all the way through and lasts indefinitely, allowing you to keep a good supply of flowers on hand at all times. Boiled icing also lasts well, but under its crisp exterior stays soft and will crumble after a time. Buttercream icing is for one-performance flowers. A buttercream blossom must be refrigerated or frozen if made even a day ahead, then consumed with the cake. Thus, for large cakes that take several days to complete, royal or boiled icings are usually best. Choose according to the cake and the occasion.

BASKETS OF BLOSSOMS—on facing page—are all of icing! A testimonial to the startlingly real look piped flowers can have. Directions for making all on following pages. Anchor to icing mounds in baskets.

108

Easy Drop Flowers

These quick, one-squeeze blossoms can be used with handsome effect on the most lavish cakes! So they are a logical starting place for the budding flower-maker. To make them, select a drop flower tube from one of the twelve noted below, or from the huge variety in Chapter One. Fill bag with royal icing, stiffened a bit so petals will hold their shape. (See Chapter Two for recipe.)

Attach a sheet of wax paper to back of cookie pan with lines of icing. Rest tube on surface, holding cone straight up. Let other hand guide tube, or, as in this picture, press fingers against paper to assure taut surface. For open petal, just press, stop, lift tube away. For swirled petal, turn hand with cone as far left as possible, press icing out gently, then (still pressing) turn cone to right as far as possible. Dry, run spatula under paper, peel off.

TUBE 217   TUBE 108   TUBE 136   TUBE 191   TUBE 109

TUBE 190   TUBE 2C   TUBE 193   TUBE 2F

TUBE 2D   TUBE 1C   TUBE 194

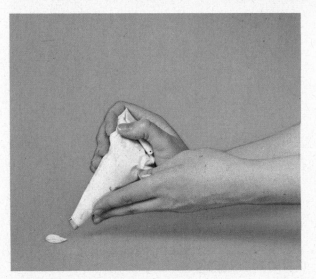

Flowers Made on a Flat Surface

Flat-surface flowers are a natural second step in the art of flower-making. They help you learn to form petals and they're simple to do. For the ones on facing page, use tube 104 for petals and tubes 3 or 4 for stem and calyx. Illustration at left shows the correct way to hold the decorating bag (at a 45° angle). To form petals, touch wide end of tube to surface, slant small end up and out. For a cupped or standing petal, hold small end almost straight up. It's a good idea to practice on a pan first, and make all flowers in advance for most cakes. (That way, the imperfect ones can be discarded.) For your practicing, use a stiffened hard-drying royal icing for best results. Attach wax paper to pan as for drop flowers, then begin with the sweet pea.

THE SWEET PEA. Hold decorating bag as shown at bottom of facing page, wide end of tube 104 touching surface, narrow end held slightly above it, pointed out. Press out back petal first, moving hand in half circle and jiggling slightly for ruffled effect. Then pipe two cupped petals on top with small end of tube straight up. For center stand-up petal, use position at top of facing page. Touch tube between cupped petals, lift slightly as you press then ease pressure as you move down. Pipe calyx with tube 4.

THE ROSEBUD. Hold decorating bag in position at bottom of facing page, wide end of tube 104 touching surface, narrow end straight up. Squeeze bag as you turn hand over to form a small cup, pulling toward you at finish for a high, sharp right edge. Touch tube just inside this edge and press lightly, lifting tube slightly. As icing catches petal edge hesitate for a second (still pressing) to let it roll itself into a spiraled inner petal. Then move back to right and down. For flat outer petal, bring hand straight over. Pipe calyx with tube 4.

HALF ROSE. Start with tube 104, position on bottom of facing page. Pipe a single flat petal like back petal of rosebud, but wider. Then do a full rosebud in center. Pipe a pair of petals over bud, swinging one in from left, the other from right. Finish with two outer petals that overlap. Hold bag almost straight up and turn hand all the way over. Important: as you pipe outer petals, push them up against bud. This will make rose stand higher. Finish by piping calyx with tube 3.

HALF CARNATION. Use a very stiff icing to create the important effect of broken petal tips. Begin with a single petal, holding tube 104 as on bottom of facing page. Jiggle gently as you press out icing, moving from center point and lifting hand slightly. Return to center, stop pressure. Repeat for fan of petals. Do second shorter row of petals over first. Repeat for four or five rows, making each row of petals shorter and more upright, until rounded half flower is complete. Pipe calyx with tube 3.

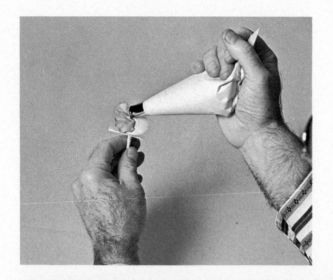

Flowers Made on the Nail

A flower nail is a tiny turntable upon which you can pipe flowers of all kinds in full, natural dimension. Practice makes this easy to do.

You simply hold nail between thumb and forefinger of left hand and roll it slowly counter-clockwise as you press out icing with right hand. Your right hand moves in or out, up or down, as it holds decorating bag and tube at just the right angle (in most cases, 45 degrees as at left) and keeps icing flowing at just the right even speed.

To start, attach a 2-inch square of wax paper to a number 7 flower nail with a dot of icing, and try the wild rose below. When complete, slide off nail on wax paper, dry. Peel off paper, place on cake.

WILD ROSE. Use tube 103 and hold cone as shown above. Have wide end of tube touching surface, narrow end lying almost flat. Begin at center of nail and press out first petal, turning nail as you move hand out to edge and back again, curving slightly upward to create a cupped shape. Repeat four more times. Pull out tiny stamens with tube 1.

IMPATIENS. A very pretty flower with wide, curved petals. Use tube 59 and form in a similar fashion to the wild rose, but make three top petals in a heart shape. As you reach outer edge of nail, do two short curves. Pipe a single short curve for the two bottom petals. Pipe tube 1 center stamen.

POINSETTIA. The Christmas-time favorite! Use tube 74 and deep color method for a dark red icing. Pipe a dab in middle of nail to center petals. Then pull out four petals about 1⅛ inches long. Add four more petals between these and pipe a second layer of five petals about ¾ inches long. Use tube 1 to pipe tiny green dots at center and same tube to do tiny yellow dots atop green ones.

PRIMROSE. A very graceful blossom with five scalloped petals, separated and identically-sized. Use tube 102, position on facing page and easy pressure. Start at center of nail, move out about ¾-inch as you curve, dip, curve and return to center, turning nail all the while to form the petal. Press out a small star at center with tube 14, dot with tube 1.

APPLE BLOSSOM. A small flower with five identically-shaped, rounded petals. Use tube 101s, position on facing page and an easy pressure. Start at center of nail, move hand out about ½-inch, curve around and return, letting spin of nail form petals. Let petals lie separately, not overlapping. Pipe small dots for stamens with tube 1.

FORGET-ME-NOT. Tiny, pretty little blooms piped very much like the apple blossom above. This time use tube 101 and move out just ⅜-inch from center, curve around and return, letting the turn of the nail form petals. Dot center with tube 1. Use large flower nail 7 and do several at once!

VIOLET. Tiny, bright flower that's a favorite symbol of love and spring. To form it, hold tube 59° in position on facing page, with wide end touching center of nail, narrow end slightly out. Press and move tube out ½-inch, turning nail as you go to shape the little petal. Do two more petals same size, then finish with two shorter petals about ¼-inch long. Pipe dots for stamens with tube 1.

WILTON'S FAST TECHNIQUE
FOR A PERFECT ROSE

Most beautiful and popular of all icing flowers! And here is a wonderfully quick and easy way to make a perfect one. First, be sure to choose the proper-size petal tube: for a small rose, use tube 102, for a medium-sized one, tube 104 and for a very large rose, tubes 125 or 127. Then just drop tube 12 into your decorating bag, fill with royal icing that's stiffened enough to make a stand-up petal, and attach a wax paper square to a number 7 flower nail. Begin by piping out base as shown in Step One. To follow these photographs accurately, work before a mirror with this page in front of you.

STEP ONE. Hold decorating bag fitted with tube 12 straight up and pipe a dome-shaped mound of icing on nail. Begin with firm pressure, gradually decreasing pressure. Keep tube buried as icing mounds.

STEP TWO. Hold second bag with tube 104 as above. Press tube lightly into mound close to top, with narrow end up and in. Turn nail counterclockwise as you pipe a ribbon of icing, swinging it up, around, back down to starting point to form bud.

STEP THREE. Hold bag so it points straight from shoulder, with narrow end of tube turned out slightly. Starting halfway up, pipe a row of 3 standing petals, turning nail counterclockwise as you move tube up and down in half-moon arch.

STEP FOUR. Pipe second row of 4 petals under first row, still turning nail counterclockwise. Pipe petals so they overlap spaces between petals in first row. Turn narrow end of tube out even more as you go, so petals appear to be opening slightly.

STEP FIVE. Pipe last row of 7 petals under the second row. Start under petal centers, pointing narrow end of tube quite far out. Again turn nail counterclockwise as you press out petals, overlapping as you go. Slide perfect rose on pan to dry.

114

THE ROSE—most cherished of all flowers, blooms in great variety of color and form.

ROSEBUD ON A NAIL—easy to do, now that you've mastered the full-blown rose. Use tube 104 and begin with a coil of icing rather than a mound. Touch wide end of tube to nail and point narrow end inward. Press out icing, moving hand up and down slightly, and let turn of nail twirl icing into a spiral bud. Add two upright petals that overlap. Add the sepals with tube 67.

MAKE TINY ROSES ON TOOTHPICKS!

Push one-inch wax paper square to center of toothpick. Hold decorating bag as in step two, facing page, small end of tube 101s up, in and just below tip of pick. Pipe icing on tip, pull ribbon straight out. At same moment, begin to lower pick and roll it counterclockwise as you return tube to pick. Icing will spiral around pick, form a bud. Finish like full-size rose. Push wax paper up to remove. Over-size at left. Actual size at right.

dampen pick

PANSY. Bright ruffles of color! Use tube 104 and pale purple icing. Hold decorating bag in usual flower nail position and pipe two back petals first, making a wide curve for each with one slightly behind the other. Then pipe two more petals atop first two as shown above. For bottom half of flower, press out a single full petal, using a slight back-and-forth motion for ruffled effect. Brush dark veins into petals with a fine brush and purple food color. Let dry, add yellow tear drop with tube 1.

DAFFODIL. Sunny flower of the early spring! To do, use tubes 104 and 2, flower nail 7 and usual flower nail position. With tube 104, pipe out six separate petals, all equal size. Start at center of nail, move out to edge (about ⅞-inch), curve and return to center as you turn nail. Pinch petals into point with fingers dipped in cornstarch while icing is still wet. Then with tube 2, do fluted center by pressing out a coil of string and complete lovely flower by piping tiny zigzag ruffle around top.

NARCISSUS. A small, dainty flower shaped exactly the same as daffodil, except for size. So make it same way, using tube 102 for petals and keeping them all the same size—just ¾-inches long. Pinch petals into points, same as daffodil. Use tube 1 for coil center, but do not add ruffle. Make the narcissus in two colors as shown.

DAISY. The cheerful flower everyone loves! To pipe, use a 1½-inch square of wax paper, tube 103 and usual flower nail position. First press small icing dot in middle to keep petals centered. Then touch wide end of tube to outer edge of nail and press out icing, moving in to center dot. Ease off pressure so petal narrows slightly at base. Turn nail, repeat for 12 petals in all. Then press large yellow tube 2 dot in center. Pick up yellow sugar on damp finger, touch dot carefully to simulate pollen.

MARIGOLD. Rich, golden puffs with a color bright as a gold coin! To pipe, use tube 101s and press out a tiny petal, just half an inch long, narrow at center and curved at outer edge. Try to maintain a continuous back-and-forth motion, moving hand out, then back, then out again, as you press out a circle of overlapping petals. Do three rows of petals, one on top of the other, making each row shorter than the last. Fill center with tube 13 stars.

FULL CHRYSANTHEMUMS. You'll need a very stiff icing to create broken petal effect. First pipe tube 6 mound in center of nail. Then, with outer curve of tube 81's half-moon opening held down and at a 90° angle, press out short ½-inch petals. Pipe next row between petals of first, making these slightly shorter and pulling tips up slightly. Continue until mound is entirely covered, with each row slightly shorter and more up-tilted. Pipe tiny stamens at center with tube 1.

BACHELOR BUTTON. Like the chrysanthemum, start with a tube 7 mound of pale blue icing. Pipe a cluster of short pointed same-color dots on center top with tube 1. Last, with tube 14 and darker blue icing, pull out tiny star petals, going round and round until mound is completely covered. Add more petals here and there for a fluffy, fully-shaped life-like flower.

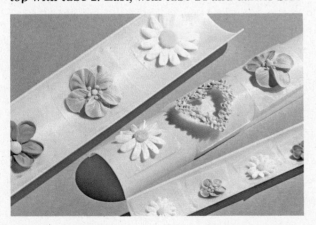

CURVE PETALS FOR A NATURAL LOOK

This is easily accomplished by drying them on a curved surface. Use concave or convex curve, depending upon the way you want flower petals to go. Slip your completed flower from nail onto or into the curved surface to dry. Use the same technique for curving delicate icing laces and other equally decorative cake trims.

FULL CARNATION. Use stiff icing, same as for half carnation. Hold tube 104 in usual flower nail position and begin to press out icing. Move out about 1⅛ inch, jiggling gently as you go and lifting slightly as you reach petal tip. Curve round, return to center, stop pressure. Repeat for a full circle of petals, then do two more rows, making each shorter. Fill center with petals that stand almost straight up.

DAHLIA. Hold tube 103 in usual flower nail position. But this time, start petal on outer edge of nail, easing off pressure as you move to center. Turn nail slightly and repeat for second petal, then continue all around nail for first row. Start second row about ¹⁄₁₆ of an inch in from edge of first. Do final row in same manner with petals begun inside previous row and standing a bit higher. Pipe tube 2 center.

ASTER. A flower full and lavish as the chrysanthemum. To pipe it, begin with a round base using tube 7. Do a row of sharp, short petals all around edge with tube 75. Do second row with petals shorter and points placed between those in first row. Repeat for third row, with still shorter petals. Fill in center with petals almost straight up. Let dry and brush petal tips with darker color, if desired.

ASTERS—glorious, many-petaled perennials that appear in the early summer. They gladden the eye and the heart with vibrant reds, pinks, blues and purples, each plant becoming a natural bouquet of blooms. Make them in icing, to add great drama to a festive cake for any occasion.

CHAPTER TEN
Making Flowers on the Lily Nail and Piping Leaves

Many flowers in nature's garden are shaped with bell-like centers or high-curved petals. To do them, it is necessary to start with the bell-shaped lily nails shown at lower right. When piped properly, these very graceful blossoms are actually no more difficult to do than flowers on a flat nail. But it is important that your icing be stiffened a little so flowers will hold their shape.

And to provide a natural framework for all your flowers, this chapter also shows how to pipe leaves of many varieties. Some long and slender like the leaves of the gladiola and fern—others tiny and pointed, round or ragged-edged. Study flowers in the garden or pictures in seed catalogs so the leaves you pipe resemble those belonging to the particular flower you are using on your cake.

The following pages show favorite flowers to make on the lily nail. Once you have done them successfully, you can do just about any other bell-shaped flower. Just carefully observe the bloom itself or a good illustration, for size, petal shape and color.

CLASSIC LILY NAIL

A one-piece nail, 1¾″ diameter. Line first with a two-inch square of aluminum foil, pressing foil down smoothly. After piping flower, lift out on foil cup to dry, freeing nail for another flower.

TWO-PIECE LILY NAILS

You may prefer the two-piece lily nails that form the aluminum foil square into a cup shape more quickly. Just place foil on bottom half of nail, press in with top half. Pipe flower in foil cup same as for classic nail above, then lift out for drying, use nail again. 2-piece lily nails come in four sizes—½, 1¼, 1⅝ and 2¼-inch diameter—to make various sizes of blossoms, from very tiny to 2½ or 3 inches across.

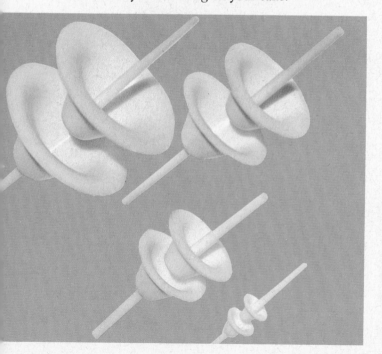

BLUEBELL. Exquisite little flower with long petals that form a pretty bell shape. To pipe, first press a square of foil into cup shape in 1¼-inch two-piece lily nail. Then with leaf tube 66 and bright blue icing, press out a ¾-inch petal, pulling it up over edge of cup into a point. Do two more petals spaced around cup as shown in second illustration above. Then pipe three more petals in spaces between first three. Dot center, attach short artificial stamens.

EASTER LILY. Press foil into the classic lily nail (or the 1⅝-inch two-piece nail). With tube 74 and white icing, pipe a long petal, pulling it out over edge of nail into a point. Pipe two more petals, spaced around nail as shown in second illustration above. Then pipe three more petals in spaces between first three, overlapping slightly. Press a tube 14 green star into center, push in red artificial stamens.

PETUNIA. Popular flower that adds color everywhere —from window boxes to garden paths! To pipe it, first line a 1⅝-inch lily nail with foil. Then with wide end of tube 102 held down, narrow end up, start piping icing deep inside nail. Move up to outer edge as you turn nail, jiggling hand slightly all the while to form ruffled petal edge, then go back to starting point. Pipe 5 separated petals in all. Add tube 14 green star, push in artificial stamens.

SHAMROCK FLOWER. The very beautiful little blossom that grows amid the famous "good luck" leaves! Press foil into a 1¼-inch lily nail and, using tube 101, pipe five ¾-inch petals very much like petunia, except narrower. Start in center, move up and over outer edge of nail as you turn it, jiggling for ruffled effect, then return to center. Dry, paint tiny ribs with deep food color and small pointed brush. Add yellow dot with tube 1.

MORNING GLORY. Line a 1⅝″ two-piece lily nail with foil. With tube 104 and white icing, form a hollow cup within nail. Keep wide end of tube down. Pipe second cup slightly above first. With blue icing and tube 103, pipe a ruffle around edge, increasing pressure at five points to form angled shape. With damp artist's brush, brush blue icing down into cup, then brush white icing up to form star shape. With tube 1 and thinned white icing, pipe five lines from base of flower to edge. Add a tube 2 stamen.

NASTURTIUM. A flamboyantly colored flower! Begin with a 1⅜ inch lily nail and bright tinted icing. Place wide end of tube 103 deep inside nail. Start with a light pressure, then pull icing out long enough to curl over edge of nail. Turn nail as you dip hand about 4 times for a deeply ruffled petal. Then return as close as possible to starting place for a very narrow point. Do 5 petals, keeping all completely separated. Brush in food color veins, join petals with tube 6, push in artificial stamens.

HOW TO MAKE A GLADIOLA

Line a 2¼ inch lily nail with a 4-inch foil square, use tube 112 and tinted royal icing. Start at center of cup to press out a small petal, pulling icing up toward edge of foil about an inch. Do second small petal, overlapping first. With tube 113, pipe large center petal over first two petals to top edge of foil. Push foil forward to curve petal up. With same tube, pipe lower center petal. Bend foil under it to curve petal down. With tube 112, add final pair of small petals. Brush center into cone-shaped well. Dry 12 hours, attach gray stamens made with tube 65-A. Push 2½ inches of white wire ½ inch up into tube. Press bag, slowly pull out wire to form stamen. Make three, dry ½ hour. Then twist stamens together partway, hook plain ends, bend in half with hooked ends highest, attach with icing.

EASY GLADIOLA CAKE. Make it in a long loaf pan, 16 x 4 x 4 inches. Frost green, edge bottom with tube 16 shells. Add tube 18 zig-zag garlands and fleur-de-lis to sides. Do gladiola blossoms as above, but use tubes 67 and 70. Pipe long stem for spray with tube 9. Make leaves right on cake, as directed on page 125. See page 146 for directions for making buds, and guide for spray.

122

HOW TO MAKE AN ORIENTAL POPPY

Line a 1⅝ inch lily nail with foil and use deep color method in Chapter Three for a scarlet icing. Hold wide end of tube 104 down, narrow end up and out and begin piping deep inside nail. Press out a large, rounded and ruffled petal as in step one above, jiggling hand as you move it up and out to edge of nail, and down again into a point. Repeat for second separate petal, as step two. Do four petals in all.

Push foil forward to make petals stand up a bit. Then pipe a second row of smaller, cupped petals inside first row, starting first petal between the ones underneath, as in step four. Repeat for four petals all around as in step five. Pipe a tube 2 center and while icing is wet, push in black artificial stamens. Dry, then paint petal bases with food color.

ORIENTAL POPPIES are very large and showy garden flowers that bloom in early summer, grow in nearly any sunny spot. The silky, ruffled blossoms are 4 to 6 inches across, with stems as much as 3 feet tall. They're a brilliant scarlet for the most part with black markings and stamens, but also come in orange, pink and white.

123

How to Frame Your Flowers with Leaves

Piping icing leaves is fun, as they emerge completely formed and so real-looking. Do make them with care, however, as poorly-done leaves will certainly detract from the beauty of nicely-done flowers. Remember, you are imitating nature. Do it well and the effect will be breathtaking! Soften icing first with a few drops of water, so leaves may be drawn to a point. But keep it firm enough to hold a true shape. Many of the leaves shown here can be piped on the cake, but the last five must be done on a flower nail. At right, a leaf tube alternative.

To cut leaf tip. First roll parchment decorating bag with needle-sharp point and fill with icing. Flatten tip and cut into arrow shape (snip from right to point, and from left to point). This will pipe leaf with center dip. For leaf with center rib, cut a tiny slit into point of arrow.

SMALL LEAVES. For flower sprays or rambling vines. Hold tube 65 at a 45-degree angle, touch to surface and squeeze to build up a base for your leaf. Then gradually pull away, relaxing pressure at halfway point. Discontinue pressure completely as you lift tube away from surface to draw leaf to a point. Practice a few small leaves, then pipe some stems with tube 3 and add small leaves to tips as shown.

LARGE LEAVES. To frame large dramatic flowers, complete elaborate decorations. Use tubes 67 to 70 and same technique as for small leaves, but this time, pipe with a heavier pressure, draw leaf out longer. Try a variety of leaf shapes, then move your hand back and forth to produce a ruffled leaf.

HOLLY LEAVES. With Color Flow icing, not thinned, and tube 70, pipe a medium-sized leaf on wax paper. Use same method as for small and large leaves above, but while icing is still wet, pull out tiny points around edge with a damp artist's brush for a true holly leaf look. Add short stem with tube 3.

Long leaves. To do on cake or off (see gladiola leaf on wire, Chapter Eleven). On cake, use tube 70 and pipe same as regular leaf, drawn out as shown. To ruffle, make back-and-forth movements as you go.

Fern. For realistic fern, pipe tube 3 stem. Then add short strings, going gradually shorter at top. For stylized fern, use tube 1, squeeze-stop motion for a curve of tiny mock leaves. Taper at top.

Primrose leaf. To pipe it, you must use a flower nail and tube 104. Begin piping the ruffled curves starting with wide end of tube touching center of nail, small end pointed out at a 45-degree angle. Press out icing, moving a little beyond edge of nail and jiggle hand up and down for three ruffles as you turn nail. Then bring hand back to starting point before cutting off pressure. Pipe five ruffled petals, brush together. Do lily pad petals same, only round and smooth.

Violet leaf. Another graceful leaf to do on a flower nail. This time, use tube 103 to press out a single ruffled shape that covers just top half of nail. Begin at center, move out toward edge of nail and immediately begin jiggling out ruffles, gradually moving hand upward as you turn nail. After curve is formed, move hand back down to starting place and end in point. Brush "veins" and "stem" sharp.

Do many other leaves in the same way. Leaves for many other flowers can also be done in a realistic fashion with the petal method shown here. Try the last three leaves above, using tube 103 and flower nail again. Do first two with motion similar to violet leaf, but describe oval shape for first, pointed, triangular shape for second. Do last leaf like the primrose, with center leaf ruffled, others smooth.

A Portfolio of Cakes Abloom with Flowers

And what glorious flowers! This collection shows fresh and happy ways to use icing flowers on cakes —to blossom on loving occasions the year around. Featured, just a sampling of the more than fifty colorful flowers given step-by-step in this book.

SWEET PEA GARLAND. Pour shiny fondant on an 8″ x 3″ cake. Edge with tube 401 ribbon. Top with sweet peas, made ahead with tubes 101, 102, 103. Add leaves with 66, 67, tendrils with 2. For butterfly on wire, see Chapter Fourteen. Serves 12.

A GARDEN CART of wild California poppies—on a sunny cake for a birthday, shower or Mother's Day. A vivid Color Flow butterfly, looking astonishingly real, flutters above to complete the pretty picture.

Prepare both butterfly and poppies ahead. For ease in cutting the cake, it is suggested poppies be made in buttercream and frozen, using tube 102 and directions in Chapter Eleven. Make butterfly on wire as shown in Color Flow Chapter Fourteen.

Now, bake a cake in a pair of oval pans, fill and ice pale yellow. Border the bottom with a tube 16 zigzag, draped with tube 104 ribbon swags. Do side stringwork garlands and accent dots with tube 3; pipe top shell border with tube 16. Finally arrange poppies on icing mound and pipe the fern-like poppy leaves with tube 2. Serves 12.

127

BLOOMING BIRTHDAY CAKE, garlanded with gay blossoms! Serves 34. To begin, pipe many yellow and pink drop flowers ahead in royal icing, using tubes 131, 190 and 224 with tube 3 green centers. Next, ice and assemble two tiers baked in 9 and 12-inch petal pans. Do blossoms "growing" on sides of bottom tier first, piping tube 3 stems, tube 65 leaves and topping with drop flowers. Then attach borders of drop flowers in garland fashion to both tiers as shown. Finally, crown cake with birthday candles, pushed into largest drop flowers while icing is still wet. Add tall center candle, more flowers.

A SHAMROCK CAKE, just right for St. Patrick's Day! Bedecked with traditional shamrock leaves and the rarely-seen, but beautiful shamrock flowers, both done in icing. To fashion, first pipe the flowers as shown in Chapter Ten, using 1¼-inch lily nail and tube 101. Then do shamrock leaves in Color Flow, using method in Chapter Fourteen, and dry on a curved form. Bake 3 single-layer cakes in 9-inch heart-shaped pans, and one cake in a loaf pan to cut into a "stem". Frost all in green, place together and border with tube 18 shells. Attach shamrock flowers and leaves where cakes join. Serves 20.

CHRYSANTHEMUM BOUQUET. A pretty centerpiece for autumn showers or parties. Bake a cake in a dome-shaped pan. Trim off top for a more rounded look, coat with icing and place on a ruffle-bordered cake circle. Make chrysanthemums in three sizes with tubes 79, 80 and 81 and primroses with tube 104, using buttercream icing and directions in Chapter Nine. Freeze flowers until just before serving time, then attach to cake with dots of icing. (They'll soften in a few minutes.) Pipe leaves with tube 67, finish with real ribbon bow. Serves 12.

BLUEBELL WEDDING CAKE. A tower of flower cakes decked with dainty bluebells. Easy to decorate because you can make all your flowers weeks in advance, then complete cake with simple one-step borders. Make flowers in three sizes as directed in Chapter Ten and reserve. Then bake three cake tiers in 6, 9 and 12-inch petal-shaped pans and ice all a snow white. Assemble tiers using a blue foil-covered board as base and 10 and 8-inch separator plates with 7½-inch long plastic twist legs. Pipe shell base borders around all three tiers, using tube 17 for bottom tier, tube 16 for other tiers. Edge all tier tops with tube 87 zigzag borders. Mound icing as base for flower clusters and place flowers, attaching some to ornament. Add tube 67 leaves. Serves 72.

LILY OF THE VALLEY CAKE. A small wedding cake with big-cake flair! Serves 98. Ice and assemble two cake tiers, a 12-inch round, 4 inches high and an 8-inch round, 3 inches high. At bottom of 12-inch tier, pipe groups of three circular motion bulbs with tube 8, add tiny tube 65 leaf between. Do tube 6 circular motion side garlands, tube 4 string. Edge tier top with tube 8 bulbs and do tier top scallops with tube 4 bulbs. Now pipe lily of the valley on sides as directed in Chapter Eleven, using tube 67 for leaves, 79 for blossoms, 3 for stems. On 8-inch tier, add bottom bulb border with tube 10, full top garlands with 8, string with 4, tier top scallops with 3. Pipe lily of the valley on top of 8″ tier, arranging in circle to frame ornament.

DAISY CHAIN. Marguerites, shastas, wild field blossoms—a wonderful variety of sizes and colors for any cake. Make them of royal icing days or weeks ahead—then decorate a simple oval cake very quickly just before the party. For your daisies, use tubes 102 and 104 as directed in Chapter Nine. Pipe large center dots with tube 3 and place on curved surface to dry for natural-looking curved petals. When thoroughly dry, achieve two-color effect by brushing base of petals with contrast food color straight out of the bottle. Use copper for orange daisies, dark gold for yellow ones. Experiment with other colors, too if you like. They'll blend beautifully! Now bake a two-layer cake in oval pans and frost with pale yellow buttercream icing. Pipe top and bottom shell borders, the elegant double fleur-de-lis and the single star that accents each, with tube 16. Pipe stems with tube 6, attach daisies with dots of icing. Add the green leaves with tube 65. 12 servings.

AUTUMN LEAVES. A wedding cake decked with vibrant color of maple leaves! Serves 182. To decorate, first prepare leaves as directed in Chapter Eleven. Then ice three round tiers pale gold—16″ x 4″, 10″ x 4″, 6″ x 3″. Assemble on a foil-covered 22-inch board, with 5-inch tall pillars, 12-inch round separator plates. On 16-inch tier, pipe bottom shell border first with tube 17. Next, pipe zigzag garlands around sides with tube 19 and use tube 17 again for pretty fleur-de-lis between. Then with same tube, pipe top shell border and edge separator plate. On 10″ tier, do fleur-de-lis first, then bottom border, then zigzag side garland and finally top shell border, using tube 17 for all. For 6″ tier, pipe fleur-de-lis, next bottom, then top shell borders, all with tube 16. Arrange leaves around cake base; scatter a few more around petite bridal couple glued between pillars. Pipe icing inside of small vase and press in iced styrofoam half ball. Push in leaves on wires. Set on top of cake.

CARNATION CAKE. Lovely Mother's Day tribute serves 14. Pipe 10 icing carnations ahead as directed in Chapter Nine. (These are full, not half carnations.) Then ice a 10-inch round, 4-inch high cake pink and make a pattern for cake top using method in Chapter Seven. Pin to cake top, use toothpick to trace and to mark cake into 8ths. Then outline in zigzag and pipe fleur-de-lis with tube 14. Next, pipe upright shells at each 8th of base with tube 199, and keeping even pressure, draw up into "posts" as shown. Now, with tube 14, pipe zigzag scallops between posts and edge base of cake with more zigzag. Next, pipe small shells above and below base zigzag and around top edge of cake. Now use tube 5 to pipe bulb of icing on backs of flowers and spray of stems on cake top. Attach flowers, pipe leaves with tube 65.

NOSEGAY WEDDING CAKE. Dainty icing bouquets make charming keepsakes! Cake serves 150. First make nosegays as shown in Chapter Eleven. Then ice three cake tiers, 6″ x 3″, 10″ x 3″, and 14″ x 4″. Assemble with 3-inch pillars, 8 and 12-inch separator plates. Using pillars as a guide, divide tiers into fourths (mark directly in line with pillars on top and bottom tiers, midway between pillars on center tier). At each fourth, drop a large tear-shaped string—longest one first—using tube 2. Then do two more over first one and add dots. (Make four tear-drops on base tier.) Next, outline separator plates with tube 2 dots. Now ring all tiers with bead borders, a triple row at bottom of tiers, a double row at top. On 14-inch tier, use tube 6 base, tube 5 top. On 10-inch tier, use tube 5 base, 4 top. On 6-inch tier, use tube 4 base, tube 3 top. Attach nosegays.

134

TIFFANY ROSE WEDDING CAKE. Petitely-tiered to serve just 90 guests. Bake three top tiers, using set of miniature tier cake pans, 5, 6½ and 8 inches round, 1½ inches deep. Use 12-inch round pan to bake two-layer base tier. Make flowers first, using tube 102 for solid-color rosebuds, 103 and 104 for two-toned Tiffany Roses. Pipe inner Tiffany rose petals pink, outer petals pale gold. Attach a few roses and buds to short florist's wires with icing. Pipe pointed green sepals under each rose with tube 2, let dry.

Next, ice, assemble, decorate all four tiers. Pipe "e" motion base borders, using tube 20 for lower tier, tube 18 for top three tiers. For rippled top borders, use tube 74 for bottom tier, tube 75 for top three tiers. Attach floral trims. Position wired flowers on cake top, add leaves with tubes 65, 67.

For table vases, cut a hole in each of four styrofoam balls. Ice balls green. Place in small vases, push candles in holes. Attach flowers with icing, add tube 67 leaves.

THIS DELFT TULIP CAKE was inspired by the famous blue and white Dutch pottery. Serves 20. To make it, first prepare 7 icing tulips as directed in Chapter Eleven. With tube 112 and royal icing, pipe 12 leaves from 1 to 2 inches long on wax paper, dry and set aside. Next, make extended circle for cake top, 8 side panels and base bevels, using a pattern and Color Flow technique shown in Chapter Fourteen. Outline, fill in designs, then overpipe outlines of petals and center circles on side panels with darker icing.

Next, prepare cake 12 inches square, 4 inches high. Chill, pin pattern to top, cut into 8-sided octagonal shape. Frost, then attach side panels, matching evenly with cake sides and securing with dots of icing. Next, attach bevel panels, piping a rope of icing around base first to lift bevels at top. Then pipe large beading around side panels and between bevels with tube 4. Add tiny beading between side panels with tube 1. Attach top piece to cake on small mounds of icing, to lift about ⅛-inch above surface. Edge with tube 2 beading and use same tube to bead bottom edge of bevels.

Arrange a circle of 6 tulips at cake top on small icing mounds. Add 7th tulip on center mound. Ice base of leaves, attach between tulips.

HYACINTH KEEPSAKE. Lovely favor or prize! Make an icing hyacinth as directed on page 145. Then pipe long icing leaves on florist wire using tube 79 and technique on page 146. Directions for butterfly are in Chapter Fourteen. Paint a small vase with softened royal icing, fill with stiffened royal icing and pull into points with wet spatula for "grass" effect. Push flower, leaves into icing, add butterfly on wire.

CHAPTER ELEVEN

Flowers made with Special Techniques

When you want a very large flower or one that stands on a stem or stalk for the closest imitation of nature, some special techniques are needed. A few must merely be piped in a unique way. For some, you must make each petal and part separately to assemble later. Of these, several take the Color Flow method described in Chapter Fourteen. For others you will pipe lacy patterns on net.

For flowers of this special sort, it is best to use only royal or Color Flow icings. Then they will stay in shape and position indefinitely because they dry firm and hard and never crumble. Extra-large flowers are usually made more for display or as keepsakes, rather than to be consumed. Such unusual icing flowers are not easy to do, but they are so very impressive, they are well worth the effort.

CALLA LILY. This dramatic flower takes a special "pivot" technique. Hold tube 124, wide end down at a 45-degree angle to surface and move it upward to lay out a ribbon of icing as in first picture above. When ribbon is about 3½ inches long, lift tube, turning narrow end almost straight up and continue to squeeze out icing for a cupped and curved-over top, as in second picture. Then continue downward to ribbon's starting point, forming a large oval cupped flower as in third picture. Next, use deep color method in Chapter Three for a bright yellow icing and slip tube 8 into base of flower. Squeeze out icing, moving upward, for a long bulb center as in fourth picture. Pipe tube 7 stem.

HOW TO MAKE A SPRAY OF LILY OF THE VALLEY

There's no lovelier trim for the sides of a towering wedding cake than sprays of that traditional wedding flower—the graceful lily of the valley. And it's one of the few you can pipe directly on the cake. Once you get the knack of piping the blossoms, the rest is really easy.

THE FLOWER. To make the tiny white, bell-like blossoms, fit a decorating bag with tube 79, 80 or 81. Touch the curved end of the tube to decorating surface and press out a tiny curve of icing. Continue squeezing and moving in a slight circular motion. Stop pressure and move away. The result should be a tiny bell as in first step above. Pipe a

curved stem with tube 2 and add alternating blossoms on tiny tube 1 stems as in second step.

THE LEAVES. The lily of the valley has broad curving leaves which are quite simple to pipe, using tube 67. As you press out icing, let it build up slightly for a broad width, jiggling your hand very gently as you move upward. Curve to right and gradually stop pressure to bring leaf to a point. Go back to base and pipe second leaf over first. With tube 2, pipe a trio of stems, beginning between the two leaves and arching out as in third step. Then add blossoms as in the fourth step.

Flowers and Leaves on Wire

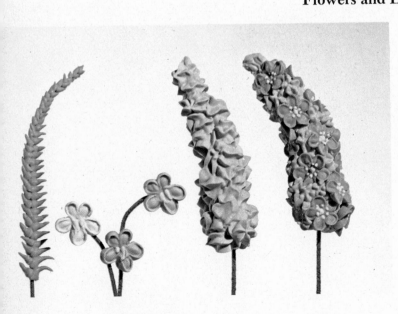

Many flowers and leaves are clustered or simply poised at the top of a long, slender stem. Start with a cloth-covered florist's wire pushed into a styrofoam base. Curve the wire for a graceful natural look and then apply icing and blossoms or leaves as follows:

TO MAKE FERN. Rub wire with icing, then pull out little points all around with tube 1, tapering to top.

TO ATTACH TINY FLOWERS TO STEMS. Rub wire with icing. Prepare flowers ahead (forget-me-nots, apple blossoms, violets), then attach with a dot of icing.

TO MAKE LARKSPUR. Pipe many tiny blossoms same as forget-me-nots in Chapter Nine and dry thoroughly. Rub wire with icing, then cover with tube 14 stars, tapering to top. Add blossoms all over with dots of icing.

140

Flowers Made in Color Flow

With this technique, petals and leaves of a flower can be made according to the Color Flow method described in Chapter Fourteen and put together with icing after drying. Color Flow enables you to make flowers of almost any size or variety in colors as brilliant and beautiful as nature. You can combine Color Flow petals and leaves with other flower parts piped in icing or molded of sugar. On this and the next two pages, you will see some of the exciting possibilities Color Flow affords.

POINSETTIA. Draw pointed oval patterns for 8 petals, 2 inches long and 1-inch wide. Cover with wax paper rectangles, outline and fill in with red Color Flow icing according to directions in Chapter Four-teen. Dry on curved form, curving 4 petals up, 4 down. Pipe a mound of green icing on cake with tube 8 and attach petals around it. Use tube 11 to dot center, first with yellow, then red.

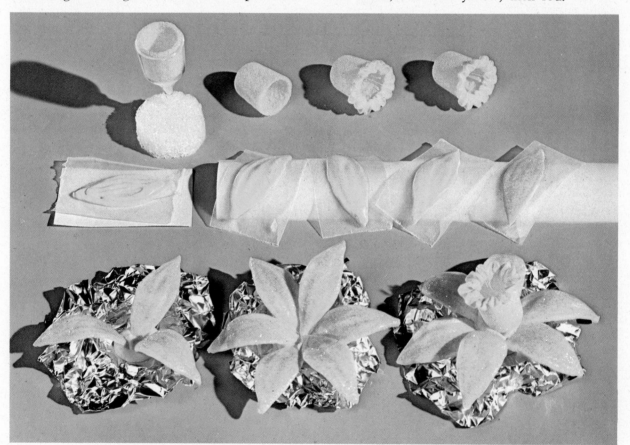

DAFFODIL. A full 3¾ inches across! A good size for large and dramatic cakes. Mold center bell first of tinted sugar in a miniature toast glass or an extra large thimble. (See Sugar Mold directions in Chapter Eighteen.) When molded sugar is partly dry, scoop out center, leaving just cup-shaped shell. Let dry thoroughly and add ruffle with tube 101s and royal icing. Pipe a small mound of icing inside and push in artificial stamens. For Color Flow petals, draw 6 petal patterns, 1¼ inches long. Tape a wax paper rectangle over each, outline and fill in as directed in Color Flow Chapter Fourteen. Dry petals over a curved shape. To assemble, shape a "nest" of foil, put a bulb of royal icing in center. Attach 6 petals in a circle, add a bit more icing to center, attach sugar bell.

HOW TO MAKE AN ORCHID

Just make petals, assemble as directed below and shown step-by-step at left.

FOR SMOOTH PETALS. Outline shape, 3 inches long, ¾ inch at widest part on a rectangle of paper. Attach to 3 inch jumbo flower nail with icing dot, cover with wax paper. Then, with unsoftened Color Flow icing, mixed according to directions in Chapter Fourteen, fill in, going up one side, down the other. Icing will ripple a bit, so smooth with damp brush, insert florist's wire, smooth again. Make 3 petals, dry over curved form, attaching one to edge with icing so it goes into an S-curve.

FOR RUFFLED PETALS. Draw outline 3 inches long, 1¼ inches at widest part. Attach to jumbo nail, cover with wax paper and fill with tube 104 ruffles. Smooth center with brush, insert wire, smooth again. Do two, dry on curve.

FOR BIG CENTER PETAL. Cover a 4½ inch tall plastic or paper cone with wax paper. Then describe a rounded triangle about 3 inches long and 1½ inches wide at base on the cone with a broad stripe of icing, using tube 104. Add another stripe down center, smooth with damp brush to fill area of triangle. Let dry on cone, then pull out cone with a gentle twist. Peel wax paper from petal. There will be a small opening for pistil at point. Hold point of petal, pipe tube 104 ruffled edge. Prop to dry.

TO MAKE PISTIL. Insert wire into tube 7, pull out as you squeeze bag for icing bulb. Brush into slim shape, dry.

TO ASSEMBLE. Insert pistil into large center petal, wind its wire around a heavier length of wire, bind together with florist's tape. Now lay all petals in position as shown. Wind rest of petals onto main stem, bind with more tape for a single stem. Carefully brush icing on orchid back to conceal joinings. Bend stem in circle, press into crumpled foil inside small cup. Dab icing inside all petals on main stem to secure. Dry in cup. Orchid's complete!

HOW TO MAKE A TULIP

Shape this stately, colorful flower of icing, with petals almost as thin and delicate as on a real tulip.

TRACE PETAL PATTERNS. With a nail, etch 4 large and 4 small petal patterns on reverse side of egg-shaped cupcake pan. Trace large 2⁵⁄₁₆ x 1⅞-inch petals on full half of egg and small 2¹⁄₁₆ x 1⅝-inch petals on narrower half. Lightly cover with shortening.

OUTLINE DESIGN. With unsoftened Color Flow icing (see Chapter Fourteen), and tube 2 or 3, outline petal design. Dry about 20 minutes.

FILL IN PETALS. Use tube 104 and more unsoftened Color Flow icing. Work from bottom up, picking up any icing overflow with a brush. Smooth petal with moistened brush, add vein with tube 2, dry 4 hours. Place in preheated 250° oven for 30 seconds to melt shortening, loosen petals, so you can gently remove them. Now you are ready to put your tulip together.

ASSEMBLE, PETAL BY PETAL. Place aluminum foil on inside of a small tapered cup or shot glass. With tube 8, pipe a mound of stiffened Color Flow icing in bottom. Push in 3 large petals as shown and brush icing up on them to smooth joining. Add more icing, 3 smaller petals. Brush smooth again.

MAKE STAMENS AND PISTIL, shown at left. Trim tips from artificial stamens. Using tube 65, dark icing, insert ½-inch of stamen into end of tube. Slowly squeeze bag and pull stamen from tube, let dry. With tube 9, green icing, pipe center pistil in tulip. (Pistil is shown separately, so you can see its shape.) Fasten 6 stamens at pistil base with icing. Dry overnight.

FOR VASE OF TULIPS. Make 5 tulips. Pipe 12 leaves, 1 to 2 inches long with tube 112, royal icing on wax paper. Place tissue paper ball in vase, level with top, cover with green icing. Arrange tulips and leaves in icing mounds on top.

Flowers To Assemble

Among the prettiest of flowers are those formed of clusters of tiny blossoms. To re-create them in icing requires more care in the putting together than in the piping. It is not really difficult to do, however. Simply pipe the simple blossoms in quantity, as directed below, then attach to flower heads of styrofoam or icing, or to wire stems. Be sure to make all the individual blossoms very, very small—the largest no larger than a dime when completed, with petals no longer than ¼-inch.

FIRST MAKE INDIVIDUAL BLOSSOMS

PHLOX. Stripe a bag, fitted with tube 101, with pink icing to narrow end of tube. Fill with white icing. Start at center of nail, pressing out 5 rounded petals, overlapping slightly. Center with a tiny tube 1 dot.

GERANIUM. Use bright icing, tube 101. Start at center of nail, move out ½-inch, turning nail as you go to shape little petal. Do two or more same size, two ¼-inch. Pipe tube 1 dots for stamens.

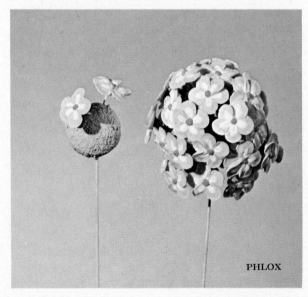

PHLOX

GERANIUM

THEN ASSEMBLE THE FLOWER HEAD

Both phlox and geranium are done in a similar fashion. First, pipe a green calyx for each blossom, inserting wire stem, same as for Queen Anne's lace, page 148. Attach with icing to back of blossoms, cut stems to one inch. Push length of heavy florist's wire into a styrofoam ball, about 2½ inches in diameter; ice ball green. With tweezers, push stemmed blossoms into ball all around, letting them stand out ¼ inch. Shape clusters as shown—geranium with flat base, phlox rounded.

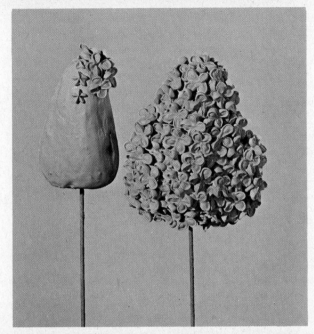

HOW TO MAKE A LILAC

FIRST MAKE BLOSSOMS as shown step-by-step, upper left. Pipe four tiny rounded petals with tube 59°. You can use a jumbo flower nail and pipe several at a time if you like. Do *not* put on calyx and stem. Pipe many blossoms, dry thoroughly and reserve.

NEXT MAKE CONE BASE. Start with a styrofoam cone about 3½ inches tall, with base 2 inches in diameter. Push in a length of heavy green florist's wire. Ice cone thickly and add on an extra thickness of icing all around base to increase width to about 3 inches in diameter. Push in styrofoam block to dry.

ASSEMBLE FLOWER. With tube 14, pipe a tiny star on iced cone as shown. While it is still wet, press on a blossom. Pipe another star, add another blossom and so on, until entire cone, bottom and all, is thickly covered with tiny lilac blossoms.

HOW TO MAKE A HYACINTH

FIRST MAKE BLOSSOMS as shown step-by-step at left. Use the smallest two-piece lily nail and line with foil. Then, with leaf tube 65, pull out six tiny pointed petals. Repeat for many, many blossoms. Dry and reserve while you go on to next step.

Now MAKE CALYX of same color on a length of light-weight white wire, same as for Queen Anne's lace, page 148. Make one for each blossom and when dry, attach with a dab of icing to back to produce a small flower with a long fluted shape. Dry and prepare to assemble.

ASSEMBLE FLOWER. Position one blossom at top of a length of heavyweight green florist's wire pushed into a styrofoam block. Use green florist's tape to bind it in position as shown. Then, tape on another blossom, letting stem extend about ¼-inch from main stem. Continue to tape on blossoms in this manner, going around and around, and allowing some air between blossoms to give the natural "see-through" appearance of the flower, until a long oval shape is achieved. (Wind in top and bottom blossoms closer to stem to taper flower.) Wind tail of tape around main stem to bottom to finish off.

HOW TO ASSEMBLE A GLADIOLA SPRAY

First make gladiola blossoms in large and small sizes as in Chapter Ten, and add a green calyx to each with icing (made as for Queen Anne's lace, on page 148). For long leaves, use tube 70. Insert medium-weight, 16-inch long florist's wire into top of decorating bag until it protrudes 3½ inches from tube. Close bag tightly, squeeze as you slowly pull wire out of tube to form leaf. To curve, bend wire as you pull. Dry in styrofoam block hung upside down so leaves will not droop. (Place block at edge of shelf, secure with weight.) For closed buds, insert 1½ inches of a 6-inch length of wire into tube 8. Squeeze slowly, draw out a long bud, brush into oval shape. Hold like a flower nail and revolve as you swirl a leaf around it with tube 67.

For open bud, use peach icing, tube 104. Pipe two or three spiral buds on 6-inch lengths of wire, partially encircle with leaves.

To assemble spray, straighten a wire coat hanger, cut to 28-inch length. Cover with florist's tape, push into 4-inch deep styrofoam block, begin assembling flower as shown above. Using a single long piece of tape, wind on smallest green bud at top, slightly to left. Wind in second green bud, below it and to right. Continue to alternate, going from small closed buds to open buds, from small to large flowers. Add leaves, taping two or three high enough to rise above lowest flowers on stalk, with other leaves below. Brush icing on any tape that still shows.

HOW TO MAKE AN AUTUMN MAPLE LEAF

Color Flow makes it easy! And so very real-looking. Trace a real leaf or use pattern and tape a piece of clear plastic wrap over it, smoothing so no wrinkles remain. Mix Color Flow icing, tint it an Autumn hue and soften as directed in Chapter Fourteen. Fill a decorating bag half full and cut a very small opening. Trace the pattern very roughly to outline the leaf—then immediately fill in with same icing and pull out points quickly with a small damp artist's paintbrush. (You'll notice this procedure is different than the usual Color Flow method.) Carefully lift wet leaf on plastic wrap and place inside or over a curved form to let leaf dry in a natural position. Mix copper brown paste color with a drop of water and paint in veins. Tint water copper color and dip cloth-covered florist's wire for stems. Dry, attach to back of leaf with matching, unsoftened Color Flow icing.

HOW TO MAKE CHRISTMAS MISTLETOE

For centuries, a magical symbol of love and peace! To do in icing, first make leaves. Attach wax paper to curved surface, as shown at right. Pipe small green dot with tube 2, push in short length of fine florist's wire while icing is still wet. Let dry, then with tubes 7 and 9 (for 2 sizes), pipe elongated leaves over dots, brush to taper at wire. When dry, cover stems with green florist's tape. For single spray, tape stems of 3 or 4 leaves together, center one, alternating others below it. Pipe white icing "berries" with tube 2. For multiple sprays, not shown, tape 2 or 3 single sprays together. See a beautiful mistletoe cake on page 185.

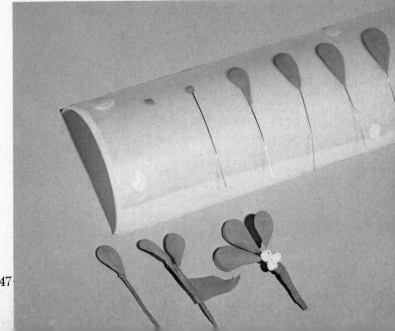

Net Flowers

A very lovely accent for cakes of any size, done with a technique adapted from faraway Australia. Cut out net petal shapes. Draw a petal pattern, about 2 inches long and ¾ inches wide in center and cut out. Fold several thicknesses of fine white tulle or net and pin pattern to them, so you can cut out several net petals at one time. Use the same shapes for both petals and leaves.

Attach each net petal shape to a rectangle of wax paper with a bit of royal icing. Outline shapes in more royal icing (for both petals and leaves) with a zigzag motion, using tube 1. Do lace cornelli work, described in Chapter Twelve, inside petals and veins inside leaves with same tube. Lift completed petals and leaves on wax paper and place over curved form to dry. Then assemble. Pipe a large bulb of icing in the center of a wax paper square. Push in two or three leaves first as shown, then five petals over them. Finish with 8 yellow artificial stamens in bulb, and flower is finished!

A Nosegay of Roses
and Queen Anne's Lace

An exquisite touch for any cake! First, prepare roses of royal icing, doing smallest with tube 101s on length of fine florist's wire, same as toothpick roses in Chapter Nine. Pipe 5 tiny points for sepals under each rose with tube 1 or 1s, push into styrofoam to dry. Do larger rose with tube 101, then make long-stemmed calyx for it. Pipe a pale green royal icing bulb on wax paper with tube 1 or 1s. Bend top of a length of florist's wire into tiny hook, push down into bulb. Lift upright, brush into cone shape. Dry 12 hours, attach to rose with dab of icing, pipe on sepal points with tube 1. Make white stemmed calyxes for lace flowers at this time.

For Queen Anne's lace, cut out dime-size circles of fine net. Attach net to wax paper squares with icing, attach square to flower nail. Fill circles with cornelli lace as described in Chapter Twelve and edge with zigzag, doing both with tube 1. Sprinkle with edible glitter, dry, attach to calyxes with icing. Press out small leaves on wax paper—½-inch long with tube 65, one inch with tube 67. Immediately, push florist's wire stem into each, dry. To assemble, push stemmed roses, lace flowers and leaves into a florist's nosegay holder. Attach to cake with hat pin, pipe bulb of icing to hold stems together, press on ribbon bow for finishing touch.

To Make in Icing: Wild Flowers

What a lovely and unusual touch for your cakes—the beautiful wild flowers that brighten woodland, meadow and mountainside! Now create them in icing for back-to-nature party centerpieces.

BROWN-EYED SUSAN. A native American flower that adds golden beauty to meadow and roadside alike—bright-eyed touch for a summer cake. To make: first pipe a cone-shaped mound of dark brown icing on a wax paper square as in bottom row of illustrations at left. Sprinkle with brown-tinted sugar and let dry.

Next, attach a second square of wax paper to a flower nail and pull out long slim petals from center of nail to edge as in step 1 of center illustration at left, using tube 103 and same motion as for daisy petal. Complete circle of petals as in step 2 at center left, then while icing is still wet, draw 2 narrow grooves in each petal with damp artist's brush. Immediately, press reserved brown cone into center, as in step 3 at center left and lift completed flower onto curved surface to dry, directing petals up or down as desired.

CLOVER. The colorful meadow flower that scents the summer air with its fresh, sweet fragrance! To fashion it, first pipe a shell-motion bulb of green icing with tube 12 as shown in first step above. Lift tapered end slightly upward. Next, starting center top as in second step, pipe tiny string-like petals down and around with tube 2. Continue until bulb is covered with petals as in third step. Do buds same way, but smaller and all green as in final fourth step. To use on cake shown on page after next, pipe a spray of stems with tube 4, starting at side of cake and fanning across top. Attach blooms and buds with icing, pipe leaves with tube 67.

QUEEN ANNE'S LACE. This delicate meadow flower has great flat clusters of white petals, so pin-point tiny, they seem to float about the stems. You can pipe them right on the cake for an effect that's positively breathtaking. Begin by piping a spray of two or three main stems with tube 4. At top of main stems, pipe a sunburst of narrower stems with tube 1. Then, over and all around these smaller stems, pipe minute white blossoms with tube 2, each a "wheel" of tiny, tear-shaped petals. Fill center of each with dots using tube 1. Continue for great clusters of flowers that nearly hide the stems.

WILD SWEET PEA. Its Latin name compares it rightfully to a butterfly! In nature, it clings to a vine which you can reproduce on any cake. Hold decorating cone at 45-degree angle with wide end of tube 104 touching surface, narrow end slightly above it, pointed out. Pipe ruffled heart-shaped back petal first. Next, do a smaller cupped petal, then a second small cupped petal within the first. Finally, pipe tiny stand-up white center petal and add green calyx with tube 2. Pipe white crescent shaped buds with tube 3 and when dry, brush on streaks of lavender and green thinned royal icing.

WILD CALIFORNIA POPPY. Press foil halfway into 1¼-inch lily nail, use stiff royal icing, tube 103. Touch center, pull icing over edge, straight across, back to center for square, cupped petals. Smooth, fill centers with damp brush. Add dot, artificial stamens (tops cut and brushed with orange icing).

THE WILD FLOWER CAKES on facing page will create a sensation at any springtime gathering. Bake cakes in simple shapes—round, petal or hexagonal—and ice them in colors that set off flowers. Add very simple borders—small neat shells, ribbons, dots or zigzags. Then let the wild flowers star!

CHAPTER TWELVE
Special Decorating Techniques

LATTICE, FILIGREE, LACEWORK, OVERPIPING, BASKETWEAVING

Now you are ready for new decorating adventures. The skills you have learned and practiced so far have given you the fine control you need to accomplish the advanced decorating techniques described in this chapter. They bring within your reach cake designs of the most intricate variety—and give your work an elegant and expert look. They take time to perfect and time to do, but mastering them is vastly satisfying.

As with other advanced techniques, these utilize many of the basic skills you've already learned and practiced. Lattice, filigree, lace and overpiping, for example, begin with simple stringwork. And basketweaving is merely a combination of strings or bands of icing. However, when used for such intricate designs, these simple techniques require nearly perfect control. But, as with the basic decorating techniques you've mastered, continued practice should give you equally pleasing results with these more advanced techniques.

BELOW: SUMMER STAR, a festive little cake that serves just 12 at a small wedding reception or bridal shower. It demonstrates beautifully, two basic lattice styles—surface and draped. Draped lattice is demonstrated on page 87. Surface lattice is shown on the facing page, where you will also find directions for decorating this cake.

Lattice—Icing Strings Form Elegant Designs

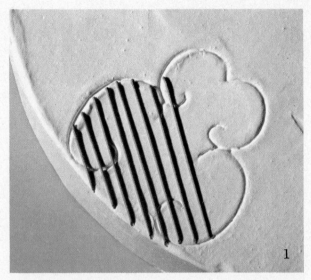

1

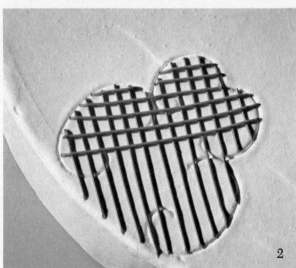

2

3

The simple strings of icing that you press through tubes 1 or 2 can be turned into designs as delicate as spider webs and graceful as Grecian lyres. Pipe them across the surface of your cake for exquisite and airy shapes. Or drape them from cake top or sides for a magical 3-dimensional effect. Wherever you use it, lattice adds a lavish look.

To frame your latticework, you can create your own designs. Just draw them first on paper, measuring carefully, of course, to fit the space on cake. Or use one of the pattern presses that offer a variety of designs shaped in hard plastic. These let you press a design right into the iced cake. At left is one example of surface lattice to try.

1. CUT A SCALLOP DESIGN out of paper and trace on iced cake with toothpick. Or use a plastic pattern press as we did. Now drop diagonal lines of string with tube 2, starting at center with longest line and working down or up. Then go back to first line of stringwork and drop more lines until design is filled.

2. NEXT, DROP LINES of tube 2 stringwork across the ones you have just piped. Begin at center again and go diagonally in opposite direction, working down or up from first, longest line, as in second step at left. Keep lines as straight and even as possible.

3. OVERPIPE original outline with tube 16, using "e" motion as you go, as shown in third step. This will conceal rough ends of latticework and make a pretty frame. A beautiful touch for top or sides of any cake.

To DECORATE SUMMER STAR, on facing page, ice a two-layer cake that is 8 inches square, 4 inches high. Fold a piece of paper same size as cake top into thirds (see page 94) and use to mark each side into thirds. With toothpick, draw guideline for scrolls from mark to mark on top and between two center marks on sides. Then with tube 2 do green lattice design on cake top in same manner as lattice design on this page. Overpipe guidelines with scrolls, using tube 17. Do side scrolls with same tube, using zigzag motion, then overpipe a second scroll on top of each. Drape lattice from top edge of cake to scroll, then overpipe one more scroll to conceal lattice edges. (Page 87 shows this step-by-step.) Use tube 17 again for "C" scrolls and to do shell border at top edge. Also use same tube for rosette-and-shells that form star on cake top. Pipe bottom shell border with tube 20.

Filigree—Lacy Icing Decorations for Your Cake

Filigree is actually a form of latticework done off the cake. Once mastered, this technique lets you create stand-out cake trims, as well as your own ornaments, centerpieces and displays. All from little more than icing and your own imagination.

For filigree, you'll need an icing that flows easily, but dries to a hard shape that will not crumble. Royal icing, thinned with lightly beaten egg white instead of water is the perfect one to use. Tape wax paper or clear plastic wrap as smoothly as possible over design, trace with plain round or star tube sized to suit design. If you are working with a fine line of icing, using tube 1, 1s or smaller, overpipe for strength. Then let dry, peel off paper, turn over and overpipe again. For designs 1 through 7, no overpiping is necessary.

FILIGREE CAN BE FLAT OR CURVED

The designs at left were piped on both flat and curved surfaces. Design 2 is piped on a flat surface. (1 and 3 are the same design, but 3 was turned upside down and piped with a circular motion for variety.) Designs 1, 4, 5, 6 and 7 were piped and dried in a curved position. The umbrella was done on plastic wrap, stretched over a small novelty umbrella which provided the size and shape. The simple design was outlined in tube 2 zigzags. Scalloped edge was overpiped in lavender and drop flowers attached while umbrella was still on curved surface, to prevent breaking. Lollipop stick handle was attached with dot of icing. Triangle, heart and oval were piped with star tube 14, using dots, tiny stars, shells and other motions to complete designs.

FILIGREE CAN BE ASSEMBLED

To create a special effect with filigree, put several sections together with icing. Examples at left were created for cake on facing page. Designs 8 are done on a flat surface by first tracing the joined series of curved "S" shapes with tube 2, then adding the curlicues and overpiping "S" shapes. After drying, turn over and overpipe "S" shapes once more to add strength. Do designs 9 and 10 in the same fashion. On facing page, top ornament has arch formed of filigree 10 in front, joined to two filigree 8 arches in back. Filigree 9 becomes standout trim for side of cake.

Here are three dramatic ways to use filigree described on facing page.

THE DAISY DREAM cake below is edged with filigree arches (designs 8, 9 and 10). Design 10 becomes front arch of ornament and two design 8 half arches are attached on a slant to back of it. Design 9 filigrees hook to tier sides. Icing dots secure all.

SWAN LAKE WEDDING cake at right is frilled with filigree scrolls (design 2). On base tier, two scrolls are joined facing in opposite directions to form long arched scrolls at top and sides of cake. Scrolls are secured with icing dots.

THE VASES OF VIOLETS shower cake below flaunts a filigree parasol. Top is design 5, handle a lollipop stick dipped in icing. After drying, it was attached to the parasol top with dab of icing. Filigree vases (design 7) adorn sides.

155

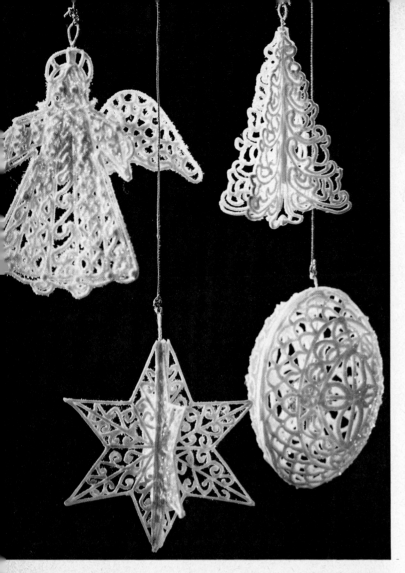

FILIGREE SHAPES MANY THINGS

Filigree constructions take care to make and greater care to assemble. But what beautiful bits of fantasy they are! For Christmas ornaments and village, use patterns and royal icing thinned with egg white. Be sure all lines connect, so designs hold together.

Cover angel, star and tree patterns with wax paper, pipe with tube 2. Spray with glaze, sprinkle with glitter. Add cord or ribbon to hang.

TREE, STAR. Trace one whole pattern of tree or star with icing. Outline two half patterns in same way. Dry, peel off paper, attach a wire down center of whole tree or star with line of icing. While still wet, press center edge of one of halves along it to attach. Prop with cotton balls to dry. Turn over carefully, repeat on other side with second half.

ANGEL. Trace lace angel and wings in icing. When dry, peel off paper, turn angel over, pipe a line of icing halfway down center of back. Press short wire, looped at top, along this line so loop is above angel's head. Touch center edges of wings here also, at 45-degree angle. Prop with cotton balls to dry thoroughly.

CHRISTMAS EGG. Grease outside of top halves of two plastic egg molds and place next to pattern for reference. Then pipe filigree design free-hand on molds with tube 2. After drying, place in warm oven to melt grease (about ½-minute), then slip mold out. Let harden, round side up. Push a short wire through a tiny golden ball, loop both ends. Pipe line of icing along edge of one egg half. Lay wire at heavy end so only top loop extends outside. Immediately, press both halves together, let dry.

FILIGREE VILLAGE. With building sections piped on net for extra strength! For snowy setting, swirl boiled icing on a 24″ x 24″ piece of styrofoam with "hill" carved into one end. Use shiny foil or mirror for "pond", sprinkle all with glitter. Next make houses. First, pin smoothly-ironed fine nylon net over patterns, cut out building sections. Then cover pattern with wax paper and attach net shapes with dots of icing. With tube 1, outline and add inner lines and designs, dry thoroughly. To assemble, pipe a strip of wet icing on joining parts of each piece, put together at right angles. Assemble walls, then add roofs and chimneys (put chimneys and church belfry together first). Cut paper in shapes of houses, place on setting to plan layout. Position houses, secure with icing swirls. Spray with glaze, sprinkle with glitter.

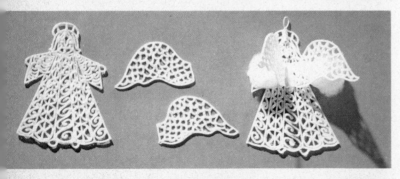

Lace Adds Such A Dainty Touch

Lacework is really the same technique as filigree—a string of icing piped into original or traditional lace designs. Pretty for bridal or shower cakes.

Use royal icing thinned with egg white as before and patterns to make lace edging for 'Happy Hearts" wedding cake below. (Complete decorating directions for cake are on page 257.) Use tube 2 for large and medium hearts, tube 1 for small heart and tiny scroll. Make many more pieces than cake requires as lacework is very fragile and may break easily in the handling. To attach, pipe string guideline on cake and press in lace pieces while icing is still wet. Do just one curve at a time, so icing won't dry before you get to it.

For larger pieces of lacework, you may want to pipe your designs on net for added strength. A book of lace patterns will suggest all kinds of ideas for adding lacy touches to cakes, favors and displays.

A TINY, LACE-DECKED BRIDE makes an exquisite top piece for a wedding or shower cake—or a unique individual cake for each shower guest.

FIRST MAKE LACE. Using smallest pattern on facing page, make 25 tiny hearts in egg white royal, plus extras, adding tiny dots around point of each.

THEN MAKE DOLL. Bake skirt in miniature doll cake pan, and when cooled ice white and push in mini doll pick. Ice torso of doll to match skirt, then brush thinned icing on arms to give impression of sheer fabric. Pipe cornelli lace (directions below) all over bodice, arms and skirt, except for v-shaped panel at skirt front, 2½" high, 3" wide at hem. To this, attach lace hearts, point of top heart down, rest up, for six rows in all. To attach, first pipe 3 tiny dots of icing, then carefully push heart on them while icing is still wet. Tip hearts out to look like rows of lace ruffles. Complete doll with veil, bouquet. Use tiny ring of pearls for cap, glue on two gathered lengths of net (for double veil). Pipe border of tiny dot scallops along edges. For bouquet, pipe 7 tiny tube 101s daisies as directed in Chapter Nine, attach to tiny puff of net along with white satin bow, using icing. Tie doll's hands together, pipe on bulb of icing, add bouquet.

Cornelli Lace—Easy Magic

DO IT FREE-HAND, using tube 1 and thinned royal icing. Pipe a meandering line of string, zigging and zagging along for a kind of jig-saw puzzle effect.

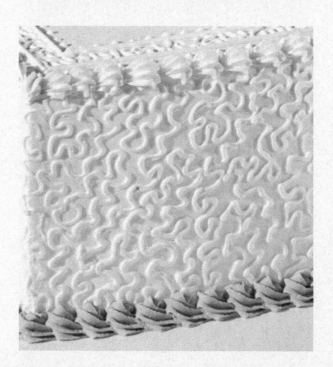

Important: make certain never to let lines touch or cross. Dry before adding trims.

LACY DAISY WEDDING CAKE, shown on page 160. Sunny touch for a reception. Serves 110.

FIRST MAKE DAISIES in 3 sizes with tubes 101, 102 and 103. Pipe tube 4 centers, sprinkle with glitter. Dry daisies on curve to lift petals. Put some daisies on wire stems: push short lengths of fine wire into tube 3 and green icing, pull out stems, then add tube 65s leaves. Attach flowers with dabs of icing.

THEN PREPARE CAKE, making base tier 14" square, 4" high, two-layer heart tier, 4" high. Ice white and assemble as shown. Next cut scallop patterns for tier sides, as directed on page 96. Pin to cake sides, outline with toothpick. Use outline as guide for other scallops and ribbon garlands.

Now DO CORNELLI LACE and frame with tube 2 beading. Bead bottoms of both tiers also, using tube 4 for heart, tube 9 for square. Drape tube 104 ribbon scallops over both, add daisies to points. Pipe tube 3 stems on tier tops, then add clusters of daisies, using some on wire stems. Then pipe tube 65s leaves. Position wire stems upright here and there for spray effect. Add daisies to petite ornament at top.

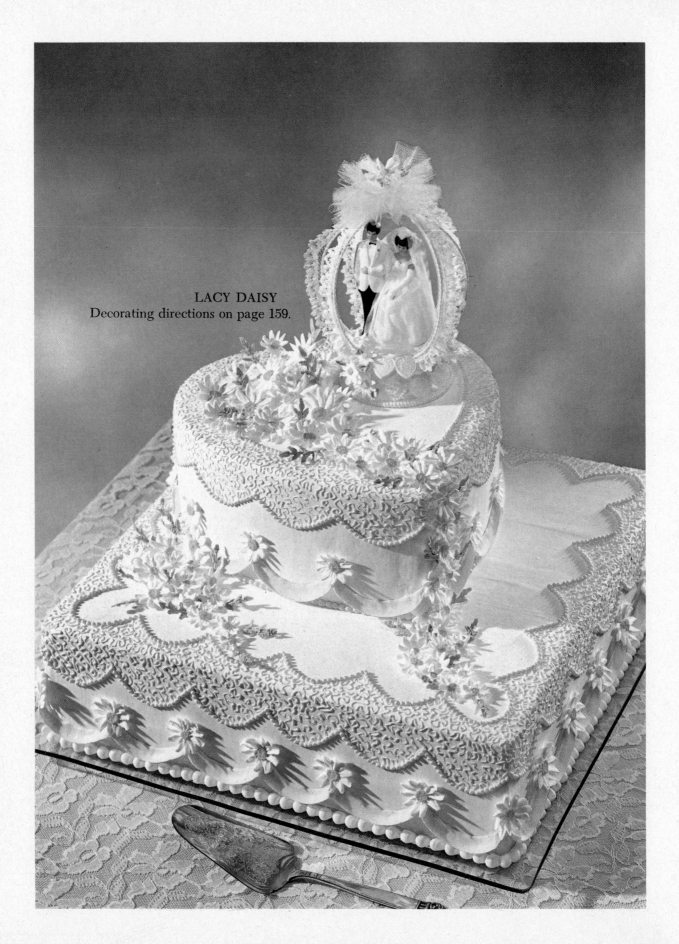

LACY DAISY
Decorating directions on page 159.

Overpiping Adds Dimension

To give a raised or dimensional look to filigree or stringwork designs, you simply pipe one line or curve of icing directly on top of another. This is the supreme test of pressure control, so much patience and practice is required to master it. It's a skill worth acquiring because it opens the way to the fabulous sculptured decorating shown next, the kind seen in decorating competitions. You've already done some overpiping by practicing borders, but fine geometric designs such as these require even greater control. The slightest variation is immediately noticeable.

Here are two examples of simple overpiping—one done on a flat, the other on a curved surface. At right, an example of curved work. A snowflake design is pinned to styrofoam cake dummy the same size as cake it will later adorn. It is covered with wax paper, then design is piped once as in first picture and overpiped as in second picture. It is kept on the dummy to dry, so it will fit curve of cake.

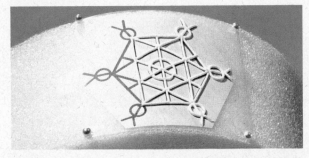

OVERPIPED SNOWFLAKE sparkles on a winter cake. Designs were traced with tube 2 and all main lines overpiped with same tube. Side pieces were dried on curve. Attach snowflakes with icing.

OVERPIPED FILIGREE adds drama to a gay fiesta cake. Filigree pattern was inspired by Spanish grillwork, piped and overpiped with tube 1. Filigree is attached with beads of wet icing at sides to stand free.

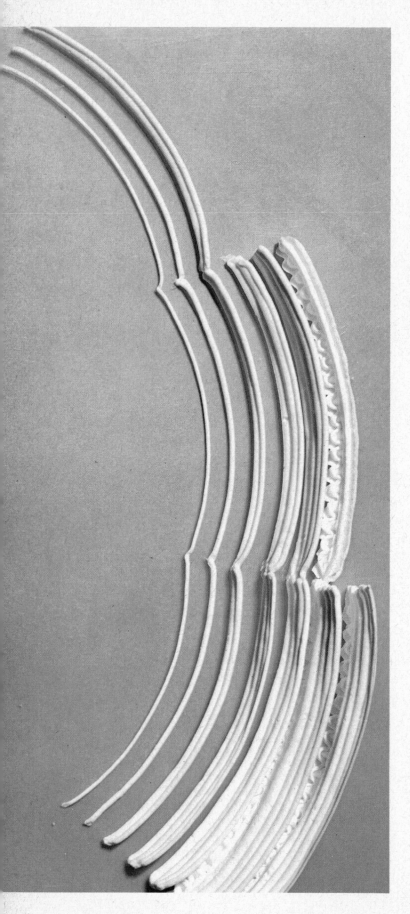

OVERPIPING CAN ADD A
DRAMATIC SCULPTURAL EFFECT

Here row after row of precision-piped (and over-piped) scallops make magic use of light and shadow for a breathtaking final effect. What appears to be rows of stand-up icing ribbons are actually rows of one icing string piped atop another!

The practice scallops shown at left are the ones used on bevel edge of lovely "Forget-Me-Not" cake on facing page. Don't let them frighten you. Just follow the step-by-step guide below, take heart and plenty of time and patience—and begin.

Draw a row of three scallops for a guide on back of a large sheet cake pan or practice board. For cake itself, you'll follow a "template" or pattern. Then draw six more scallop rows outside first, about ¼ inch apart. For this design, your scallops will begin with a single piped line and rise higher and higher until they end in the high curve at outer edge. (Always start with innermost scallops for decorating ease.)

Begin by outlining first row of scallops with a narrow string of icing, using tube 1. Go on to second row of scallops. Pipe a single line with tube 2.

In third row of scallops, overpiping begins! Outline scallops with tube 3, let dry, overpipe with tube 2. Be sure each row of string is dry before adding another atop it. As you overpipe, lift tube slightly to let icing drop for better control. Also, position icing along outer edge of string below it, to give completed scallop a slight outward slant. If done correctly, finished work will blend so smoothly, individual strings will be nearly invisible.

The fourth and fifth rows of scallops are string again, the fourth row beginning with tube 4, then 3 and 2. For fifth row, begin with 5, then 4, 3 and 2.

The last two rows rise very high, so they require a firm foundation. To provide this, outline the sixth row of scallops with a ridged line, using tube 14. Keep a groove of your tube facing up at all times and you will provide a perfect guideline for the overpiping that follows. Now overpipe four more times, with tube 5, then 4, 3 and 2.

For seventh or outer row of scallops, do outline with a tight, narrow zigzag using tube 14. Overpipe this with a plain tube 14 line. Then overpipe 4 more times, with tube 5, 4, 3 and 2. Finish with a tiny line of tinted icing, using tube 1.

"FORGET ME NOT"—OVERPIPING MAKES IT A STANDOUT

A decorator's masterpiece for a shower or small wedding! Serves party slices to 26 and wedding slices to 68.

To decorate: first make flowers and flower hearts. Pipe many tiny forget me nots as directed in Chapter Nine, in two sizes using tube 101s. Then draw patterns for edge-of-cake hearts, cover with wax paper squares, outline with tight, tiny tube 4 zigzag. Lift while wet, place over curved surface to dry. Add flowers with dots of icing, tube 65 leaves.

Prepare 12 inch round cake, 4 inches high and a 14 inch base bevel layer. Fill, ice white. Fold and cut scalloped, heart-shaped pattern using directions in Chapter Seven. Pin to cake top, trace around with a toothpick, remove pattern. Cut heart-shaped piece of cake an inch high for center, secure

in position shown and ice same as rest of cake. Pipe tube 1 cornelli lace within heart design.

Next, do overpiped scallops on cake top similar to those on facing page, except start with highest scallops at center, end with single string at outer edge. Top inner scallops with dots instead of string.

Then pipe large tube 199 puffs around top edge. Add blue crossed-over stringwork with tube 2 and tube 14 zigzag scallop around each puff. Overpipe with tube 14 line, then 5, 4 and finally 2 in blue. Secure flower hearts over puffs, then ring cornelli heart on cake top with more flowers.

Do base bevel scallops exactly as those on facing page. Add tiny forget me nots between scallops and circle entire bevel with tube 14 shells.

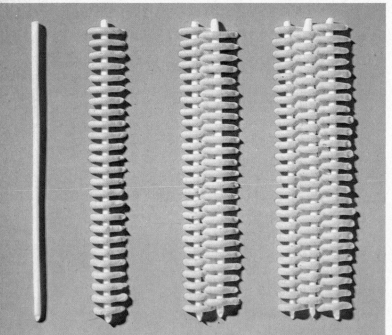

Basket Weaving
Fascinating, It Looks So Real!

Your skill with icing string brings you to another accomplishment—weaving with icing. For cake sides, try this style first—and remember, precision and neatness count. Fit one decorating bag with tube 5 and fill with white icing. Fit another with same tube and fill with yellow icing. Then practice on a board or back of cake pan as follows:

1. With first bag, pipe a vertical line of icing about 5 or 6 inches long as in first step at left.

2. Then with second bag, pipe horizontal rows of icing about ½ inch long across vertical line. Begin at top and leave about ¼ inch space between each as you move down, as in second step.

3. Pipe a second vertical line where horizontal lines end and pipe more horizontal lines over it. Work between first row of horizontal lines as in third step shown at left.

4. Repeat vertical lines, then horizontal lines until you achieve basket effect in fourth step.

NOW MAKE A BUNNY BASKET AND A BASKET OF ROSES

Do bunny, basket and eggs separately, put together. Ice two 9″ x 13″ x 2″ sheet cake layers, top with green icing patted with damp sponge for "grass". Build up top edge with two tube 30 lines, basket weave sides using tube 48 and single color only. Pipe tube 30 top rope border. Bake bunny in bunny pan, swirl with tube 17. Shape sugar eggs in plastic molds, add tube 1 trims, drop flowers. Serves 36.

A quick and easy cake to decorate with your new basket weaving skills, perfect for any occasion. Simply pipe big open roses with tube 127 and buttercream icing. Freeze until you make the two-layer, 10 inch cake. Then do basket weaving around sides, using two wide bands of icing, tubes 47 and 48. Add rope and star borders with tube 44-B, then heap with roses and tube 67 leaves. Serves 14.

A CAKE TOP FLOWER BASKET

A rich, 3-dimensional effect that will win applause. So simple with the basket weaving technique shown below. Just pipe your basket right on an iced round cake top, following the steps shown below. Be sure to leave at least half the cake top for handle and flowers. Then attach California poppies, made ahead in bright colors as directed in Chapter Eleven. Press each flower into an individual mound of icing and tip up slightly, positioning them so they appear to be curving out of basket in a natural way. Then add leaves with tube 65. Curve a leaf-decked vine all around sides of cake, using tube 2 for vine, tube 67 for leaves. Edge top of cake with rope border, bottom with ball border, using tube 9.

You can vary this basic idea many ways, perhaps filling your basket with sugar molded flowers from Chapter Eighteen, or using other varieties of flowers—roses, daisies, daffodils or the many others shown in Chapter Nine. The choice is up to you!

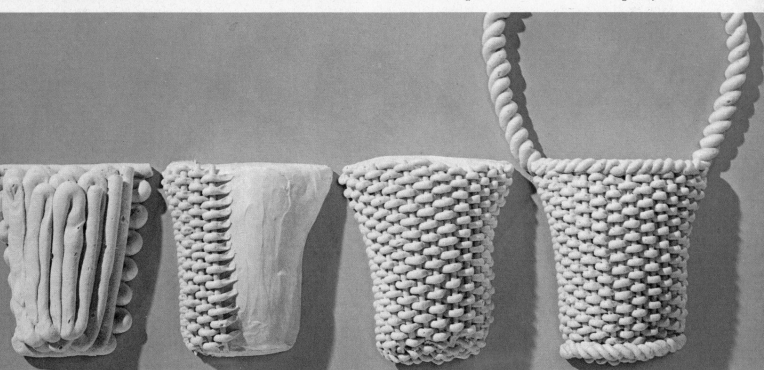

HOW TO WEAVE A CAKE TOP BASKET

1. Draw outline of basket in size and shape you prefer with toothpick, then fill in with tube 9 and several layers of zigzag, going across, then up and down. Smooth surface with damp brush or spatula.
2. Draw vertical line at one side with tube 7, following curve of basket. Then pipe short horizontal lines across it with same tube down to edge of base about ⅛" apart. Pipe a second vertical line where horizontal lines end. Then add more horizontal lines, working between first row.
3. Continue vertical and horizontal lines until basket is filled. To weave basket bottom, begin at bottom edge and work upward.
4. Pipe tube 7 rope for top and base rims. Add a rope handle to basket with tube 9.

165

CHAPTER THIRTEEN

The Techniques of Lettering

Writing with a decorating tube is a great deal easier than it appears. In fact, even if you have less than perfect handwriting, you can still do a very satisfactory job of writing on a cake top.

There's a good reason for this. When you write with a pen, you use only the movements of your fingers to control the curves and lines of the letters. When you write with a decorating bag, you use the movements of your entire arm. After you become practiced enough at tube writing, you may even develop a writing style for decorating all your own.

There are two basic requirements to keep in mind. Your icing or piping gel must be thinned enough so you can pipe long, thin lines that won't break off. And you must practice until you can control the string perfectly as you curve it into uniformly shaped and spaced letters and words.

Once you've mastered script, you'll see how you can fancy it up a bit by adding "decorative build-up". You'll also discover how to print with block letters, and even how to add drama by outlining your block letters and filling them in with bright Color Flow icing.

A few easy exercises will help to get you started correctly. You'll find them on the next page.

HOW TO DECORATE BOOK CAKES

STORYBOOK CAKES. Adding a Color Flow message to the curved surface of a book cake is very effective, but takes a rather special technique. First you will need to tape a pattern for the design to the curved top of book cake pan, making sure it follows curves smoothly. Next, tape wax paper or clear plastic wrap just as smoothly over pattern. Then outline and fill in, using Color Flow icing and technique described in Chapter Fourteen. Let design dry in position on pan, so it will fit curves of cake, and when you remove it, release it very carefully, sliding wax paper off pan, up or down—never to the side. Color Flow figures are also made and dried on pan. Stringwork and leaves are piped on, drop flowers made ahead and added to the iced book cake at same time as letters and figures.

CHRISTMAS STORY CAKE. This time, the message is written in icing, right on the frosted and trimmed book cake. You must carefully follow curve of page as you "write". Make poinsettias and holly leaves ahead as directed in Chapters Nine and Ten.

First Practice Basic Movements

When you stop to think about it, all written or printed letters are simply combinations of straight and slanted lines, circles or half circles. So it makes sense to get some control of these movements before practicing the actual letters. Fit a decorating bag with tube 3 and fill with thinned icing. Do your practicing on the back of a cake pan and you'll be able to scrape off your first efforts and try again immediately. Hold bag nearly flat and parallel to the pan and use a light, even pressure as you glide along. Practice everything shown at left, then practice again and again. If you do, you'll soon see some pleasing results.

FIRST, TRY "UP-AND-DOWN" MOTION. Press icing out lightly and draw tube along as you move your hand first up, then down, all across the pan. Try to keep lines an even size and thickness and also try to keep icing flowing evenly out of tube.

THEN, THE "C" MOTION. Rest tube lightly on pan and press evenly while doing a series of circular movements. Describe a "C" with your hand as you move along, then another and another. Join one to the other, striving for a smooth, unbroken line and even spacing.

NOW, THE "E" MOTION. Now you're ready for a double curve. Begin as before, this time describing two shorter curves before gliding upward. Do some joined "e's," breaking each off at end of long tail before starting next "e", but keeping close together for a joined look.

DO " E "AND "C". This is an excellent exercise in both concentration and control. Do an "e," then a "c" and then continue to alternate all across the pan. Again break off long tail of each letter before starting the next, but begin next right on top of tail, for unbroken joined look.

TRY SOME "L's". This time the up-and down motion takes on a curve, and again, the challenge is to make the loops all of an even size and length. Move along in a single, continuous motion.

FINALLY, STRAIGHT LINES. Though these look simpler, you will find they are not easy. It is necessary to pipe them equally sized and spaced, and to break each line off cleanly. Practice, and you will soon be turning them out perfectly. Now, try a slanted row. Many letters you will be printing in block lettering have diagonal strokes. Try some horizontal lines. Practice until you feel you have control, then go on to the next page and block lettering.

Block Lettering

Now you are ready to print with icing. An easy way to practice is to print your message on a piece of paper and tape clear plastic wrap or wax paper over it. Then trace the letters in icing. For an actual cake, print your message on iced cake top with a toothpick. Then trace with icing as before.

FLOWER-RINGED CAKE above adapts to dozens of occasions with just a change of message. The cake itself is 10″ round, 4″ high, serves 14. Drop flowers are piped ahead with tubes 217 and 224. Side border is done by the same method as Rose Ballet border on page 103, using just single rows of tube 3 dots as a frame. Pipe top vine with tube 3, leaves with tube 65, ball borders with tube 10 at bottom, 8 at top. Print message with tube 3.

Lettering in Script

To practice script, write message on a piece of paper, cover with plastic wrap or wax paper, trace with icing. Try to glide over the surface smoothly without digging in, and use your whole arm to make the various curves and swings. As soon as you feel yourself gaining control, try lifting tube slightly as you go along. You'll write more quickly, easily.

Practice the familiar phrases shown above, first tracing them in icing on the back of a pan. Then write message on cake top with a toothpick, trace as before. In time, you will be able to write your message free-hand in icing on your cake top just as easily as you now write in ink on a piece of paper.

When you start free-hand lettering, write the message on the cake top first, then add other trims. This insures plenty of space for your message.

LETTER IT SIMPLE— on a round birthday cake, sure to please anyone of any age. The cake is 10″ x 4″ and bordered with circular motion swirls piped with tube 22. Double rows of draped stringwork are started just below the top border and piped with tube 3, then accented with loops and circles at points. String designs and message are added with tube 3. Complete with novelty trim. Serves 14.

Decorative Build-Up

This is done the same as the regular script on facing page, except for extra flourishes added. Once you have gained good control with regular script, try a few phrases this way. Go along as usual, but on the downstroke, pause slightly while using the same pressure and make a slight back and forth movement as the icing builds up. This will produce an attractive rippled effect.

Decorative build-up is most frequently used for capital letters, although you can use it effectively for any letter with a long ascender or descender. To add even more swing and drama to your lettering, swing tails of first and last letters into a deep scroll-like curve, coming back down from point with a circular motion. Small scrolls can also be used to cross "t's" or as bars for "A's" and "H's."

LETTER IT FANCY—on a party cake fit for a king, or queen. To make it, first pipe several tube 190 drop flowers with a tube 4 centers and reserve. Then ice an 8″ square, 4″ high cake a pale pastel. Edge with shells, using tube 21 at bottom, tube 16 at top. Use tube 16 again to drape zigzag scallops around sides and frame them with tube 4 dots. Add tube 3 script, reserved drop flowers, tube 65 leaves. Serves 12.

Color Flow Lettering

This is a very colorful and attractive way to do lettering that uses the Color Flow icing and technique described in Chapter Fourteen.

Color Flow lettering is always done off the cake with a pattern. It is basically an outline-and-fill-in technique and makes it possible for you to spell out your message in a very artistic and unusual fashion. Using Color Flow, you can actually make your lettering an important part of the cake's design.

You can also outline and fill-in a lettering pattern with royal icing. Use a medium consistency royal for the outline, let dry and fill in with a softened royal. The Color Flow method has a higher sheen and smoother finish. Also, because Color Flow has strength, you can do stand-up letters with it.

HAPPY BIRTHDAY, PAPA. A cake with a message especially for dad, decorated with a "tweed" technique that will fascinate him. First prepare Color Flow message, using a pattern and technique in Chapter Fourteen. Outline letters with brown icing, then fill in. When completed, dry thoroughly and reserve. Then fill and frost a 10" round, 4" high cake with light chocolate icing. Next pipe tweed design. Raise cake to eye level and press out vertical lines all around, about ½ inch apart, using dark chocolate icing and tube 3. Then add chevron stripes. Finish cake with shell borders, using tube 21 for top, 199 for base. Attach Color Flow message with dots of icing.

A Portfolio of Christmas Cakes

Christmas time is more merry and bright with cakes as enchanting as the season itself. In this portfolio are cakes decorated with holiday fruits and flowers, sugar-sweet santas and best wishes for the new year. There are tiered cakes for winter weddings and jovial gingerbread cookies to delight the young.

HOLIDAY WREATH, the cake pictured below, is one that truly reflects the Christmas spirit. The cookies, which are baked first, are brushed with softened icing and then decorated with holiday motifs using tubes 2 and 3 for faces, writing and designs. The cake, a 12″ x 4″ on a 16″ bevel, bears Color Flow holiday wishes trimmed with wavy piping gel lines. The wreath is also piping gel that's spread to ring the cake top and then brushed to leaf points. The tube 2 piping gel vine is trimmed with tube 67 leaves, again feathered to points. To finish, tube 3 berries and ribbon bow are added. Serves 22.

HORN OF PLENTY, a cake that's truly holiday bright with its richly colored Color Flow cornucopia. To decorate, make the horn of plenty by taping wax paper over pattern and outlining with tube 2. Fill in each section with appropriate shades of Color Flow icings, referring to basic Color Flow technique in Chapter Fourteen. When Color Flow decoration is dry, ice a 9" x 13" x 4" high rectangular cake white and place on a foil-covered board cut to a slightly larger size rectangle. Frame cake base with tube 18 zigzag garlands, overpiping with tube 3 scalloped stringwork. Fill in spaces between garlands with tube 16 upright shells and stars, and use same tube to pipe shell border around cake top. Now position Color Flow cornucopia with icing. Serves 24.

HOLIDAY STAR, at right, in dazzling white and gold reflects its name. To decorate, tape wax paper over patterns for starburst top and side trims. Trace full starburst with tube 3, overpiping twice, and half starburst rays with tube 3, overpiping once. Sprinkle with edible glitter. Next, outline and fill in patterns for Color Flow star and triangles with tube 3. (Refer to Chapter Fourteen for basic Color Flow directions.) When all trims are dry, ice a two-layer star-shaped cake and place on a foil-covered board cut to slightly larger star size. One by one, carefully peel starbursts off wax paper and attach Color Flow star and triangles with icing. Position sunbursts with more icing and edge cake with tube 3 beading. Serves 12.

DELLA ROBIA WREATH, a cake as festive as Christmas itself! To make, shape assorted colorful marzipan fruits following basic directions in Chapter Twenty. Glaze fruits and trim some of them with artificial leaves. Ice a 10″ x 4″ round cake white and position fruits around cake top with icing for a lavish wreath-like effect. Now pipe a ruffle around cake base with ripple tube 402 and attach clusters of fruit. Trim all arrangements with tube 67 leaves, top cake center with a tall candle and light up your decorative efforts for the holidays! Serves 14.

SNOWBALL, a cake that's topped with a wintry scene to delight little ones around the house at Christmas time. To decorate, shape marzipan children following basic techniques in Chapter Twenty. The snowman's body is formed of two iced cupcakes, his head is a marshmallow—all assembled with toothpicks. Figure pipe arms with tube 6. Pipe features and buttons with tubes 2 and 3; then fasten candy corn snowman "nose". Now ice a 10" x 4" cake, swirling icing with a spatula to effect snow. Edge cake base with tube 9 icing snowballs and position merry figures atop cake with icing. Serves 14.

SWEET SANTAS gayly dance around cakes as festive as the holidays. Pipe Santas using pattern with tube 2 and Color Flow icing following basic technique described in Chapter Fourteen. Do six Santas for each cake. (Each cake is a 10″ x 4″, iced white.)

For cake at left, pipe tube 74 leaves on a cone-shape, starting at base and working upward. Dry thoroughly. Then pipe tube 3 scallops around top, and add tube 21 zigzag garlands and top border. Use the same tube to frame cake base with shells; then top cake with tree, attaching Color Flow Santas to cake sides with icing. To finish, pipe tube 21 rosette, push in candle, dry and set on tree.

To decorate cake at right, pipe tube 9 beads around base, topping with tube 104 ribbon and more beads. Position dancing Santas on cake top with icing, then pipe tube 9 beads around edge. Add a tube 22 rosette on cake center, push in candle and light up for celebrating. Each cake serves 14.

SNOWSHINE. Three tiers of cake for a wintry white wedding. Assemble 16″ x 4″, 12″ x 4″ and 8″ x 4″ tiers with 14″ separator plates and 5″ iridescent columns, placing base and center tiers on double ruffle edging which has been lined with twinkle lights. Now refer to Chapter Seven for pattern making directions and trace scallops on base and center tier sides. Overpipe tracing with tube 16 and a circular motion, adding hearts on center tier where scallop points would be. Use same tube to pipe scallops around these tier tops. Pipe tube 21 reverse shells at base and tube 21 shells at top of 16″ tier, and tube 21 rosettes at base and tube 17 shells at top of 12″ tier. For top tier, use tube 17 for garlands and top shell border and tube 4 for string-work. Frame base with tube 75 reverse shells, then position iridescent bells, birds and grape trims with icing. To complete the shimmering effect, top cake with iridescent column ornament lit with more tiny lights. Serves 215.

178

SNOWSHINE
Decorating directions
at left

183

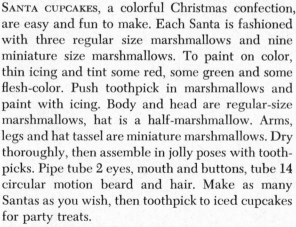

SANTA CUPCAKES, a colorful Christmas confection, are easy and fun to make. Each Santa is fashioned with three regular size marshmallows and nine miniature size marshmallows. To paint on color, thin icing and tint some red, some green and some flesh-color. Push toothpick in marshmallows and paint with icing. Body and head are regular-size marshmallows, hat is a half-marshmallow. Arms, legs and hat tassel are miniature marshmallows. Dry thoroughly, then assemble in jolly poses with toothpicks. Pipe tube 2 eyes, mouth and buttons, tube 14 circular motion beard and hair. Make as many Santas as you wish, then toothpick to iced cupcakes for party treats.

JOLLY SANTA CAKE. Make color flow eyes and mouth, referring to basic directions in Chapter Fourteen. Then bake and ice a dome-shaped cake and position eyes and mouth with icing and tinted marshmallow "nose" with toothpick. Figure pipe tube 12 cheeks

and press flat, then pipe tube 19 circular motion hair, beard and eyebrows. Top cake with red construction paper hat, adding tiny styrofoam ball covered with tube 76 icing frills for tassel. Serves 12.

CHRISTMAS TREE CAKE sweetly trimmed with candy canes is a centerpiece that's as delicious to look at as to eat! To decorate, make marshmallow Santas following directions given on this page. Then use tube 5 and the basic rope border technique described in Chapter Six, page 81 to pipe about forty tiny red and white candy canes on wax paper.

When Santas and candy canes are dry, bake a tree-shaped cake and cover with tube 74 green icing leaves, starting at the cake base and working up. Overlap leaves as you pipe so no cake is left exposed. When you finish piping leaves, attach candy canes with icing and secure a marshmallow Santa with toothpick for a jolly top ornament. Set more Santas around tree. Serves 12.

HOLIDAY POINSETTIA. Make the poinsettia and holly leaves following basic directions for making net flowers on page 148. Pipe petal edges and veins with tube 1 and stiffened royal icing. Place all petals on a curved former to dry. To assemble, pipe large green center dots and push in petals, propping with cotton. When dry, pipe poinsettia stamens with tubes 3 and 2, holly berries with tube 3. To decorate cake, ice a 12" x 4" round and 16" bevel and place on a foil-covered board. Make scallop patterns for cake top and sides following basic pattern-making directions in Chapter Seven. Trace patterns with toothpick, then pipe free-hand tube 1 cornelli lace designs within tracings. Pipe tube 14 zigzag around edges. Overpipe zigzags with tube 14 straight lines, then overpipe with tubes 4 and 2. Pipe second row of scallop tracings with tube 14 overpiping with tubes 4 and 2, then pipe third row of tracings with tube 4, overpiping with tube 2. Finally pipe over outer row of scallop tracings with tube 2. Now divide bevel into 24ths, piping tube 16 garlands be-tween marks. Trim garlands with tube 74 and edge bevel base with tube 14 shells. Position poinsettia on cake top and holly leaves on cake sides with icing, and present this stunning holiday treat. Serves 22.

GINGERBREAD COOKIES shaped in a colorful collection are perfect for fanciful holiday decorations to delight young and old. Shape the gingerbread with an assortment of festive cookie cutters; then when cookies are baked and cooled, decorate.

Brush several cookies with thinned royal icing, leaving others plain. (Note: when using several colors for a cookie, let one dry before applying another). When icings are dry, pipe faces, dot flowers, hearts, string hair, outlines, beading and tree ornaments with tubes 3 and 4. Use tube 16 to pipe stars, shells and ruffled trim on cuff. For stringwork trims and outlines add a tablespoon of clear corn syrup to the icing mixture. Corn syrup gives icing designs a more adhesive quality.

HAPPY NEW YEAR HORSESHOE reflects best wishes for the holidays. Make the "Happy New Year" letters with tube 2 and Color Flow icing, referring to the basic directions outlined in Chapter Fourteen. Also in advance, make tube 217 and tube 225 drop flowers with tube 2 centers and set aside to dry.

Now bake a cake in a horseshoe-shaped pan, cool and ice a frosty white. Place cake on a shiny foil-covered board cut to same shape as cake. Edge cake base with tube 9 beading and cake top with tube 7 beading. Position the bright color flow letters with icing as shown, then pipe tube 2 scroll-like vines on cake top and sides and attach drop flowers with more icing. Decorate the drop flowers with tiny tube 67 icing leaves, then bring in the New Year with cake and celebration! Serves 12.

CHRISTMAS MISTLETOE for a holiday wedding celebration. To decorate, make mistletoe in advance with tubes 7 and 9 as directed in Chapter Eleven, page 147. When dry, assemble into single sprays with florist's tape. Make a few multiple sprays also by combining three or four single sprays.

With mistletoe decorations ready, assemble 16″ x 6″ and 10″ x 4″ tiers on a laced cake stand with 18″ and 12″ scalloped separator plates and a 13½″ center pillar. (Note: 16″ tier consists of three two-inch high cake layers with a hole cut in center of tier to fit center pillar.)

With cake tiers assembled, use a pattern press or make a pattern following basic directions given in Chapter Seven, and trace with a toothpick on tier sides and bottom tier top. Pipe over designs with tube 14, filling in tier top patterns with tube 2 free-hand cornelli lace. Cover center pillar with more cornelli lace. For patterns on tier sides, attach single mistletoe sprays with icing, framing with tube 6 dots of green icing. Next, tie single sprays of mistletoe with ribbon and tape to underside of top tier's separator plate. Edge both tiers with shell borders using tube 32 for the base and tube 19 for the top of the 10″ tier, and tube 4B for the base and tube 21 for the top of the 16″ tier. Pipe "i" motion curves of icing over base shell borders with tube 4, adding tube 9 green dots between each shell.

Now position ornament with kissing couple seated under an arched canopy trellis. Decorate the ornament with ribbon and multiple sprays of mistletoe. What a wondrous winter tribute to present to a bride and groom! Serves 175.

CHRISTMAS MISTLETOE
Decorating directions
at left

CHAPTER FOURTEEN

Color Flow..."Drawing" in Icing

This ingenious technique lets you make a perfect copy in icing of any picture, seal, emblem, design or cartoon. It was inspired by an English method known as "flow-in" or "run sugar". Here it is renamed and given a whole new dimension.

Color Flow has exciting and virtually unlimited possibilities for creative cake decorating. You can use it to bring your own original designs, patterns and ideas to colorful life.

And Color Flow is basically quite simple. Outline your design, then fill in. As with any technique, it takes some practice, first in getting the icing to flow just right, then in using a gentle enough touch, so you can fill outlines without breaking them, or fill curved surfaces and tiny spaces without overflowing. This chapter tells just how to do it all.

To make the icing, start with a powdered mix, available at decorating stores. Or, if not available, use an egg white royal, made according to recipe in Chapter Two and softened with a few drops of water. It will not work quite as well as Color Flow, but is an acceptable substitute.

Color Flow Icing Recipe

3 ounces water
1 pound confectioners sugar
2 level tablespoons Color Flow mix

Combine confectioners sugar and icing mix. Add water. Mix 5 minutes at slow speed. Use at once.

SPECIAL TIPS

SET MIXER AT SLOW SPEED to avoid whipping in too much air, or you'll have bubbles in your finished design. If tiny bubbles do appear, pop with pin while icing is still wet.

USE FIRM ICING straight from batch for outlining, tinted as you wish. Keep icing covered while you work to prevent hardening, as it is very fast-drying.

TO SOFTEN ICING for filling in outlined spaces, follow this method. Place a portion in a container and add water, a few drops at a time, stirring by hand. (Never beat!) To be sure it flows properly, spoon out a "blob" of icing and let it drop back into container. When it takes a full count of ten for "blob" to sink back into mixture and disappear completely, icing is ready and will flow in and set up perfectly.

NEVER FILL CONE over one-half full of thinned icing. It may "squish" up and drip on design.

IF YOU HAVE MORE AREA to fill than one half-full cone will cover, have a second filled and ready. Color Flow icing crusts quickly and crust lines will show in finished design.

DECORATE A FLOWER CAKE

This trio of beauties can blossom in any season, for any reason. Top designs, made the Color Flow way, can be done ahead of time and kept until you have time to decorate the cakes. Each needs a pattern, of course. On daisy cake, little flowers "growing" up sides are also Color Flow, stems and all. On sides of rose cake, stems are piped and tube 225 drop flowers added to them. On sides of Iris cake stems are piped and tube 103 sweetpeas added. Borders on all cakes are simple to let cake top designs star. On rose cake tube 18 top and 21 bottom circular motion borders are used. On daisy cake, tubes 21 top and 199 bottom shell borders make a pretty frame. Dots circle the iris cake with tube 5 used for top, 8 for base. All cakes are 10" round, 4" high, serve 14.

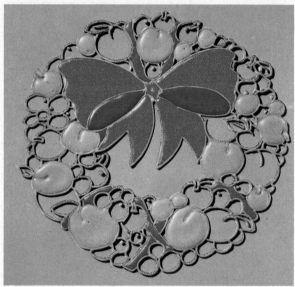

STEP ONE. OUTLINE DESIGN. Tape pattern to a piece of cardboard. Then tape clear plastic wrap or wax paper over pattern, stretching until it is smooth and wrinkle-free. Outline pattern, using Color Flow icing straight from batch and small tubes 2 or 3. Keep lines as clean and smooth as possible, as shown in first illustration at left. When color of outline is much darker than color of fill-in space (such as dark green with yellow), let dry at least an hour or two, so softened Color Flow icing won't "feather" the outline when you fill it in. For close colors (such as blue and green, red and orange), let dry just a few minutes until icing crusts, then fill in.

STEP TWO. FILL IN DESIGN. Soften icing as directed on page 187 and fill a parchment decorating cone just half full. Do not use tube, but just cut a small opening at tip of cone. (A tube might break the delicate outline.) Then, starting just inside outline, press out icing gently, letting it flow up to outline almost by itself. Do not press it out too quickly or, again, outline might break. Fill remainder of section immediately—icing crusts quickly and crust lines will show if icing begins to dry before you finish filling in. Once outline is crusted or dry, you can fill in all sections of design at once, even if they are different colors. For efficiency, do all sections the same color at the same time (for example, do all yellows, then all reds).

STEP THREE. COMPLETE DESIGN, DRY. After you have filled in entire design, dry it thoroughly. The traditional rule is 48 hours. But many decorators find that their Color Flow designs are still not completely dry after that length of time. So it is recommended that a heat lamp be used, shining it in the direction of the completed design at a distance of about two feet. Do not put design directly under lamp, or it might bubble. Dry with lamp about two hours, then let it dry without lamp about 12 hours more. Drying it quickly in this manner also gives the Color Flow icing a higher shine. Whichever method you use, make sure Color Flow design is completely dry before removing from plastic wrap or wax paper.

STEP FOUR, PEEL OFF PAPER. When design is thoroughly dry, peel away plastic wrap or wax paper very carefully. Now it is ready to place on cake.

STEP FIVE, PLACE ON CAKE. Secure on cake top or sides with a few dots of icing. Or, to make cake easier to slice, support Color Flow design on cake top on three or four flat sugar cubes or dried mounds of icing. Then just lift off Color Flow design before slicing. This is a good way to keep design intact— to use again—or give as a keepsake.

COLOR FLOW WREATH CROWNS A CAKE

As colorful as any wreath brightening the holidays, this one is set off dramatically by a snowy white cake. Make the wreath, of course, as directed step by step on the facing page. Make it a month ahead, if you like, long before the holiday rush begins. Then, when your party is near, simply frost a 10″ square, 4″ high cake white, place it on a slightly larger golden foil-covered board and trim with swirls of icing. Edge top and base with dainty shells, using tube 16. Pipe side "C" scrolls and top corner scrolls with same tube, using a decorative circular motion to complete them. Then place your Color Flow wreath on mounds of icing, or a few strategically placed flat sugar cubes (for easy removal at serving time). You're ready for the party! Serves 20.

189

COLOR FLOW MAKES SUCH BEAUTIFUL CAKES

BON VOYAGE CAKE will give someone a lovely send-off! Use pattern and method described on page 188 to turn out Color Flow top and side designs Then ice a 9″ x 4″ oval cake. Attach the Color Flow designs with icing. Finish with pretty tube 14 shell borders. Pipe tube 103 ruffles between bottom shells. Serves 12.

HEARTS AND FLOWERS. A pretty touch for a sentimental party. Use pattern and Color Flow method to complete stylized "wheels of hearts" and small hearts. For hearts at cake corners, tape pattern to curved form, then attach creased wax paper over it, so crease lies exactly over heart's center. Out-line, fill in, let dry on form. Now edge a cake 10″ square, 3″ high with shells, using tube 199 at bottom, tube 22 at top. Add tube 2 stringwork. Attach Color Flow pieces on icing mounds. Serves 20.

ZODIAC CAKE for special birthdays or to start the New Year right. Make it with pattern and Color Flow technique. When the Color Flow pieces are completed, cake's practically finished! Ice a 12″ round, 4″ high cake, pipe tube 14 zigzag at top and bottom edges to support Color Flow pieces. Pipe extra zigzag on base board to lift name panels, icing mounds for stand-away stars. Serves 22.

A truly exciting effect to add to your cakes—stand-up Color Flow figures and designs. This technique lets you express your ideas in three-dimensions—adds a feeling of movement as clowns dance, vines climb, hearts rise high. And these wonders are not difficult to perform. Just outline and fill in pattern as described on page 188. When completely dry, turn figure or design over and do back exactly the same as front. Front of design must be *completely dry* before you do back, or wet icing may seep through to soften it. When back of design is completed, dry for same length of time again and design is ready to add to cake. On large stand-up pieces, add several toothpicks to the base of the design to penetrate the cake top and give added stability. Lay toothpicks on back of design with half extending below it, and "fill in" right over them.

JOLLY CLOWNS dance a jig right on cake top. Do them in stand-up fashion described above, using Color Flow technique and pattern. Pipe small round icing balloons for cake top with Color Flow icing, tube 10. Do flat balloons by filling in circles the Color Flow way. Trim 10" x 4" round cake with tube 104 ribbon border at bottom, tube 18 rosette border at top. Pile small icing balloons into a pyramid on icing mound. Pipe a little icing on clown feet and set clowns into circle. Use crumpled foil to keep clowns upright until icing dries. Pipe tube 1 strings on cake sides, attach flat balloons above them with icing. Serves 14 circus-lovers.

CUPID'S BOW CAKE. For Mother or anyone you love! Do cupid with pattern and Color Flow technique, outlining and filling in both sides so figure can stand upright. Insert two toothpicks to point of heart at back when filling in. Prepare roses and buds ahead with tubes 101 and 102 as directed in Chapter Nine. Then circle a 10" x 4" round cake with tube 17 puff garlands, and add "e" motion scallops at bottom, stringwork at top and message with tube 3. Push heart into small 1" thick styrofoam circle iced to cake, spread on more icing and press in roses. Add rosebuds. Serves 14.

JACK AND THE BEANSTALK. Not stand-up but stand-out! Complete Color Flow pattern in usual man-net but do leaves, beans and Jack separately, or pattern will be impossible to transfer to cake top. Dry leaves and beans in and over curved form. Dry Jack flat. Edge 9" x 4" oval cake with tube 16 bottom shell border. Then using pattern for guide, find point on cake top where Jack's lower boot will

be. Pull a vine of icing up side and across top to boot point with tube 10. Pipe two more tube 10 lines on top of first one. Turn cake and continue vine down opposite side. Then pipe branch of vine. Place leaves and beans on small mounds of icing and push gently so they touch vine. Some leaves go over beans, some under. Add tube 1 tendrils. Place Jack on mound. Serves 12 enchanted children!

"PAINTING" A PICTURE IN COLOR FLOW

Since your Color Flow designs are pretty as a picture when completed, why not frame them and hang them up for a permanent source of pleasure? Do the scenes the usual way, using a pattern and the Color Flow method on page 188. When thoroughly dry, attach them to backing with Color Flow icing, slip them into a matching frame and hang them on the wall.

MAKING PLAQUES. Obtain oval frames at an art supply or frame store or paint them yourself. Cut stiff gold-colored cardboard to fit, secure with tacks or tiny nails and add a hanging hook. You'll need oval frames, about 14½" x 11¼" for the Christmas Scene and 16¼" x 13¾" for Holy Family. To attach, trace outline of pattern on transparent paper, cut out and place in position on cardboard. Use pin to mark position lightly, then pipe dabs of softened Color Flow icing inside marks at top, sides, bottom and center. Lay plaque in position, let set. Handle carefully, so you can bring your beautiful icing pictures out Christmas after Christmas for years to come. If you've favorite pictures of your own that you'd like to do this way, just follow the same general procedure. Just remember to measure carefully to fit frame.

HOW TO MAKE A COLOR FLOW VILLAGE

A charming little Christmas town that can give your home a special look at holiday time. Everything is done in Color Flow, then put together with more Color Flow icing. An example of the amazing versatility of this fun-to-do technique.

To build your village, use pattern and Color Flow technique. Since only one side of walls, roofs and other parts shows, fill in one side only. Pattern identifies each building part and tells how many to make. Then make snowy setting by cutting a piece of styrofoam 24″ x 24″ square, and icing to it a second piece about 15″ long, 9″ wide carved into a "hill". Push clusters of tiny Christmas tree lights through holes drilled in styrofoam, so they come up inside houses and church. (Cut paper in shapes of "floor plans" of buildings, plan layout first.) Use shiny foil or mirror for pond. Then swirl boiled icing over base for "snow" effect. Make trees on cone shape, bush on half marshmallow, covering with tube 74 leaves. Now assemble buildings, using unsoftened Color Flow icing in matching colors for "glue". Assemble chimneys and steeple first. Pipe tiny line of wet icing along edges, put together at right angles. Place buildings over lights, secure with icing swirls. Sprinkle with glitter. Display the village every year at Christmas!

HOW TO MAKE A BUTTERFLY

STEP ONE. To make a beautiful—and authentically marked—Monarch butterfly, you'll need to use a pattern and the Color Flow method. Tape down pattern, cover with wax paper and outline, following procedure on page 188. This is one of the rare times to use black-tinted icing, to capture the true colors of the magnificent Monarch. (Of course, you can use same technique for any other species.)

STEP TWO. Fill in center sections of wings with orange-tinted icing. Do outer "frames" of wings in two steps. First, fill completely with black-tinted icing and let dry at *least* 2 hours. Then, using unsoftened Color Flow icing (right from batch) and tube 1, pipe white dots on top of black, making those at very edge slightly larger than those on inner area by using a bit more pressure. Set aside to dry thoroughly.

STEP THREE. Now take a 6″ length of fine black florist's wire and bend in half for butterfly's "antenna". Then take a second length of wire 12″ long and wrap around bent wire, beginning about ½″ from fold and continuing for another ½″ for "body". Let remainder of wire hang down. Next, tape a piece of wax paper atop a piece of cardboard, punch hole through both and push "antenna" and "body" through hole so that they lie flat on top of wax paper. Bend remaining long piece of wire so it lies flat under cardboard and extends beyond it. Then figure-pipe a long, narrow cylinder of icing over wire "body", using unsoftened Color Flow icing and tube 3. While icing is still wet, push dry wings into it and prop immediately with cotton balls, keeping cotton away from wet icing. Let dry until firmly attached (at least overnight).

STEP FOUR. When entire butterfly is completely dry and firmly attached to "body", unbend long wire and push it very gently up to lift butterfly and wax paper off cardboard. Then take wire between fingers and pull butterfly and wax paper completely away from cardboard, and gently peel wax paper away from butterfly. Your butterfly is ready—push wire into any flower-decked cake and let him "flutter" above the blossoms.

Monarch

1

Monarch

2

3

4

JOINTED TEDDY BEAR CAKE

Here's your favorite toddler's very own teddy bear, jointed legs and all. The Color Flow technique makes it possible to capture all of teddy's chubby charm in icing for the best birthday cake ever. To make the bears, outline all pieces of teddy bear pattern separately (head and body, arms, legs) in brown Color Flow icing. Then fill with bright primary colors according to Color Flow technique on page 188. At same time, make Color Flow letters for message. When Color Flow work is completely dry, ice a 8″ square, 4″ high cake white, edge with tube 18 shells and position bears on sides. Arrange any way you want—one leg up, one leg down, arms in air, the choices are endless. Arrange Color Flow letters on top in happy random fashion. Attach all with icing. Push candles in piped rosettes. Serves 12 delighted children.

CHAPTER FIFTEEN

The Star Method of Decorating

The Star Method is always a happy discovery for the decorator. It lets you do almost any simple picture or design, mainly using the open star tubes 14, 16 and 21 and icing of a medium consistency. Use hard-drying royal icing for a star picture that will last almost indefinitely, or use buttercream icing, so picture can be sliced right along with cake. If you use buttercream, freeze your star picture right after you complete it and place on cake before serving.

Basically, the Star Method is a one-two technique. One, outline any simple picture or pattern. Two, fill in the outline with stars, using different tints of color to define areas or, in the case of a portrait, facial contours. Often, as with two of the examples given in this Chapter, you can skip the first step completely and do the entire picture with stars only. Because they require a pattern, Star Method pictures or designs are easier to make off the cake.

HOW TO DECORATE A LINCOLN CAKE

This is one of the more difficult star patterns because of the many colors used. To make it easier, color the portrait pattern first with crayons or magic markers, following the picture on the facing page.

PIPE PORTRAIT FIRST. Tape pattern flat on table, then tape smooth, clear plastic wrap over it. Do not outline, just fill in pattern with star tube 14. When filling in the face, do lighter beige areas first, then darker ones. Do white parts of eyes last, then fill in blue suit, and finally white collar. Be sure to pipe stars very close together, so portrait will not crack or fall apart after drying. Dry thoroughly, at least 24 hours, then carefully peel plastic wrap away and attach portrait to cake after decorating.

THEN DECORATE CAKE. Prepare two tiers (two layers each), 14″ and 10″ round. Frost sides of both tiers and top of 10″ tier white, top of 14″ tier red. Make Color Flow stars for sides, using pattern and directions on page 188, or draw your own star pattern, 1½″ from point to point. Attach with icing. Then pipe blue ribbed stripes on top of 14″ tier with tube 46. Pipe all shell borders, using tube 16 to frame portrait, tube 20 for both borders on 10″ tier and for blue border at top of 14″ tier. Edge bottom of 14″ tier with tube 32 shells. Add stringwork with tube 3. Serves 46.

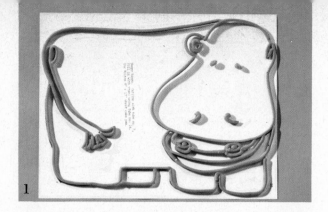

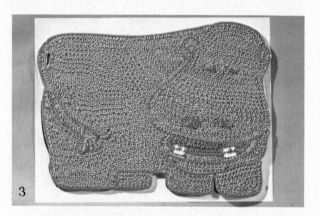

MAKE A HAPPY HIPPO CAKE

1. Tape down hippo pattern and tape a larger piece of clear plastic wrap smoothly over it. Outline with tube 6, making sure to include all features and tail. Pipe small dots for eyes and nostrils.

2. Fill in outline with stars, using tube 16. Be sure to pipe stars very close together or picture may crack or fall apart after drying. Do hippo's starry white teeth last of all.

3. Re-pipe all features, making sure to reinforce dots for eyes, nostrils and teeth. Let dry thoroughly, at least 24 hours. Then peel off backing very carefully, bit by bit, to avoid cracking.

4. Attach to decorated cake with dots of icing.

How to decorate the cake. Bake a sheet cake, 9″ x 13″. Place on a cardboard base, slightly larger, covered with gold-colored foil. Frost with bright buttercream. Then pipe border around top and down corners with tube 8, using the same motion you would use to pipe a shell. Pipe the bottom bulb border, using tube 12 and alternating two cheery colors. Add hippo star picture and serve to 24 young animal-lovers at party time. If made with royal icing, your hippo picture can be placed on flat sugar cubes instead of being iced directly to cake. Lift off before slicing and give to birthday child. Your other star pictures can be saved in the same way.

MAKE A WAVING FLAG CAKE

1. Tape down waving flag pattern and tape smooth plastic wrap over it. Do not outline, just fill in pattern with stars, using tube 16. Do flag stripes first, piping 3 rows for each, except in folds where you may have room for only one or two.

2. Next do blue field. Pipe a small area at a time and leave open spaces for stars, then go back and pipe them in. This keeps blue field from drying out and white stars from being blotted out. Pipe stars close together to prevent picture cracking or falling apart after drying. Do *not* pipe rope or pole.

3. Let all dry thoroughly for at least 24 hours. Then carefully peel off plastic backing.

4. Attach to iced cake with dots of icing, being careful to leave room for rope and pole.

To DECORATE CAKE: frost a 9″ x 13″ sheet cake white and attach star method "flag". Mark cake with toothpick to indicate position of pole, then use tube 8 to pipe it. Press out bulb for top knob, then pull a long, thick line over edge of cake and down. Add tube 3 rope, drawing a white line along flag and down to join pole. Add garland borders, using tube 16 for top, 18 for bottom, poking tube under pole to begin. Use tube 3 for stringwork and gold loops between top garlands. Pipe tube 16 stars between bottom garlands. Serve to 24 patriots.

CHAPTER SIXTEEN

Decorating Cakes without a Tube

One fast and easy way to achieve a pretty cake is not to decorate it at all. Not in the usual sense, that is. Instead, let the cake itself be the decoration, by baking it in a pan with an interesting shape and topping it with a glaze. Or keep the shape conventional and swirl the icing into fascinating patterns. Fresh flowers, fruit or cookies make attractive trims. This chapter gives many short-cuts to lovely cakes.

SHAPE AND GLAZE. Bake your cake in the classic bundt pan, in a dessert or ring mold. Then pour over one of the glazes given in Chapter Two. Here, a snowy white glaze is flecked with bits of maraschino cherries for a holiday flair. Add cherries while icing is still moist and serve immediately. Or pour on rich chocolate or tangy orange sauce. If you

want the shape to stand out even more clearly, just brush on hot apricot glaze or shake on confectioners sugar through a siften For cakes baked in high shaped pans, it is best to use a regular white or yellow cake recipe or mix. These will bake into a rich texture, much like a pound cake.

LET THE ICING STAR. Tint buttercream or whipped cream a delicate pastel and use a spatula or icing comb to make lovely, swirling designs. For the flower-topped cake on facing page, icing was simply swirled up and down sides, round and round top, and fresh flowers placed at top center. Round cake at lower right was given its distinctive look just by drawing an icing comb across top with a slight back-and-forth motion, and around sides with

a scallop motion. Tube 16 shells add a pretty finishing touch.

Trim with coconut, mints. A striking effect achieved with everyday sweets! Ice cake with buttercream icing, sprinkle sides with coconut and make a polka dot pattern (or any pattern you like) on top with colorful candy mints.

An easy way to coat cake sides with coconut or chopped nuts, is to ice just sides, hold in hands like a wheel and roll through the coconut or nuts. Ice top afterwards. Dip square cake sides.

To tint coconut, place a cupful in jar or plastic bag. Add 1 or 2 drops of food color mixed with a teaspoon of water, close jar or bag, shake until coconut is colored. Dry before using.

204

ADD COLORFUL FRUITS. If you start with a simple cake, iced white or chocolate, you can almost follow your instinct when decorating with fruits. Their colors are so fresh and bright, fruits enhance almost anything they touch. And when fresh fruits are in season, what could be more tempting and appetizing, than a light sponge or angel cake, filled and frosted with fluffy icing and crowned with these jewels of summertime. And what, as well, could be more time-saving for the busy decorator. Here are just a few of the many ways to use fruits.

SHINY GLAZED FRUIT. Frost a cake in fluffy pink and trim with sparkling glazed strawberries and grapes.

GLAZE FOR FRUITS

2 pounds granulated sugar
9 ounces water
1 cup corn syrup

Cook to 290 degrees as quickly as possible, wash down sides of pan to prevent granules from forming and dip in fruits. When cool, place fruits on cake. Because of sugar's quick-wilting nature, glaze fruits just before serving.

PINEAPPLE FLOWERS. Couldn't be simpler or prettier! Just take well-drained and dried canned pineapple wedges—or cut slices into wedges—and arrange petal-fashion on a 10″ x 4″ round cake, iced snowy white. Use buttercream icing, please, never boiled! Center with bright maraschino cherries, cut in half and serve to 14 guests. For another dramatic fruit-topped cake, try clusters of red cherries atop a dark chocolate-torte!

FRUIT-AND-WHIPPED CREAM. Set off by the rich swirls of a whipped cream icing, red and green maraschino cherries sparkle like rare gems. Here, they crown a "Zuppa Inglese", delicious treat from Italy. To make it quickly, just split frozen or bakery loaf-shaped pound cake into 3 layers, and sprinkle with rum, using about one cup for the three. Then spread layers with almond-flavored custard (the pastry cream in Chapter Two is a fine choice) and refrigerate for several hours. Just before serving, pipe swirls of whipped cream over cake, using tube 2-E. Stud with half cherries, pecans and candied violets. A rich and festive dessert treat for 12.

Fresh strawberries and raspberries are also favorites with whipped cream. Whipped cream can't be surpassed for any last-minute decorating. It's a rich, showy and very easy icing with which to work.

205

"Chocolate web" technique—quick way to trim cakes and cookies. Ice, let set, then begin.

For cakes. Fit a decorating cone with tube 1 and fill with 2 ounces of unsweetened chocolate which you have melted over boiling water and cooled. Start at center of cake top and drop a spiral line, squeezing cone very lightly and going around and around to edge of cake. Then, while chocolate is still wet, draw a line with edge of spatula from center out to edge for a fascinating web effect.

For cookies. Start as for cake, but drop circles of chocolate, or a series of straight lines. Then draw a toothpick back and forth to achieve web or chevron effect. For cookie "wheels", pipe scallops at edge, shell motion "spokes" toward center.

Clever decorators store up festive trims for the day a pretty cake is required at a moment's notice.

MERINGUE PUFFS. Crisp, melt-in-the-mouth puffs go on cake top or sides with dots of icing in seconds. Use your favorite meringue recipe and large pastry tube 6-B to pipe onto a greased and floured cookie sheet. Bake at 250 degrees for an hour, turn off oven, let stand another hour. Keep in dry, airy place (not tightly covered) for several weeks.

DIPPED COOKIES. Easy, and they give an elegant "continental" look. Fit a large decorating bag with a 4-B pastry tube and press out spritz cookie dough into shell shapes. After baking, dip rounded ends into melted sweet chocolate. They keep in refrigerator a week, but freezing is not recommended. Arrange on top and sides of iced cake as pictured.

DROP FLOWERS. One of the best ideas, because these pretty blossoms wait indefinitely. Make up lots of them as directed in Chapter Nine, using several tubes and tints of royal icing. Add contrast centers with tube 1. Then bake a 9" x 13" x 4" sheet cake, ice pastel and divide with tube 14 zigzag lines. Center each square that results with a drop flower, add leaves with tube 65. Serves 18 at a party or picnic.

MARSHMALLOW FLOWERS. Fun to make and very festive! For flower petals and leaves, dip a scissors in water and cut slices from the flat side of a standard marshmallow. (You'll get about 4 slices from each.) Cutting action will shape slices into ovals. To color, dip cut sides into tinted granulated sugar. To assemble flowers, arrange 5 petals in a spiral, overlapping tips slightly. Place ¼ of a miniature marshmallow behind petals as a base, press remainder on top for flower center. Dry in up-curved form for natural look. Then swirl a 9" petal cake with icing, add flowers and serve to 12 guests.

CHAPTER SEVENTEEN

Using Novelties to Save Time

Even for the accomplished decorator, there comes a day when there is "just no time" for elaborate decorating efforts. This is often the case with cakes for family festivities, club functions and children's parties that have a way of coming in bunches. For these occasions, just choose one of the many novelty decorations and ornaments available to highlight your cake. Trim a simple cake to go with it, and the day is saved! When it comes right down to it, most children actually prefer to have their cakes topped with "toys" which they can play with later on. This chapter shows many clever ways to use novelties on cakes, including two towering wedding cakes.

Circus party cake—looks like a real merry-go-round. You can even put it on a musical cake plate that plays "Happy Birthday" while it revolves—and the merry-go-round will go round! It's quick work to put together. Just ice a cake, 10″ round, 4″ high and push in a plastic carousel cake top. Use tube 10 to pipe the icing balloons on awning, the bottom bulb border and top zigzag border of cake. Add criss-cross zigzag side lines with tube 16. Write names on flags with tube 2. And just for fun, add brightly-colored plastic clown heads all around. Serves 12 very delighted children.

Bowling banquet cake. You're sure to score high with the league champions. This time, shaped cake pans speed the work. You bake the two shaped cakes at the same time as base sheet cake, using a 12″ x 18″ x 2″ sheet cake pan, a half bowling pin pan and a two-piece ball cake pan. Ice all three cakes (put ball together with icing and secure halves on a dowel rod first). Pipe "bowling lane" lines on base cake top with tube 1, then position pin and ball cake as pictured. Trim pin with tube 1D band and edge with tube 13 shells. For "holes" on ball cake, pipe circles with tube 1 string, fill in with more string and smooth over with damp finger or brush. Finish by framing base cake with tube 32 shells and attach bowling pin picks to cake sides. Serves 72 bowlers beautifully.

RED CARPET CAKE—for any very important person in your life. Once you have the golden coach and royal guard soldiers, the rest is simple. Just ice a 10″ x 4″ round cake white, place it on a cake plate circled with ruffled edging, then add some easy borders. Pipe the puffy rosettes at bottom of cake with tube 199 and accent each with a drape of tube 3 stringwork. Then add the "carpet"—outlined and iced-in with royal red icing. Next, pipe the rope around the top with tube 21, the double ribbon scallops and icing bows and streamers with tube 104. You'll find step-by-step directions for all the borders in Chapter Six. Place soldiers and coach in position and call in the royal guest of honor. Serves one king or queen and eleven royal subjects.

INDIAN SUMMER SCENE, surrounded by a village of tiny teepee cakes is heap big fun for a childrens' party! To make, just bake and ice a 12″ x 4″ round cake and as many dome-shaped cakes as guests, and place them on appropriately sized foil-covered boards. Decorate the large cake base with bulb borders using tube 10. Use the same tube for the top border, piping the bulbs of icing into arrowhead designs; then frame with tube 16 zigzag, overpiping with tube 5.

To decorate small cakes use tubes 2, 3, 4 and 5 to make the variety of line designs, then push in food-color-dyed toothpicks for teepee tops. To complete, position plastic teepee, totem pole and Indians and call the young braves to the table! Large cake serves 22.

BABY SHOWER CAKE. A baby angel ornament sets the theme. To make cake, pipe large and small daisies as directed in Chapter Nine, using tube 102 and 103. Then ice and assemble two tiers, 6" x 3" and 12" x 4" round. Frame bottom of base tier with tube 21 shells, tops of both tiers with tube 14 shells. Next, use tube 3 to do "i" motion scallops on tier tops and to drape stringwork at top of base tier. Join string drapes with large daisies, alternating colors. Repeat for top tier, using smaller daisies. Ring top tier base with small pink daisies. Serves 28.

ENGAGEMENT PARTY CAKE. Given special charm by old-fashioned loving couple ornament and an unusual dome canopy. Begin by baking a two-layer round 10" cake and a cake baked in half a ball cake pan. Ice and assemble with 5" tall pillars and 8" separator plates. Use ready-made design press to quickly mark heart designs on sides of round cake. Trace with tube 16, then overpipe with same tube and swirly motion. Do other hearts free-hand—1½" high on plates, 1¾" high on dome. Trace separator hearts with tube 2, do dome hearts same as base with tube 13. Edge separator plate with tube 16. Add tube 7 bulbs at base of both tiers, tube 6 shell motion for top of 10" cake, tube 3 for dome sides. Serves 20.

TULIP-TIME CAKE. For a dinner to honor the bride and groom. Spark it with a little ceramic tulip party

212

cup. Ice a cake 12″ round and 4½″ high (fill thickly to achieve additional ½″ height, so side designs will fit). Mark sides and top with design press and trace with tube 16. Use same tube for "e" motion borders. Fix candle in tulip cup with dab of icing. Serves 22.

MAYPOLE BALLERINA CAKE. Big and little ballerina dolls and lacy platforms make decorating quick and easy. Make lots of multicolor drop flowers with tube 225. Then ice a cake 10″ round, 4″ high white

and ring base with tube 16 garlands, draped with tube 3 stringwork. Press lacy shelves into cake sides, edge with tiny tube 3 ropes and secure small dolls with icing. Pipe tube 3 guidelines for flower garlands and push large doll into icing mound at cake top. Attach all drop flowers. Then wire on ribbon bow and streamers made of 3 long strands, caught at center. Serves 12.

GOLDEN COACH CAKE—to make Mother feel like a queen. A decorative coach filled with fresh flowers gives drama and importance to a simple cake. Bake a 9″ x 13″ x 4″ sheet cake (two layers) and place on a golden foil-covered base, slightly larger. Ice pale yellow and edge top with reverse shells and bottom with regular shells, using tube 18 (apply lighter pressure for top shells so they appear smaller). Pipe fluted garlands at sides with tube 103, top with tube 4 stringwork and add elongated shells to points of stringwork with tube 16. With same tube, curve scrolls on cake top. Write the message and pipe tiny heart (a pair of tear drops) with tube 1. Add coach and serve to a Mother's Day gathering of 24.

SPRING CASCADE. A real fountain adds not just sparkle, but refreshing sound to this impressive wedding cake. Lofty arched pillars and a plastic filigree frame for the fountain give further dimension to a quick-to-decorate cake. Serves 200.

To create this beauty, start by making a quantity of icing sweet peas, using tube 103 and directions in Chapter Nine. Next, bake three round cake tiers: 16″ x 4″, 12″ x 4″ and 8″ x 4″. Ice white and assemble with arched pillars and an electric fountain. Ring the fountain before positioning pillars with a circle of iced styrofoam, press on plastic filigree shields, and attach sweet peas. Edge all three cake tiers with bulb borders, using tube 10 for top and bottom of lower tier, tubes 8 for the tops and 10 for the bottoms of the center and top tiers.

For side trims, drop a tube 3 garland guideline around all three tiers. Pipe bulb garlands over the guidelines, using a circular movement and tube 9 for lower tier, 7 for center tier and 6 for top tier. Then drop 3 rows of stringwork over each garland, using tube 4 for the two lower tiers and tube 3 for top tier. Pipe icing between garlands and position sprays of sweet peas as pictured.

Use remaining sweet peas to decorate the romantic ornament that crowns the cake. More sweet peas trim the sprays that circle the filigree wedding bells at center of the two middle tier tops.

214

SPRING CASCADE
Decorating directions
on opposite page

215

SKI-MOBILE CAKE. Quick way to create a winter spectacular for your party table. All you need are two or three miniature snowmobiles, a dome-shaped cake pan and a 74 tube. Then just bake a cake, using a single mix, pile it high with swirls of boiled icing to create a "mountain" effect. Make the trees by piping tube 74 leaves on ice cream cones or cone-shaped plastic forms and place on mountain. Add miniature snowmobiles. Serves 12.

SOMBRERO CAKE. Ole! South-of-the-border charm for your fiesta. First pipe several tube 104 poppies

and tube 103 wild roses, using directions from Chapter Nine. Set aside to dry while you bake and ice a 9" x 13" two-layer cake. Edge cake with contrast borders, using tube 14 for top reverse shells, tube 21 for bottom rosettes and directions for both in Chapter Six. Attach reserved flowers with icing, pipe tube 67 leaves. Place the miniature sombreros and serve to 24 guests.

PINK SURREY CAKE. Sweet treat with a quaint, old-fashioned air. With the little surrey ornament, you're halfway there. Start with a 9" x 13" x 4" iced sheet

cake. Next pipe a tube 2 garland guideline every inch around top edge. Then drape fluted garlands over it with tube 103 as directed in Chapter Six, and drape with two rows of tube 2 stringwork. Attach tiny tube 225 drop flowers made in advance between each garland all around and finish rest of top edge with tube 14 shells. Pipe tube 105 bottom shells and drape them with tube 2 string. On top of cake, swirl little tube 14 "C" scrolls and fill with more drop flowers. Add little surrey ornament to top and serve to 24 guests.

SKIER'S PARTY CAKE. For a shower planned around the couple's favorite sport. Or without the wedding rings, display it as a conversation piece to fête someone about to start a ski vacation. Your masterpiece is truly easy to make. It's just a 10″ square, 4″ high cake that's iced and swirled with boiled icing so the top resembles a snow-drift. Then simply pipe a stand-up ribbon border around base with tube 402, stand miniature skis on top, tied with ribbons and strung with "wedding rings." Place a pair of tiny ski boots and poles at cake side. Serves 20.

MERRY MAYPOLE CAKE. One of the happiest cakes that ever centered a child's birthday party table. And it's quick to do, once you've the cake topper with its colorful ribbons and "smiley" figures. Then just pipe a quantity of one-squeeze tube 225 drop flowers in bright colors and reserve. Prepare and ice a 12″ round, 4″ high cake and push in maypole topper and figures. Trim base of cake with tube 18 shells, and mark top edge into 16ths. Using marks as a guide, pipe tube 104 ribbon garlands all around, then underscore with tube 3 stringwork. Next, starting about 2 inches above bottom of cake, and right under garland centers, repeat the border all around, but this time, pipe string on top of garlands. Finish top edge of cake with tube 16 shells, then attach flowers, putting trios at points of garlands, ringing maypole base and crowning top. Add tube 65 leaves, candles, call in the children. Serves 22.

MILITARY BAND CAKE. Stirring tribute for a little boy's birthday! And the marching band of toy soldiers that makes decorating so easy will be favorite playmates long after the party. To complete, just bake and ice a cake 16″ long, 4″ wide and 4½″ deep, using a long loaf pan. Then with tube 14, pipe half puff garlands around top edge and full garlands around bottom edge, as directed in Chapter Five. Drape tube 3 strings over top garlands, finishing each point with a tiny string loop. Position toy soldier band on top and let the children parade to the party table! Serves 16.

POP-IS-TOPS CAKE. A "gold" crown and a top hat and cane tell father you think he's debonaire and king of his castle at the same time. Ice an 8″ round, 4″ high cake and use tube 18 to do deep zigzag garlands at top edge, smaller ones at bottom. Drape stringwork with tube 3, place favors, call in dad to admire. Serves 10.

ROYAL CUPCAKES. The easiest! Dip and swirl cupcakes into tinted icing, pipe a tube 12 bulb on top and press on crown candle holder. Make one for each guest.

ROCKING HORSE CAKE. Fun merry-go-round, all lit up to celebrate a toddler's birthday. With the little rocking horses on hand, you can complete the cake in very little time. Bake and ice a 10″ round, 4″ high cake and divide into sixths, using method in Chapter Seven. Then pipe a small rosette at top center with tube 32. Use tube 46 to pipe 6 spokes from center to edge of cake and down sides to base. Ring cake with rosette borders, using tube 4-B for bottom of cake, 32 for top. Decorate rocking horses with drop flowers, piped ahead with tube 225. Insert candles, fill with candy and place on cake. Serves 14. Fill more rocking horses with candy for favors.

TUMBLING CLOWN CAKE. A birthday spectacular for the sandbox set. Circus clowns hold a cake high and animals parade around the top carrying blazing candles. To make it, gather the ready-made decorations—clown separator set, animal candleholders, clown head picks, pink elephant favors and an alphabet sugar mold, so you can mold the birthday child's name to put on side of top cake.

Then prepare and ice two tiers, one baked in a hexagon pan and the other 6″ round and 2″ high. Assemble with clown separator set, placing base cake on a ring of ruffled net. Press plastic Happy Birthday signs onto hexagon cake sides and attach sugar letters to sides of top cake. Edge bottom separator plate with tube 16. Then use same tube to pipe top and bottom star borders for both cakes, side borders for hexagon cake. Add clown heads and wooden horses. Light the candles! Serves 18.

Set the pink elephant favors around cake to complete the circus atmosphere.

219

GHOST CAKE. With everything that makes Halloween fun—a scary ghost, pumpkins, even a resounding "Boo!". First make sugar pumpkins as directed in Chapter Eighteen, using pumpkin mold, add tube 5 icing stems. Then make "Boo!" letters using Color Flow method in Chapter Fourteen and pattern. Dry on curved form or cake pan. Bake and ice a cake, 10″ round, 4″ high, trim with tube 401 bottom ruffle border, tube 18 top shell border. Attach letters with icing, position plastic ring and pumpkin picks. Then set ghost figurine and sugar pumpkins on top. Serves 14.

TENNIS TREAT. A smart serve, this cake that starts with a tennis girl figurine and a star cake pan. Make lots of tube 224 drop flowers, add tube 2 centers, reserve. Then bake star cake, cool and ice, place on cardboard star-shaped base, covered with foil. Attach flowers to top and bottom edges of cake with icing, trim with tube 65 leaves. Top cake with more flowers and tennis girl. Serves 12.

PONYTAIL CAKE. Start with ponytail figurine that looks just like the birthday girl herself, and the rest is easy! Make tube 225 drop flowers, then bake and ice a 2-layer cake 8″ round. Edge base of cake with tube 16 shells and, moving up an inch, pipe tube 103 draped ribbon border all around. Use tube 16 again to pipe zigzag garlands at top edge and "e" motion scrolls over them. Attach drop flowers between garlands, trim with tube 65 leaves. Scatter a few more flowers at feet of figurine. Add candles pushed into tube 22 rosettes. Serves 10.

FLOWERY SHOWER CAKE. This time, little watering cans make the decorating easy. Plastic panorama eggs become favors. First make tube 225 drop flowers, attaching some to florist wire stems. Divide an 8″ round, 4″ high iced cake into 12ths and add pastel borders, using tube 16 for zigzag garlands, tube 104 for top ribbon scallops. Trim with drop flowers, adding tube 65 leaves. Top with watering cans, filled with stemmed flowers. Spray plastic eggs with coating from hobby shop, dry and paint with tinted icing. Fill with stemmed flowers set in icing. Cake serves 10.

BIRTHDAY SPECIAL. It's a circus train cake, with a car for every year! To make it, you'll need a set of four 5″ square cake pans, four 5″ square cake trays with daisy wheels and a set of circus animal candle holders. Then just bake cakes, ice in gay pastels, edge with tube 16 star borders. Set animals into mounds of icing, press in tube 225 drop flowers made ahead. Add candles. Serves 12.

220

GET ME TO THE CHURCH ON TIME. That's the plea of every bridegroom and here's the cake that salutes him—a perfect centerpiece for the masculine atmosphere of a groom's party or bachelor dinner. Start with the miniature coach-and-horses and groom figure, the rest is quick and simple. Bake a two-layer devil's food cake, 10″ round. Cool, fill with creamy white filling and frost with mocha buttercream at sides, white on top. Pipe bottom shell border with tube 4B, top shell border with tube 32. Cut chocolate wafers in half and place between each bottom shell. Write the merry message with tube 2 and trim with coach, horses and brave little groom. Serves 14 sympathetic guests.

HE LOVES ME. A wedding cake ringed with hearts, that achieves a "floating" effect by the use of a center-post cake stand. So easy, the bride might even want to make it herself. Serves 176.

Shape the sugar hearts first, using heart-shaped candy molds and directions in Chapter Eighteen. Then bake three cake tiers, 6″ x 3″, 12″ x 4″ and 14″ x 4″ round, and ice a snowy white. Trace patterns on cake tops before assembling on a tiered cake stand.

Next, make a pattern for the eight-scallop design on tier tops, using pattern making directions in Chapter Seven. Trace pattern on cake tops and pipe over tracings with circular motion and tube 17.

Then remove one of the petals from the large pattern, trim off an inch from bottom and cut a heart-shaped hole in center. Trace this pattern around side of bottom tier, leaving about a two-inch space between. Pipe over these tracings with tube 15, using circular motion again and attach a sugar heart inside each design with icing.

For sides of center tier, fold petal pattern in half and trace curved end only, leaving about an inch between each. Pipe a rippled garland over tracing with tube 15 and drop two rows of stringwork within the curves with tube 2. Place pink sugar hearts between garlands. Repeat for sides of top tier, but pipe guideline over tracing with tube 4 and overpipe this with same tube and "i" motion. Drop a tube 4 string over and under each ripply curve and add icing bows to the lower string border. Again, attach sugar hearts within garlands.

For remainder of borders, pipe rosettes at base, shells at top of each tier. Use tube 32 for bottom and top of base tier, tube 32 for bottom, tube 18 for top of center tier and tube 18 for bottom, 16 for top of top tier. Drape rosette borders on base and center tiers with tube 4 string. Now, with tube 32 rosettes, ring base of pillars on center and bottom tier. Add more sugar hearts around these and to top ornament for a final sweet touch.

CHAPTER EIGHTEEN

The Art of Sugar Molds

An ingenious idea, sugar molds let you make your own sparkling trims, decorations, favors and ornaments as easily as a child makes sand shapes at the seashore. All you use are plain sugar and water and a method so simple, even the smallest children in the family can help. Yet your beautiful sugar decorations look as if they took a great deal of time and skill to create.

To turn out a sugar mold, just mix sugar and water together (or sugar and egg white, if extra strength is needed) according to the recipes given here. Tint if you wish and press into light plastic molds. Unmold immediately and the designs will dry into perfect shapes, firm as sugar cubes. You can then paint them with tinted icing, frost or decorate them with borders and flowers. Sugar molds are an easy technique that will add dazzling variety to your decorating repertoire.

The pretty sugar molds you make will inspire cakes for every mood and moment, from those that enchant children to beautiful, many-tiered wedding cakes that can star at the largest and most lavish receptions.

You can turn some into unique Christmas ornaments, from those with a quaint, old-world air displayed at left, to others in more conventional ball, star and bell shapes. It is best to make hanging ornaments so they can be viewed from both sides. To do this, mold two identical shapes for each, then put them together with royal icing, securing a wire loop for hanging into tops as you do. Then sprinkle with glitter, and pipe on trims with tinted royal icing and tube 2.

To begin the fun, select your sugar molds, then mix a batch of molding sugar in minutes to fill them.

SUGAR MOLD RECIPE

2 cups granulated sugar
4 teaspoons water

This will produce a perfect mixture to pack into all sorts of molds for holiday decorations, cake trims and table centerpieces. Just a few of the many beautiful and imaginative ways you can use them are shown on the following pages.

EGG WHITE SUGAR MOLD RECIPE

5 pounds granulated sugar
2 egg whites

Stir egg whites slightly with a fork before mixing with sugar. This recipe resists crumbling even longer than the conventional sugar mold mixture above and is best for large molds such as the Cinderella Castle, shown on page 233.

Now you are ready to mix and mold your sugar, using the step-by-step method on following page.

225

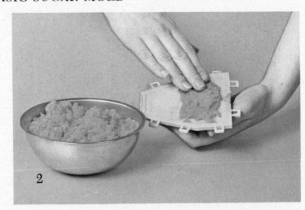

1. Knead mixture with hands about a minute or use electric blender on slow speed for larger amounts. To tint, substitute liquid color for same amount of water or egg white and blend in by hand.

2. Pack sugar mixture into mold. Press tinted portions into mold where needed, features first, then add the rest. For more than four of same mold, dust mold with cornstarch to prevent sticking.

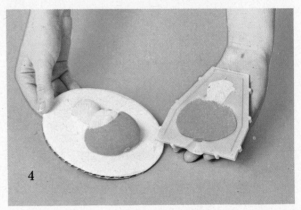

3. Scrape off excess sugar mixture with spatula. Mixture should be packed as firmly as possible into mold, with top perfectly flat and level with edge in order that you may unmold it smoothly.

4. Unmold at once. Place cardboard over mold, turn upside down, lift plastic mold off. Shape dries hard in 5 hours (longer in humid weather). Or place in 200 degree oven 5 minutes.

1. Mold two half sugar eggs in two piece plastic egg mold according to four steps on facing page. Immediately after unmolding, cut off tapered ends with pieces of string held very taut.

2. Let dry about 2 hours, then hold egg halves in palm of hand and scoop out soft inside gently, leaving shell ¼" thick. Finish drying, place figures in bottom half, secure top with royal icing.

EASTER FANTASY. Position piped or plastic bunny, chicks, drop flowers, coconut. Add top, icing trim, flowers.

EASTER FUN. To make, just mold tinted sugar egg, put halves together with royal icing. Add zigzag border with tube 14, ribbon garlands and flower petals with tube 102, leaves with 65, drop flowers with 225, dots with tube 1. Add bunnies.

EASTER TREASURE. Prepare many tiny narcissi and apple blossoms, as in Chapter Nine. Mold sugar cross, trim with tube 1 strings, dots. Make lace pieces as directed on page 158. Then mold and hollow a large sugar egg in an egg-shaped cake pan. Cut "window" at top of egg. Make curved styrofoam prop for egg about an inch high and rectangular prop for cross, same width and about 2″ deep. Pipe stems, mound icing inside, place cross and add flowers. Pipe tube 3 dots at seam and opening, set lace between while icing is wet.

228

SUGAR HARVEST. Once you've discovered how to mold the basic sugar mixture, you can shape it with any appropriate mold. For example, these little works of art—perfectly-shaped miniature pumpkins and grape clusters—were made in hinged metal gourmet molds. These molds were designed to shape butter and individual servings of ice cream, but work just as beautifully for sugar, too.

SUGAR BLOSSOMS. Quick, easy accent for the brightest cake that ever greeted spring. Mold dimensional sugar flowers at top in gourmet molds, flat side flowers in plastic sugar molds. Then simply ice a cake 10″ round, 4″ high and edge base with tube 199 shells. Trace tube 3 vine around sides, add leaves to it and base border with tube 67. Ring top of cake with tube 32 shells, attach flowers, add leaves to flowers with tube 70. Serves 14.

SMALL ROUND AND EGG-SHAPED ORNAMENTS are so easy to make with sugar. Mold round panorama balls in two-piece ball-shaped molds. Then cut "window" across top curve. Put scene or tiny plastic toys in uncut half and attach cut half with icing, adding wire hanging loop at same time. Or just scoop out half balls, put together with wire loop and trim with icing scrolls, dots and flowers. (Scooping out the centers makes ball ornaments light enough to hang.)

HUMPTY DUMPTY is made with a small egg-shaped mold. Mold sugar "body," ice together and attach to ornament base with icing. Paint "suit" with tinted, softened Color Flow icing, pipe collar with tube 104, belt with 44, hair, eyes, eyebrows, buttons and base trim with tubes 1, 2, 4 and 9. Dot cheeks and figure-pipe arms and legs with tube 10. Finish with plastic hat, banded with tube 14.

TOYLAND PANORAMAS. Fun favors for Christmas eve! Tint sugar in candy pastels, mold in two-piece ball molds, cut opening, hollow out. Put candy canes, tiny plastic toys or icing snowflake (made with method on page 156) inside. Prop on ornament base with styrofoam. Add reverse shell and zigzag borders with tube 14, shell-motion bulbs with tube 5. Add ribbon bows, drop flower trims.

PATRIOTIC CAKE is topped with the proud American eagle and stars, all molded of sugar. They're placed atop a two-layer sheet cake, 9″ x 13″ x 4″. Draped with trios of crescent garlands at top, full garlands at bottom, both done with tube 19. Rosettes and teardrop drapes between top garlands are made with tube 14. Edge bottom garland borders with tube 3 "U's." Now let guests parade to the table.

CHESS CAKE will score high! Mold a full set of sugar chessmen, dry, put halves together and paint with softened Color Flow icing. Then make 32 squares plus extras for breakage for the "board." Draw 1¼″ square patterns, outline with tube 2, fill with Color Flow icing. Ice 12″ square, 2″ deep cake, draw checkerboard with toothpick. Attach squares, pipe tubes 7 and 10 bead borders, position chessmen.

MICKEY MOUSE* and his Walt Disney character friends. Mold the 4½" tall figures in two pieces, front and back and then put them together with royal icing for full, stand-up figures. Dry thoroughly before painting the gay colors. Use an artist's brush and softened, tinted Color Flow icing (see Chapter Fourteen). Be sure to let one color dry before adding another. Or add color with tinted sugar at the time you mold figures. Press in various colors for nose, eyes and other parts of figure, working quickly, so different colors of icing adhere to each

other. For cake, use 6" and 16" round tiers.

CINDERELLA'S CASTLE* brings the fairytale to life right on the party table. All you need to make this sparkling centerpiece, are the stronger egg white sugar mixture, the mold and directions that come with it. These tell number of sections to make and how to put them together with royal icing. They also tell how to illuminate castle with tiny Christmas lights, or make a flower-covered icing "mountain" to set it on.

* © Walt Disney Productions

SHAPE A ZOO of sugar! When dry, pipe on trims, using tube 1 for bow tie, dots, eyebrows, mouths and lion's tail. Use tube 2 for lion's mane and blanket outlines, tube 3 for eyes and giraffe dots. Fill back blankets and bunny bow with Color Flow icing and pipe tube 16 rosette base for lion. Make tube 225 drop flowers ahead. Then decorate 10″ square, 4″ high cake with tube 21 rosettes at base, add curved tube 2 beading and flowers. Put lion at top, attach other animals with icing. Serves 20.

FILL A SUGAR BASKET with sugar flowers to brighten a summery cake. Mold flowers and basket of tinted sugar, dry. Trim flowers with tubes 1 and 2, sprinkle with edible glitter. Use tube 16 to give basket its zigzag base and handle, tube 1 for top string drapes. Decorate a 12″ round cake with tube 21 shells at top, tube 199 shells at base. Curve stems out of basket and vine along cake sides with tube 3, then add flowers, tube 65 and 67 leaves, finish with tube 104 bow. Serves 26.

SHAPE SPARKLING 3-D figures—using the stronger egg white sugar mixture. Form front and back halves, dry thoroughly, then put together with royal icing. To add the vivid colors, use tinted sugar for basic colors, add features, dots, stripes and other details with tinted icing and tubes 3 and 10. Or paint on colors with softened, tinted Color Flow icing, described in Chapter Fourteen.

The doll, panda, stork, tree, snowman and mushrooms make the most unusual displays, table decorations, favors or party prizes ever. Once molded and trimmed, they last and last. Make them for one party and bring them out again for another —and another! You can even change the colors, if you wish—just paint them on fresh.

They're a good size, from 5 to 7" high, so they're easy to group into eye-catching centerpieces and room trims. Wouldn't the mushrooms set a bright theme for a garden club luncheon—or a row of Christmas trees liven the holiday table?

235

CHAPTER NINETEEN
The Art of the Tier Cake

For weddings, anniversaries, formal parties and other equally elegant occasions, the tier cake has long been the eye-catching, center of attention. The artistic design, the graceful structure, the endless variety of dramatic decorating effects all contribute to the fascination of the tier cake. These combined qualities have not only made the tier cake a favorite, they assure its continuing popularity.

Impressive as they are, towering tiers of cake are well within the realm of achievement for any aspiring decorator, once the basic techniques for proper assembly are acquired. In this chapter these basic techniques will be explained. Also shown are a variety of possible tier shape and size combinations to best acquaint you with the tier cake's structural potential.

How to Assemble a Tier Cake

The tier cake is not unlike any other architectural structure in that it needs a strong foundation on which to stand. Therefore a sturdy network of wooden dowel rods and plastic pillars and separators give the tier cake its necessary solid foundation, as well as provide the framework on which to build. Cleverly designed, this network does not interfere with cake serving.

On this page are the basic steps for assembling a tier cake, each of which is important in achieving beautiful end results. Once you understand these steps you can apply them to any tiered cake, regardless of size or shape. So in learning how to lay the groundwork for towering tiers of cake, you're also creating the groundwork for exhibiting elaborate decorating effects.

1. First place the iced bottom cake tier on a sturdy base two inches larger than the tier's diameter. Using a cardboard cake circle one size smaller than the next tier, press it gently on the center of the bottom tier top to effect an outline. Within the outline, position seven, ¼" diameter dowel rods. Push rods in cake to touch base, then lift up, clip exposed portions and push back into cake so they're level with top.

2. Now center a corrugated cardboard cake circle, one size smaller than the next tier, on the bottom tier's top. Position the next tier and make an outline with another circle, again one size smaller than the next tier to be added. Position five, ¼" diameter dowel rods within this outline, clipping them level. To keep these two tiers stable, sharpen one end of another dowel rod, push through the center of both tiers and clip level.

3. Before positioning the top tier, insert the separator plate, complete with pillars, by pushing the pegs, supplied with the plate, into the cake until the plate is resting on the tier top.

4. Finally, place the top tier, which is resting on its own separator plate, on the pillars. The top tier, though securely positioned for decorating, should be removed for transporting.

The Tier Cake: An Architectural Art

As stated at the beginning of this chapter, the tier cake offers a variety of structural possibilities to the imaginative decorator. Just like any other artistically designed structure the many sizes and shapes of cake tiers, when properly assembled, exhibit all the grace and beauty of an architect's creation.

On this and the following pages, there's an assortment of tier cake combinations to best acquaint you with this type of building potential. One glance and you'll see what a dazzling vehicle the tier cake is for showing off your decorating skills.

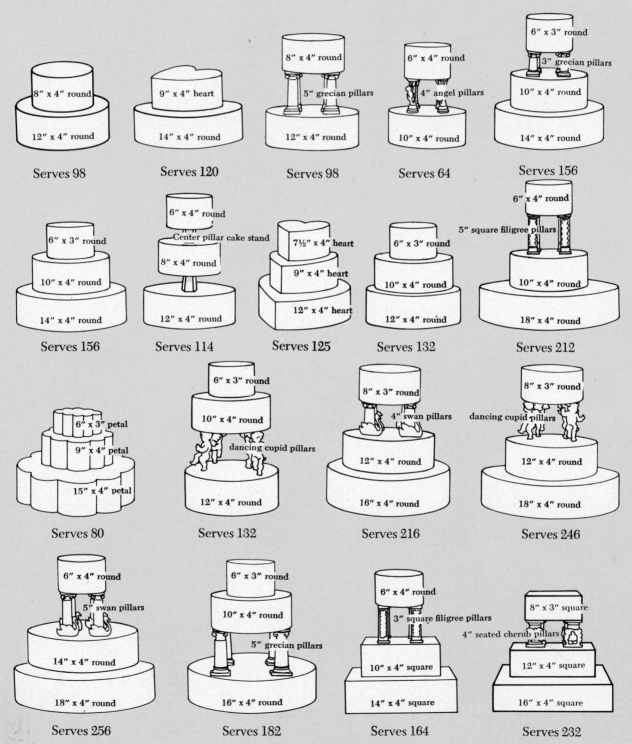

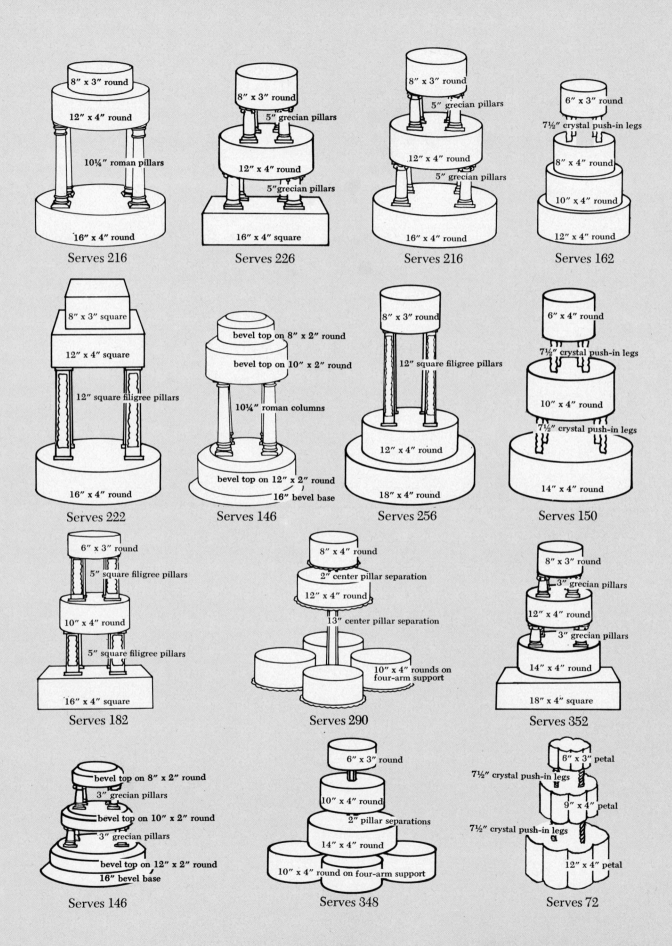

8″ x 3″ round
12″ x 4″ round
10¼″ roman pillars
16″ x 4″ round

Serves 216

8″ x 3″ round
5″ grecian pillars
12″ x 4″ round
5″ grecian pillars
16″ x 4″ square

Serves 226

8″ x 3″ round
5″ grecian pillars
12″ x 4″ round
5″ grecian pillars
16″ x 4″ round

Serves 216

6″ x 3″ round
7½″ crystal push-in legs
8″ x 4″ round
10″ x 4″ round
12″ x 4″ round

Serves 162

8″ x 3″ square
12″ x 4″ square
12″ square filigree pillars
16″ x 4″ round

Serves 222

bevel top on 8″ x 2″ round
bevel top on 10″ x 2″ round
10¼″ roman columns
bevel top on 12″ x 2″ round
16″ bevel base

Serves 146

8″ x 3″ round
12″ square filigree pillars
12″ x 4″ round
18″ x 4″ round

Serves 256

6″ x 4″ round
7½″ crystal push-in legs
10″ x 4″ round
7½″ crystal push-in legs
14″ x 4″ round

Serves 150

6″ x 3″ round
5″ square filigree pillars
10″ x 4″ round
5″ square filigree pillars
16″ x 4″ square

Serves 182

8″ x 4″ round
2″ center pillar separation
12″ x 4″ round
13″ center pillar separation
10″ x 4″ rounds on four-arm support

Serves 290

8″ x 3″ round
3″ grecian pillars
12″ x 4″ round
3″ grecian pillars
14″ x 4″ round
18″ x 4″ square

Serves 352

bevel top on 8″ x 2″ round
3″ grecian pillars
bevel top on 10″ x 2″ round
3″ grecian pillars
bevel top on 12″ x 2″ round
16″ bevel base

Serves 146

6″ x 3″ round
10″ x 4″ round
2″ pillar separations
14″ x 4″ round
10″ x 4″ round on four-arm support

Serves 348

6″ x 3″ petal
7½″ crystal push-in legs
9″ x 4″ petal
7½″ crystal push-in legs
12″ x 4″ petal

Serves 72

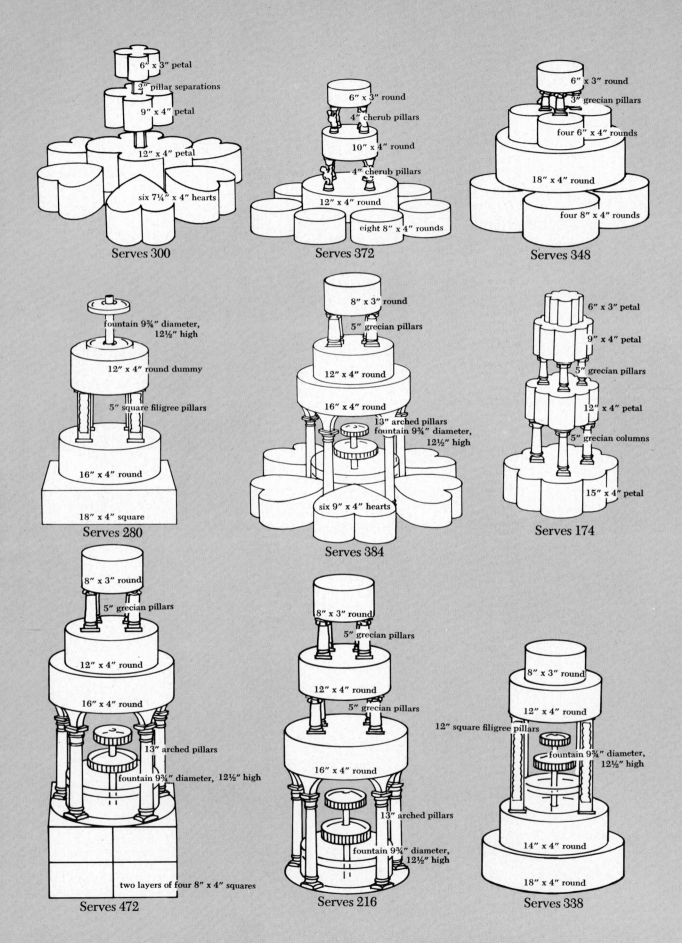

6" x 3" petal
2" pillar separations
9" x 4" petal
12" x 4" petal
six 7¼" x 4" hearts
Serves 300

6" x 3" round
4" cherub pillars
10" x 4" round
4" cherub pillars
12" x 4" round
eight 8" x 4" rounds
Serves 372

6" x 3" round
3" grecian pillars
four 6" x 4" rounds
18" x 4" round
four 8" x 4" rounds
Serves 348

fountain 9¾" diameter, 12½" high
12" x 4" round dummy
5" square filigree pillars
16" x 4" round
18" x 4" square
Serves 280

8" x 3" round
5" grecian pillars
12" x 4" round
16" x 4" round
13" arched pillars
fountain 9¾" diameter, 12½" high
six 9" x 4" hearts
Serves 384

6" x 3" petal
9" x 4" petal
5" grecian pillars
12" x 4" petal
5" grecian columns
15" x 4" petal
Serves 174

8" x 3" round
5" grecian pillars
12" x 4" round
16" x 4" round
13" arched pillars
fountain 9¾" diameter, 12½" high
two layers of four 8" x 4" squares
Serves 472

8" x 3" round
5" grecian pillars
12" x 4" round
5" grecian pillars
16" x 4" round
13" arched pillars
fountain 9¾" diameter, 12½" high
Serves 216

8" x 3" round
12" x 4" round
12" square filigree pillars
fountain 9¾" diameter, 12½" high
14" x 4" round
18" x 4" round
Serves 338

240

How to Cut a Tier Cake

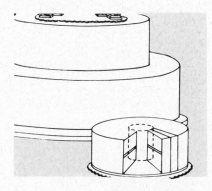
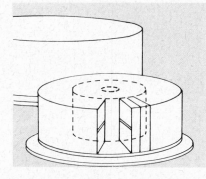
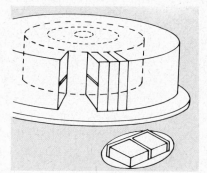

HOW TO CUT A ROUND CAKE

Since many tiered cakes consist of three round or square 14″, 10″ and 6″ tiers, these sizes will serve to illustrate proper cutting procedures.

To cut a tiered round cake, start from the top and remove the 6″ tier. Cut a circle about two inches in from the tier's outer edge and, working from this circle out, make vertical cuts about an inch apart until the ring is sliced into wedge-shaped pieces. Using the same starting procedure for the 10″ tier, cut a circle in about two inches in from the tier's outer edge and make vertical cuts, again about an inch apart, around the entire tier. Now with the remaining cake, cut another circle two inches in, again slicing the ring into wedge-shaped pieces. The 14″ tier employs exactly the same procedure except that this time there will be an extra ring from which to cut cake.

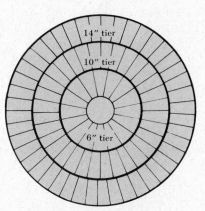

Top view of a three-tiered round cake

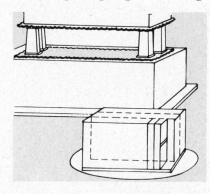
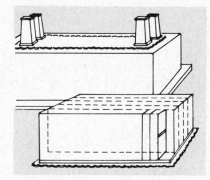
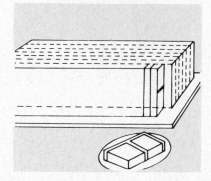

HOW TO CUT A SQUARE CAKE

To cut a three-tiered square cake, again start from the top and remove the 6″ tier. Working from any side, cut a horizontal line about two inches in from the tier's edge. Then slicing from right to left, make vertical cuts about an inch apart slicing the entire row. Now move in another two inches, cut another horizontal line and vertically slice the row into one inch pieces. This should leave one more row from which to cut cake.

Use the same procedure for the 10″ tier. Start from any side, cut a horizontal line about two inches in from the tier's edge and cut slices from this entire row before moving in another two inches. After slicing the next row there should be two more rows to cut.

The 14″ tier is cut exactly the same. Cut two inches in from any tier side and slice one row before moving in another two inches. This time there will be seven rows to cut.

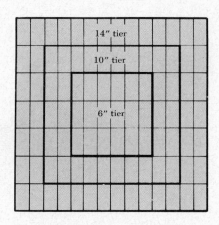

Top view of a three-tiered square cake

IVORY ROSE
decorating directions
at right

242

A Portfolio of Wedding Cakes

How fitting that the most elegant of all cakes—the tier cake—be chosen more than any other to star at the most elegant of all celebrations—the wedding! Here, in this portfolio, is the most beautiful collection of tiered wedding cakes one could imagine. Wedding cakes trimmed with filigree, flowers, flouncy borders and so many of the decorative techniques you've seen in previous chapters. So to begin this portfolio, adorned in wedding white, is a perfect tribute to nuptial bliss!

IVORY ROSE. Four 9″ x 3″ petaled cakes encircle three graceful wedding white tiers—a 12″ x 4″, 9″ x 4″ and 6″ x 3″, all prettily petaled also. The cake is supported on a four arm stand with 10″, 14″, 12″ and 8″ laced separator plates. Edge tier bases with circular motion borders using tubes 75 for the 12″, and 72 for the 9″ and 6″. Make the triangular garlands on the 12″ tier with tube 18 using a pattern outline, then add tube 5 stringwork. Pipe reverse scrolls on tier sides with tube 72, add top swirl border with tube 75.

On the 9″ tier, pipe tube 72 circular motion garlands, tube 4 stringwork and tube 72 top border. On the 6″ tier, pipe tube 16 reverse shells on sides, tube 4 strings and tube 71 top border. Next, decorate the four 9″ x 3″ cakes before placing them on their armed support plates. Edge the bases with tube 17 circular motion borders, then frame the top edges the same. Pipe smaller inside connecting cake top borders with tube 16 using back and forth motion. With cakes iced and assembled, position cupids and attach roses with icing. Serves 152.

How TO DECORATE SUNGLOW pictured on frontispiece. This gloriously golden sunshine cake is made up of three square tiers—a 14″ x 4″, a 10″ x 4″ and a 6″ x 3″ assembled with 12″ and 8″ separator plates and 5″ grecian pillars. To decorate, make lots of tube 103 sweet peas following directions given in Chapter Nine. While flowers are drying, trim tops of separator plates using tube 5 for both the center puffs and the scalloped string edgings. Now pipe tube 22 stars around the base of the bottom tier, and use tube 5 and a circular motion to drape a scalloped border around this same tier's sides. Overpipe this border with a double row of tube 4 stringwork and add tube 4 beading. Finish off the top edge of this tier with a tube 19 reverse shell border and position clusters of sweet peas with icing.

Use the same decorating tubes for the 10″ and 6″ tiers, with the exception of tube 17 for the top reverse shell borders, tube 4 for the dotted cake corners and tube 2 for the stringwork trim around the base borders. Now top the two lower tiers with a white bird figurine, and place a garden gazebo on the top tier. Serves 165.

SWAN LAKE. Pipe all the tube 80 water lilies on a flower nail. Squeeze out eight flat petals first, then eight shorter slightly cupped petals and finally six cupped center petals. Fill in all flower centers with tube 2 stamens. Pipe the tube 102 lily pad petals on a flower nail also. Pipe the tube 13 filigree trims in advance following directions in Chapter Twelve.

The cake is a 6″ x 3″ tier on an 8″ separator plate with a 14″ x 4″ base and 5″ pillars. Refer to pattern-making instructions in Chapter Seven to trace a series of four arched patterns on the 14″ cake top. Follow overpiping directions in Chapter Twelve to dimensionally decorate tracings. Use tubes 14, 4, 3, 2 and 1 for inside row of overpiping, tubes 3, 2 and 1 for next row of overpiping and finally tubes 2, 1 and then tube 1 alone for outer rows. Fill open center of the dimensional design with tinted piping gel. Edge the tiers with shells using tubes 14 for the top and 16 for the base of the 6″ tier, and tubes 15 for the top and 17 for the base of the 14″ tier. Drape tube 16 garlands around both tier bases and overpipe with tube 2 strings. Attach petals, lilies and laces with icing. Top cake with bell "fountain", trim with tube 15 shells, icing flowers and tinted piping gel. Serves 108.

DAISY DREAM
decorating directions
page 246

245

DAISY DREAM (shown on page 245) blushes with wedding bliss! Pipe the variety of assorted pink daisies with tubes 101s, 101 and 103 referring to the directions in Chapter Nine, page 116. Pipe the bright floral centers with tube 2, then dry daisies on a curved form to gently shape petals. Make the tube 2 filigree pieces following the detailed directions in Chapter Twelve. Dry the filigree at least twelve hours before overpiping on reverse sides.

The cake itself consists of 8″ x 3″, 12″ x 3″ and 16″ x 4″ round tiers assembled on 10″ and 14″ separator plates with 5″ pillars. Frame the separator plate tops with tube 16 zigzag icing curves, then pipe tube 2 stems from the plate centers out. With icing, attach ready-made daisies to stems and pillar bases, trimming with tube 67 leaves. Now edge the cake tops and bases with shell borders using tube 16 for the top tier, tube 17 for the middle tier and tube 18 for the bottom tier. Position daisies around tier bases with icing, encircling the entire bottom tier base with daisies side by side. Trim the daisy border on the bottom tier with tube 67 leaves, piping one in between each petaled flower. Attach clusters of assorted size daisies to the sides of each cake tier with icing, again trimming with tube 67 leaves.

Next, attach the filigree side pieces to the tiers with icing. Assemble filigree arch following directions in Chapter Twelve, pages 154 and 155. "Glue" arched filigree over the bridal couple proudly standing on a daisy-trimmed ornament base. Place the ornament atop the cake to complete the daisy dream come true! Serves 215.

HEART CHIMES, with cherubic figures piping sweet strains and wedding bells ringing out best wishes! To decorate this tiered trio, make the flowery hearts first. Refer to Chapter Nine, page 113 and make the apple blossoms with tube 101s, setting aside to dry. When flowers are dry, pipe tube 4 zigzags on wax paper over heart patterns, place on curved surface and attach ready-made apple blossoms with dots of icing. Trim with tube 65 leaves and let dry.

While floral hearts are drying, assemble the 8″ x 3″, 12″ x 3″ and 16″ x 4″ round tiers on 10″ and 14″ separator plates with 5″ grecian pillars. Glue clusters of white plastic bells on separator plates of lower two tiers. Attach flower hearts to bells with icing. Glue cherub above bells on next-to-top tier. Divide the 8″ tier into 24ths, the 12″ tier into 36ths and the 16″ tier into 48ths. Edge with the elegant "La Mer" border following directions in Chapter Eight, page 102. Use tube 199 for the puffs, tube 2 for the "three bears" stringwork and tube 14 for the zigzag scallop frame around each puff. With the same tube 14 overpipe the scallops with grooved lines, then pipe scrolls on puff tops. Finally overpipe scallops and scrolls with tubes 4 and 2, adding tube 14 shells to finish off border base. Now, with the exception of the stringwork, pipe the same border around the tier bottoms, this time trimming the border base with a double row of tube 14 shells. With icing, attach curved flower hearts to tier tops and bases. Trim the top ornament with more flowered hearts. Serves 215.

HEART CHIMES
decorating directions
at left

CLASSIQUE. A romantic, white cake with 16″ x 4″, 12″ x 4″ and 8″ x 4″ tiers assembled with 10″ separator plates and 5″ grecian style pillars. Position bells, net and lacy base atop separator plate; then at base of 16″ tier pipe tube 22 stars, framing each with tube 3 string. Drop a guideline around tier top, then pipe tube 2 latticework using directions in Chapter Twelve. Add tube 3 stringwork. Finish tier's top edge with tube 15 reverse shells, trimming with tube 14 zigzag. Edge separator plate with tubes 13 and 2. For 12″ tier, pipe tube 17 bottom shell border, adding tube 102 ruffles. Pipe tube 18 upright shells at tier top, and tube 14 zigzag trim above shells and around plate and pillars. Decorate shells with tube 2 stringwork. For 8″ tier, do same base border as for bottom tier. Pipe tube 3 guideline around tier's top side, then add tube 14 garland and tube 3 strings. Pipe tube 14 shells at top and tube 14 inside curves. Add cherub ornament. Serves 215.

LOVEBIRDS alight on a lavish cake that displays the art of figure piping. To decorate, assemble 14″ x 4″, 10″ x 4″ and 6″ x 3″ round tiers with 8″ and 12″ separator plates and 5″ grecian style pillars. Pipe floral trims using tube 127 and varying pressures for large and giant roses and rosebuds. Refer to directions in Chapter Nine. Next decorate all three tiers with tube 2 freehand icing lace designs and position flowers on separator plates of bottom and middle tiers. With tube 103 and a circular motion,

pipe rosebuds onto pillars, trimming with tube 65 leaves. Referring to directions in Chapter Twenty-Two, figure pipe pairs of lovebirds with tube 10 on top of base tier. Then using the same tube and a heavier pressure, pipe an icing "nest" and two more lovebirds on the top tier. Use tube 7 to figure pipe hearts, then with icing position sugar bells and flowers. Frame with tube 70 leaves and figure pipe tube 4 chimes into bells. Serves 155.

GARDEN GLORY
Decorating directions
on page 252

HERITAGE
orating directions
on page 252

251

GARDEN GLORY. Pipe tube 103 wild flowers, then assemble 18″ x 4″, 12″ x 4″ and 8″ x 4″ tiers with 10 separator plates and dancing cupid pillars. To decorate, divide 18″ tier into 5″ wide sections and pipe tube 199 long upright shell "posts" at each division, filling in sections with regular tube 199 reverse shells. Next drop a tube 5 guideline and overpipe with tube 7 zigzags. At ends of garlands add tube 4 bows and attach drop flowers between trimming with tube 66 leaves. To finish, pipe tube 21 shells at top adding tube 4 stringwork. For 12″ tier, attach flower garlands with icing above each 18″ tier shell "post", adding tube 4 bows. Frame tier top with tube 21 shells, tier base with tube 17 shells. For 8″ tier sides pipe tube 3 vine and stems, trimming with tube 66 leaves and attaching flowers with icing. Frame tier base with tube 18 reverse shells, tier top with tube 17 shells, and ornament. Serves 245.

HERITAGE, pictured on page 251. A tier cake with a charming colonial air. The cake itself is an 8″ x 3″ tier on a 12″ bevel, a 12″ x 4″ tier on a 16″ bevel and a 16″ x 4″ tier on a 20″ bevel. (If tiers are not baked in bevel-edged pans, mark base of tier one inch up all around and mound icing from that mark down to edge of base and separator plates, smoothing into slope with a spatula.) Place the 16″ tier on a 22″ cake board, the 12″ tier on a 16″ separator plate and the 8″ tier on a 12″ separator plate so you can decorate the tier tops before assembling them with 3″ clear plastic twist leg pillars. Referring to the directions in Chapter Seven, page 97, make patterns for all tier tops and for sides of 12″ tier. Attach patterns with pins and outline with a toothpick. For the 8″ tier top, trace innermost scallop with tube 4, overpiping with tube 2. Use tube 2 again to pipe the next scallop; then pipe the third scallop with tube 1. Use same tube to edge outer scallop with picot, piping first three dots, then two, then one.

For the 12″ tier top, trace over innermost scallop with tube 14, overpiping with tubes 4 and 2. Pipe the next scallop with tube 4, overpiping with tube 2; then edge with picot trim as before.

For the 16″ tier top, trace over innermost scallop with a tube 14 zigzag line, then a tube 14 straight line and overpipe with tubes 4 and 2. Cover next scallop with tube 14 again, overpiping with tubes 4 and 2 once more. Pipe over third scallop with tube 4, overpiping with tube 2; and finally pipe fourth scallop with tube 2. Edge with picot.

Before adding the pretty side borders, use the tier top designs as a guide to mark off side sections. Divide the 8″ tier and bevel into eighths, then divide the 12″ tier into eighths with the bevel in sixteenths, and finally divide the 16″ tier and bevel

into sixteenths again. With these divided sections defined, refer to the directions in Chapter Eight, page 105, to pipe the dainty picot lace and loop borders on the sides and bevels of the 8″ and 16″ tiers. Use tube 1 to drop six short loops across the top of each section. Then drop a loop from the center of each of these top loops, add four more, then three, then two, then one. Add tube 1 picot trim to frame each looped section, by piping clusters of tube 1 dots—three, then two, then one. Next, pipe double picot trim at top points of loop border sections on tier and bevel sides, and add more double picot to join tier top and bevel borders.

To decorate side of 12″ tier, follow pattern tracings with tube 1 beading, then add picot edging as before along with picot dot flowers. For scallop trim on all bevels, mark off guidelines with a toothpick, then trace with a tube 14 zigzag line, a tube 14 straight line and finally overpipe with tubes 4 and 2. To finish bevel decorations, add tube 1 picot dot flowers and shell borders piping a double row with tube 14 on the top tier, a double row with tube 15 on the middle tier and a single row with tube 16 on the bottom tier. To finish, top middle and bottom tiers with cherubs and place a bowl of fresh flowers on the top tier. Serves 215.

CHANTILLY. (Opposite page.) A cake that's intricate lacework in icing! The tiers are an 18″ x 4″ square, a 16″ x 4″ round and a 12″ x 4″ round assembled with 14″ separator plates and clear plastic twist leg pillars. To decorate, make a pattern referring to directions in Chapter Seven, or use a pattern press, to mark off top of round tiers and top corners of square tier. Pipe a tube 3 string guideline for scallops on sides of center tier and bottom tier. Pipe the same guideline for sides of top tier, only leave a one-inch space between scallops. Over all tier guidelines starting with bottom tier, pipe a tube 18 zigzag, overpiping each scallop twice with the same tube. Then refer to directions in Chapter Twelve to pipe tube 3 latticework from tier tops to zigzag scallops. Use tube 14 zigzag to cover the rough ends of latticework at tier edges and on scallops. To pipe latticework within tier top patterns use tube 3, then once again cover rough edges with tube 14 zigzag. Use tube 14 to pipe fleur-de-lis trims on top tier.

To finish cake, pipe shell borders at the base of all three tiers using tube 18 for the top tier, tube 20 for the center tier and tube 4B for the bottom tier. Frame this latter shell border with tube 14 zigzag, then top the cake with a delicate cupid ornament. Serves 350.

253

CHANTILLY
Decorating directions
on opposite page

RUBY ROSE
Decorating directions
on page 256

STARSHINE
Decorating directions
on page 256

RUBY ROSE. (Shown on page 254.) A beautiful tribute to a fortieth anniversary. Vary the color and trim to mark other important milestones. The cake consists of three round tiers—an 8″ x 3″, a 12″ x 4″ and a 16″ x 4″. The bottom tier is placed on an 18″ laced separator plate with a 14″ separator plate placed on top. Before assembling the other two tiers, use a pattern or make your own, following directions in Chapter Seven, and trace it on top of the 16″ tier's separator plate with a pencil. Then with a toothpick, trace patterns on all three tier sides. Cover plate's pattern tracings with tube 13 zigzag, then overpipe with tube 1 piping gel beading. Position anniversary emblem on center of separator with icing, framing its base and pillars with more tube 13 zigzag. Now edge the outside of the separator plate with zigzags this time using tube 16. Assemble the top tiers with 10½″ roman column pillars, then on the bottom of the 14″ separator plate glue a plastic bell that's been decorated with tube 1 piping gel beading.

For all three tier sides use the same tubes as for the separator plate to outline and overpipe pattern tracings. Be sure to fill in all "ruby" side designs with tube 3 and red piping gel before framing with tube 13 zigzag and piping gel beading. With side designs complete, pipe puffy garland borders around all three tier tops and bottoms using tube 18 for the base tier, tube 17 for the center tier and tube 16 for the top tier. Use tube 1 to pipe red piping gel stars between each garland, then add more tube 16 zigzags around middle tier's separator plate. Now to complete the decorations, trim a decorative bowl with tube 1 red gel beading, fill it with fresh flowers and place it atop the cake for a stunning anniversary gem. Serves 215.

STARSHINE. (Pictured on page 255.) A cake that's truly as bright as its name! Before assembling the 16″ x 4″, 12″ x 4″ and star-shaped 4″ high tier at top, make the tube 2 filigree icing shields. Make a pattern, trace it several times, tape patterns to canned fruit cans, cover with waxed paper. Trace patterns with tube 2, dry and remove. Repeat until you have made 46 shields, plus extra for breakage. Make filigree star designs, and when dry turn them over to pipe on opposite sides. When dry again, attach filigree star parts one at a time to a lollipop stick with icing. Place in styrofoam to dry.

With filigree trims complete, assemble the cake tiers with 5″ grecian pillars and 14″ square separator plates. On the center of the 14″ plate attach a filigree star with icing and frame separator plate with tube 16 scallops, then position two top tiers.

Pipe shell base borders around all three tiers using tube 18; then on the two square tiers drape zigzag garlands using tube 18 for the 16″ tier and tube 16 for the 12″ tier. Pipe tube 21 zigzag garlands of icing around each tier top, then carefully position filigree shields over garlands with icing. Next add scallops of beading under each filigree shield using tubes 2 and 4. Top each tier with tube 16 zigzag borders, push filigree star into cake top and Starshine's complete. Serves 220.

HAPPY HEARTS. A cake consisting of 6″, 9″, 12″ and 15″ petal-shaped tiers, each 4″ high. To decorate, make drop flowers with tubes 193 and 224, adding tube 3 centers. Attach some of the flowers to tinted florist wire with icing. When dry, push into small circle of iced styrofoam.

Next, referring to Chapter Twelve, pipe lace hearts using tube 2 for large and medium size and tube 1 for small size. Use tube 1 also for tiny lace scrolls. While icing laces are drying, assemble cake tiers. Place base tier on a scalloped foil-covered board, 20″ in diameter. Top with 12″ and 9″ tiers. Position drop flower bouquet in center of 9″ tier. Place 6″ tier on a 7″ scalloped board covered with foil. Ice 5″ iridescent pillars to top of 9″ tier and place 6″ tier on top, securing with icing.

To decorate, edge all tier tops and bases with shells using tube 21 for the bottom of the 15″, 12″ and 9″ tiers, tube 16 for both bottom and top of the 6″ tier. Use tube 19 for the top of 15″ tier, tube 17 for the tops of the 12″ and 9″ tier.

With shell borders complete, attach lace pieces and drop flowers with icing. Position them in a garland fashion curving around each petal of cake. (If you wish, draw toothpick guidelines first.) Use three large flowers at center of garlands, two small ones at ends and finish with tiny tube 65 leaves at points. Attach lace hearts the same way, with the largest at the center of the garland, finishing with tiny scrolls. Trim board at base of cake with drop flowers and tiny scrolls.

The top ornament is a cluster of iridescent bells gathered with tulle for a fitting finale! Serves 134.

HAPPY HEARTS
Decorating directions on
opposite page

257

COLONIAL BOUQUET
Decorating directions on
opposite page

258

COLONIAL BOUQUET. Make the violets with tube 59° following directions in Chapter Nine. Bake 8″ x 3″, 12″ x 4″ and 16″ x 4″ tiers and ice white. Assemble with 14″ and 10″ separator plates and 3″ pillars. Make a scalloped pattern for each tier, referring to Chapter Seven for instructions, and secure patterns with toothpicks. With a small spatula ice lower part of tiers orchid, let dry and remove patterns. (Do not be concerned if edges are rough where colors meet. The ruffle trims will cover them.) Drop a stringwork guideline all around tiers where icing colors meet, then overpipe with tube 104 ruffles. Pipe tube 124 ruffles at each tier's base and top with tube 7 beading. Attach violets with icing and trim with tube 65 leaves. Now ice a half styrofoam ball, cover with violets and place atop bottom tier. Adorn other tier tops with cherub musicians and more violets. Serves 216.

ROMANTIQUE. To decorate, make tube 225 drop flowers and two cake tiers—a 9″ x 3″ heart and a 14″ x 4″ round. Ice and assemble so point of heart is about three inches away from round cake edge. Use templates or make patterns following directions in Chapter Seven and trace on cake tops and sides. Pipe over heart top and scalloped round cake top tracings with tube 3 stringwork, filling in with tube 1 free-hand cornelli lace and framing with tube 1 dots. Pipe cake side and heart-top petite heart pattern tracings with tube 14, again filling in with tube 1 free-hand icing lace. Then for round cake borders, pipe tube 21 circular motion base, tube 19 top shells and frame hearts with tube 3 stringwork. For heart cake, pipe tube 1 cornelli lace on sides, tube 17 circular motion base and tube 17 shell top border. Attach drop flowers with icing, trim with tube 67 leaves. Serves 120.

LOVELIGHT. Flowers strewn on a candlelit pathway give this cake its soft romantic glow. To decorate, make tiny drop flowers with tubes 190 and 225 and set aside to dry. Then assemble 6" x 4", 10" x 4" and 12" x 4" round tiers on a ruffle trimmed cake board. Edge all three tier bases with tube 22 shell borders, framing each with "s" curves of tube 14 zigzag. Then on the side of the base tier, pipe tube 14 garlands and fleur-de-lis, draping garlands with a triple row of tube 2 stringwork. Use tubes 14 and 2 again to pipe garlands and stringwork on the middle tier. Now, with a toothpick, trace a scrolled guideline around the sides of the top tier and over-pipe with tube 14. Add tube 2 stringwork around the top of this same tier. To finish, pipe tube 20 shells around the top of each tier and push stairstep candleholders into all tier sides. Position drop flowers on the stairs with icing and trim with tubes 65 and 67 leaves. Place candles in holders. Crown the cake with a petite bride and groom ornament and light the candles for a fitting finale. Serves 130.

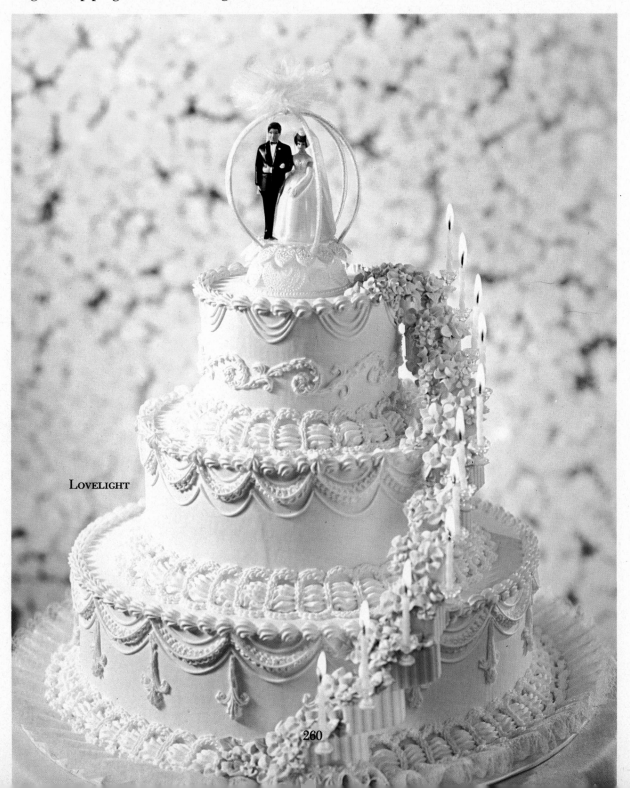

LOVELIGHT

260

CELESTIAL BLISS
Decorating directions
on page 262

261

CELESTIAL BLISS (page 261), a cake that's truly heavenly! To make, assemble three tiers (a 16" x 4", a 12" x 3" and an 8" x 3") with 10" and 14" separator plates and dancing cherub pillars. Now referring to directions in Chapter Nine, make the blushing roses using tubes 101, 102 and 103. When flowers are dry, pipe a mound of icing on centers of separator plates, along with tube 2 stems, and attach assorted size roses. Trim flowers with tubes 67 and 68 leaves. Now around the base of each tier pipe tube 199 puff borders using tube 14 for the zigzag trim and stars between puff tops.

Before piping the top borders, divide the bottom tier into sixteenths, the top tier into eighths. Then for each of these two tiers, use tube 17 to pipe the side garlands which are filled in above with tube 17 zigzags for crescent-shaped effect. For scrolls on these same two tiers use tube 17 zigzag overpiping with tube 14. To finish off these lavish borders drop a triple row of tube 2 stringwork over each adding tube 65 leaves. See page 101 for detailed instructions. Now for the 12" tier, drop a triple row of tube 2 stringwork adding tube 199 puffs above and once again framing them with tube 14 zigzags. Ornament the cake with a cherub and lacy look-through heart to top off the blissful decorations. Serves 216.

TOWER OF LOVE (facing page), a trio of tiers as romantic as its name. The cake is a 6" x 4" tier, a 10" x 4" tier and a 14" x 4" tier assembled with a 16" laced cake stand base, 12" separator plates and 5" filigree pillars. To decorate, pipe shell borders around all tier bases using tube 32 for the bottom tier, tube 20 for the middle tier's reverse shells and tube 19 for the top tier. Now around the top of the largest tier, drape tube 75 garlands using a circular motion and leaving about an inch space between each. Drop a double row of tube 4 stringwork above this, and top the tier with a tube 76 reverse shell border. For the middle-tier top, again drape tube 75 circular motion garlands, adding tube 4 stringwork and tube 18 fleur-de-lis. To finish, frame this tier's top edge with a tube 73 reverse shell border. Next for the smallest tier top, drape a tube 73 circular motion garland border adding tube 4 stringwork above and below, and once again topping with a reverse shell border using tube 17. Now, mound icing between garlands on the sides of the bottom tier and attach clusters of artificial roses. Position a few more roses around the base of this tier and with icing add roses to the tops of the other two tiers. Place a trio of cupids posed on pedestals atop the separator plate and crown the cake with a garden tower housing a bridal pair. Serves 155.

NUPTIAL NOSEGAY. Shown on page 264. A cake that's freshened with flowers to celebrate love in bloom. To make, pipe scalloped icing lace and flowers first. Refer to directions in Chapter Twelve for lace technique and pipe scalloped lace with tube 1, overpiping once for strength. Refer to Chapter Nine for flower making instructions and pipe daffodils and daisies with tube 104, red wild roses with tube 101 and blue bachelor buttons with tube 14. When dry, attach some flowers to florist wires with icing and push into gathered net ruffle. Attach lace to ruffle edges with icing, trim flowers with tube 67 leaves and tie bouquet with ribbon streamers. With more icing, "glue" nosegay to a lacy ornament base and reserve for cake top.

Now assemble the cake tiers, (a 6" x 3", a 10" x 4" on a 14" bevel and a 14" x 4" on an 18" bevel), with 14" separator plates and 10¼" grecian pillars. (Note: if cakes are not baked in bevel-edged pans, mound bevel shape with icing and smooth with spatula.) To decorate bevels, divide into twelfths, piping three rows of scallops in each division. For the scallops first pipe a row of tube 1 beading, then a row of tube 2 beading and finally a row of tube 4 beading. On outer edge of bevels, trace triple swirled scrolls with a toothpick and cover with tube 14 zigzag, overpiping with tube 14 ribbed lines. On the border of the 14" bevel, attach laces with icing and above pipe a double row of tube 14 shells. To decorate the base of the top tier, the one without a bevelled edge, pipe a triple row of tiny tube 14 shells.

On the sides of all three tiers pipe parallel rows of tube 14 shells adding tube 13 colonial scrolls between rows on the top and bottom tiers. Then with icing, attach laces to the top edge of the base tier and frame all tier tops with tube 14 triple shell borders. Add a final double row of tube 14 shells around the 18" bevel edge and with icing position four clusters of assorted icing flowers, trimming them with tube 67 leaves. With icing, attach more flowers to a bridal couple ornament and center on top of the separator plate. Now place the nuptial nosegay of icing blossoms atop the exquisite tiers of cake and the garden fresh decorations are complete! Serves 155.

TOWER OF LOVE
Decorating directions on
opposite page

NUPTIAL NOSEGAY
Decorating directions
on page 262

264

WEDDING WATERFALL. Assemble 16″ x 4″ round and 18″ x 4″ square tiers with 5″ filigree pillars and 14″ separator plates. Use a 10″ x 4″ hollowed-out cake dummy for top tier. Place fountain inside, using cake circles to raise fountain to proper height. Place cherubs on separator plate top; then edge base of bottom tier with tube 21 star drop border. Pipe side garlands and scallops with tube 15, drop stringwork with tube 4 and attach sugar-coated

bells between garlands with icing. Top tier with tube 16 reverse shells and inside scallops.

For center tier, pipe tube 32 reverse shells around base, tube 16 reverse shells around top. Position shields, angels and roses with icing. Pipe borders of top tier with tube 19, adding tube 2 stringwork. Then trim tier sides with tube 80 lily of the valley. Serves 280.

BAHAMAS TRIBUTE. This towering cake, decorated especially for the Bahamas' Independence Day Celebration, is one that truly exhibits the many exciting architectural possibilities of the tier cake! Although the decorations—the coat-of-arms, the national flower, the sun and palm leaves—all apply to a specific event, the basic construction of the cake could be used to serve a variety of festive functions—a community celebration, a fund-raising benefit or an equally large event.

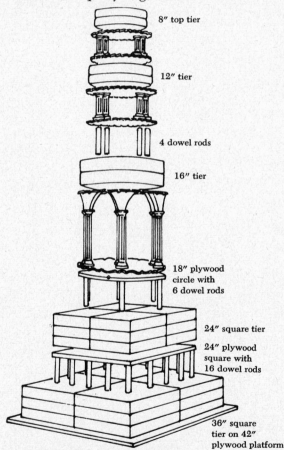

8″ top tier

12″ tier

4 dowel rods

16″ tier

18″ plywood circle with 6 dowel rods

24″ square tier

24″ plywood square with 16 dowel rods

36″ square tier on 42″ plywood platform

THE FIRST STEP: PREPARING OVERSIZED TIERS. The 36″ square, 6″ deep base tier is made up of 12 layers, each 18″ square and 2″ deep. The second 24″ square, 6″ deep tier is made up of 12 layers, each 12″ square and 2″ deep. The next tier up is two 16″ round, 2″ deep layers; the next 12″ round, 4″ deep and the top 8″ round, 4″ deep.

THE SECOND STEP: ASSEMBLING THE CAKE. The base tier is placed on a ⅝″ plywood platform, 42″ square. Dowel rods, (1″ in diameter and 6″ long), are then nailed to a 24″ plywood square so the rods can be pushed into the base tier to support the next addition. The 24″ tier rests atop this plywood form.

Next, six more dowel rods, the same size as before, are nailed to an 18″ round plywood circle so they will stand underneath each of the 13″ pillars to be placed above. With dowel rods in place, the circle is pushed into the 24″ square tier and the 13″ pillars and 18″ separator plates are positioned. The 16″ tier then stands upon this separator and four dowel rods are positioned for next tier.

With the 12″ tier assembled with 14″ separator plates and 5″ pillars, the cake is ready for the finishing 8″ tier, positioned with 10″ separator plates and 5″ pillars. The construction complete, the cake is now ready for decorating.

THE THIRD STEP: DECORATING THE CAKE. Although these stunning decorations apply to a specific occasion, the basic techniques could be adapted for a variety of decorating effects. For example the coats-of-arms are done in color flow on plexiglass so it can be beautifully illuminated. (For basic color flow instructions refer to Chapter Fourteen.) For this cake the plexiglass was cut into shields the exact size of the patterns to be piped. Then the patterns were taped to cardboard and the plexiglass placed over pattern to outline and fill in design. When color flow designs are dry they're positioned on cake in front of tiny twinkle lights to illuminate their beauty!

The national flower of the Bahamas is the yellow Elder, and, a decorative trim for any cake. To make use tube 104 and a large lily nail. Start at center of nail with a light pressure and pull icing up over edge. Turn nail to form a wide, curved petal, then return to nail's center. Make five separate petals in all, then smooth center with damp brush into glossy hollow. Let dry, attach blossom to calyx and you have a flower delightful enough for any cake, including a tiered wonder like the Bahamas Tribute!

BAHAMAS' TRIBUTE
Directions on opposite page

INDEPENDENCE OF THE BAHAMAS · JULY 10, 1973

FORWARD
UPWARD · ONWARD
TOGETHER

267

Marzipan Christmas Wreath
described on page 272

CHAPTER TWENTY

Molding with Marzipan

Marzipan is a rich confection that can be tinted into a rainbow of colors and modeled easily into an endless variety of realistic shapes. It is thought to have originated in ancient Persia and, for centuries, has been a traditional holiday treat.

Once the secret of highly-skilled confectioners and chefs, marzipan is really a simple mixture and its modeling an art anyone can master. And your marzipan masterpieces can be used for cake trims, ornaments, centerpieces, displays or gifts.

MARZIPAN RECIPE

1 cup almond paste (8 ounce can)
2 egg whites, unbeaten
3 cups confectioners sugar
½ teaspoon vanilla or rum flavor

Knead almond paste by hand in bowl. Add egg whites, mix well. Continue kneading as you add sugar, 1 cup at a time and flavoring until marzipan feels like heavy pie dough. Stored properly, marzipan dough will keep for months. Cover with plastic wrap, then place in tightly-sealed container in refrigerator. After storing, let stand at room temperature until soft enough to work. If still stiff, soften with a drop or two of warmed corn syrup.

Add colors by kneading them into basic mixture or painting them on finished pieces. To knead colors in, work in one drop of liquid food color at a time until natural shade is achieved. For dark chocolate color and flavor, work in powdered, unsweetened cocoa until dark as you wish. For deep golden color and coffee flavor, use powdered instant coffee. If these make marzipan dough too stiff, soften with a little extra egg white or a few drops of corn syrup.

To paint colors on, dilute food color with any white brandy, such as kirsch, until you reach desired shade. Try colors on white paper first, then using a nearly dry sable brush, paint colors on marzipan pieces. Alcohol in brandy helps colors dry quickly.

To glaze marzipan pieces, lightly brush on glaze solution (mix ½ cup corn syrup, 1 cup water, bring to boil). This gives a soft shine. For a high shine, cut water to one or two tablespoons, simply heat.

To put marzipan pieces together, touch piece to a sponge soaked with egg white, then fix to second piece with a turning motion.

All the tools you will need for marzipan work are an orange stick, sharpened to a point at one end, and a small kitchen knife with a pointed blade.

FOR GARDEN HARVEST vegetables, colors were painted on, cabbage, cauliflower leaves shaped separately.

How to Form Marzipan

Though it is basically simple, modeling marzipan does take practice. Below are most of the basic shapes you will need to make. Practice until you can do each well. Begin by dusting table with powdered sugar, then with palms of hands, roll mixture into 12″ length, ⅞″ diameter. Cut 1″ pieces, roll all into balls first. After practicing, try simple fruits on facing page. For uniformity, cut and model all similar shapes at once. For example, for apples, cut 1″ pieces, larger for pumpkins, smaller for strawberries.

1. FOR EGG SHAPE, roll ball into a point at one end. Place between heels of hands, holding hands level with shoulders. (You'll find this easier to do standing up.) If you find marzipan difficult to work with, practice first with a softer material such as modeling clay, until you get some control.

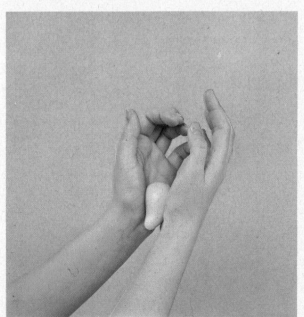

2. FOR PEAR SHAPE, begin with basic egg shape just practiced, model pointed end a little longer and sharper, then turn up. This is the shape to use for bear's head, and with slight variations, for polar bear and panda. Always try to model animal head with slight lift in front for a young look.

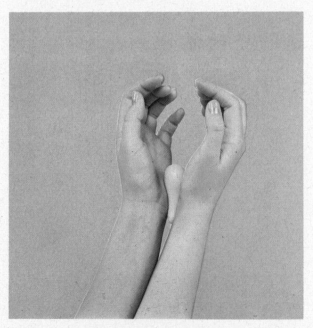

3. FOR ELEPHANT HEAD, roll ball into egg shape again, then extend pointed end into an elongated stem. To give head a youthful look, keep head round, forehead large and trunk slender. Hold heels of hands slightly apart when modeling trunk to shape it without crushing.

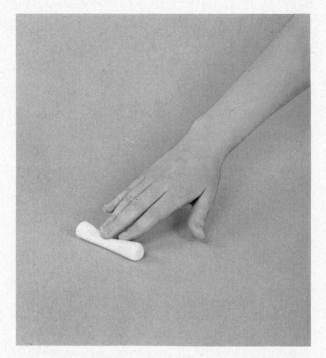

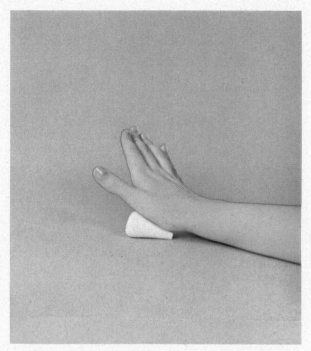

4. FOR PAWS, ARMS, LEGS, shape a narrow cylinder. Form a rough cylinder in palm, then roll out on marble slab or mar-proof table, first between two fingers, then three. This will produce a shape slightly thicker at ends than in middle, perfect for forming limbs as you will see later on.

5. FOR CONE SHAPE, you must roll ball under hand on slab. Roll into cylinder, tapering one end as you do. This is the shape you can use for many animal figures that stand upright. Thick end is used for back paws, tapered end is split and cut pieces bent outwards to help figure stand upright.

BEGIN WITH FRUITS AND VEGETABLES. Model pre-colored marzipan mixture into natural shapes, then add indentations, color, glaze or texture, stems and leaves as shown left to right. Press small holes with point of orange stick. Cut grooves with knife blade. Blush or mark with food coloring on damp cloth, then lightly brush on glaze. Add stems and leaves —marzipan, royal icing or artificial. For texture, roll potato in powdered cocoa, add "eyes" with orange stick point. Roll strawberry in red-colored granulated sugar. Roll orange (not shown) over grater, add clove stem.

A SUGAR BASKET OF FRUIT.

One of many beautiful ways to use your marzipan fruit! Put it in a basket shaped of lacy caramel. There's a cake inside, too, so it can be a fabulous finale for any sort of celebration.

First make the marzipan fruit as directed on page 271, including grapes and cherries, if you wish. Shape cherries round and use florist's wire for stems. Shape grapes slightly oval, attach to small pear-shaped marzipan base for cluster look.

Next make caramel basket. Cover a turned-over 1½ quart bowl smoothly with aluminum foil, making sure bowl has flat rim. Grease well. Prepare caramel, using ⅔ cup water, 1¼ cups granulated sugar and ½ cup corn syrup. Boil mixture until bubbles are thick and a light brown color. Cool until bubbles disappear, and, using a greased tablespoon, dribble over foil-covered bowl to make a lacy pattern. Let dry until hard, but still warm and grasp foil with fingers to lift basket off bowl. Then gently remove foil and finish cooling.

Now make cake. Bake it in a dome-shaped pan and cut ⅛ from top and bottom. Use center portion for inside basket (test fit first by placing it in the bowl you used as mold). Cut small piece of left-over cake into mound for top of basket cake to raise fruit, put together and ice.

Then assemble. Attach basket to cake plate with dab of icing. Carefully place cake inside and arrange marzipan fruit on top, attaching pieces with toothpicks. For handle, twist two 12-inch pipe cleaners together for 22-inch length and ice by pushing down through icing bag and out tube 32. Squeeze, slowly pull out handle. Push into cake.

If piece of basket breaks off, touch broken piece to candle flame, press back on.

MARZIPAN CHRISTMAS WREATH
(Illustrated on page 268)

A beautiful conversation piece at holiday time!

First, model fruits according to directions on page 271. Use artificial marzipan leaves for fruits. To make larger leaves, roll marzipan mixture thin and cut with a 1″ to 1½″ long leaf cutter. Mark veins with back of knife and dry over and inside a curved form. Glaze fruits and leaves.

Then assemble. Cut a ring of styrofoam, 10″ in diameter, 2″ wide and 1″ thick, ice in green royal icing and dry thoroughly. Push a wire hanging loop through back of styrofoam ring before attaching fruit and spread protruding ends to secure, adding a bit of icing for extra strength. Arrange fruits and leaves all around ring, attaching those with icing that you want to lie flat, others on toothpicks to stand out slightly. A dab of icing on toothpicks will help to secure them. Dry, attach ribbon and bow, hang up to be admired.

STRAWBERRY BUCKET

A cake that looks like a real strawberry bucket with blossoms, fruits and leaves growing from its top and sides!

Begin by making marzipan strawberries as shown on page 271. Form berries and insert a hooked 4″ florist's wire into each one before rolling in red-tinted sugar. Leave three-fourths of wire exposed so fruit can be hung on cake. Make ¾″ marzipan leaves as directed in wreath description above. Insert florist's wire in leaves before drying. When dry, assemble in trios with florist's tape.

Pipe blossom petals of icing same as apple blossoms in Chapter Nine. Pipe large center dot with tube 4, press lightly with finger to flatten. Dry on curved form, attach wire stems with icing.

For cake, assemble three 8″ x 2″ layers, chill and carve to a 7″ diameter at base for bucket shape. Ice cake chocolate, using a spatula to make board marks. Pipe gold bands around with tube 45. Place a mound of icing on top of cake and attach the "growing" berries, blossoms and leaves. Attach some berries, leaves and blossoms to cake sides, as if they were growing out of holes in bucket.

ACTUAL SIZE, 2" TALL

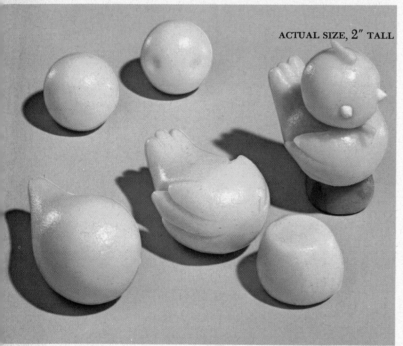

ACTUAL SIZE, 2" TALL

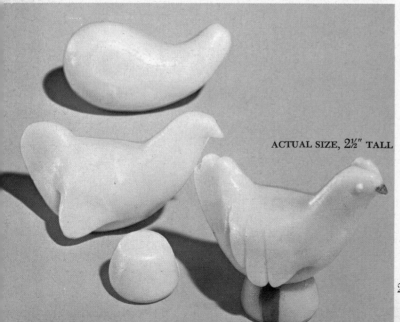

ACTUAL SIZE, 2½" TALL

Storybook Figures in Marzipan

These charming, whimsical figures will delight the children in your life. Try to give each a characteristic expression and you will capture their appeal easily. To make figures that are in perfect proportion, cut all pieces needed for each before you model it. When making several figures, use the same amount of marzipan dough for each.

For each of these figures (except Winter Playmate) roll out 2½-ounce piece of marzipan dough to the length of your middle finger, or about 3½". To divide, you must use your judgment. Look carefully at picture and estimate how much to cut off roll for body, head, base and other pieces. After one or two figures, you will be able to judge. If you use both hands to shape similar small pieces, you can keep them sized alike more easily.

After measuring off the portions needed for head, body, and other parts of figure, color by kneading-in method given on page 269. *Then* divide colored dough again as needed. This will keep the figures in proportion. Note: "Winter Playmate's" (page 278) bright colors are painted on.

Now you are ready to begin modeling the figures on these pages, using directions given with each and the tools and techniques on pages 269 and 270.

DUCKLING. A toddler's favorite, to sail perhaps, across his very first birthday cake. You will need to form three pieces—a ball for head, larger ball for body and a small ball for base. Model body into pear shape, lifting point for tail. Flatten tail slightly and make two small cuts with knife to simulate "feathers." Make head perfectly round and press in "eyes" with blunt end of orange stick. Model a small ball and flatten it for base. Leave body and head natural color, paint color on base. Use a half-almond for bill, glazing it to a high shine. Assemble, pipe icing bulbs for eyes, black dots for pupils. If doing several, a cute touch is to turn one duck's head to the side.

CHEERY CHICK. As sweet as the baby whose cake he will decorate, he takes just three pieces to complete. Model a ball for head, a slightly larger one for body and small one for base. Make two indentations for "eyes." Model flat-topped cone for base and pear shape for body, lifting point for tail. Flatten back portion of body and tail and cut V's into sides of body for wings. Cut shallow notches for wing and tail "feathers." Put all pieces together, glaze and pipe icing dots for eyes. Attach high-glazed almond slivers for comb and beak.

HENNY PENNY takes just two pieces of marzipan

dough. Cut most of roll for body, small piece for base. Model body piece into long pear shape, pinch thick end into a point and flatten at sides. Then cut a flap at either side of body with scissors for wings so they point down. Pull narrow end of pear shape into head, forming a tiny beak at tip. Next, with knife, cut three vertical slashes for wing feathers, making them appear to overlap. Cut two slashes in top of tail. Mold back into shape pictured. Pipe comb with tinted icing. Finish by painting beak and base only, dry and glaze. Pipe icing dots for eyes.

MR. RABBIT. Cunning bunny for an Easter cake. Begin him by rolling a 2½ ounce cylinder of marzipan dough and measuring off amounts you need first, for back legs, front paws and nose, then body, head and tail (8 pieces in all). Knead in cocoa and instant coffee to tint, then divide portions again as needed, roll into balls and proceed to model.

For head, model ball into long pear shape, press narrow end somewhat flat and cut down center for two sections. Model these into ears, using blunt end of orange stick at center, sharp point at ends of depressions. Roll body portion into egg shape, press in a curve where head will fit. Roll tail portion into pear shape, turning point down and flattening where tail will attach to body. Roll long cones for back legs, flatten thick ends and bend for haunches. Flatten tips of thin ends and cut notches for back paws. Roll smallest pieces into egg shapes, flatten and cut notches for front paws. Roll tiny ball for nose. Assemble all pieces. Pipe icing dots for eyes, add tiny marzipan dots for pupils. Glaze.

TEDDY BEAR—simply adorable! Little pink bear has the familiar "jointed" look, tiny toenails, too. For teddy, cut your roll into eight pieces—largest for the body, then a smaller one for head, the next four, smaller still for front and back paws, and finally, cut piece to roll out flat and cut into circles for ears. Roll body in egg shape, then make indentation in thick part with blunt end of orange stick for "belly button". Model head into pear shape and lift pointed end for snout. Form four legs into cylinders, two slightly longer than others, then flatten and widen one end of each to join body, turn other into tiny paws. Flatten and model two slices of dough for shell-shaped ears, working with two hands at once to make them even-sized. Glaze pieces, put bear together. Pipe icing dots for eyes, tiny black dot for nose, tiny black teardrops for toenails. Teddy's ready to love!

ACTUAL SIZE, 2½″ LONG

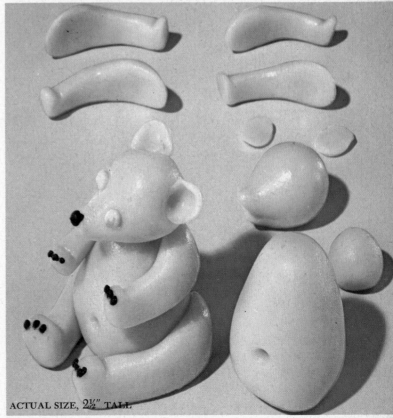

ACTUAL SIZE, 2¼″ TALL

275

ACTUAL SIZE, 2¼" LONG

ACTUAL SIZE, 3" LONG, 2¼" TALL

PLAYFUL PANDA. Favorite of children everywhere. To make him, first cut largest piece for body, next largest for head, two smaller pieces for hind legs, two smaller still for front legs, a small piece for tail and two tiny pieces for ears from your roll. You'll also need some small bits for eye circles and nose.

Color leg, tail, ear, eye and nose portions with cocoa, then roll and divide again as needed.

Model natural-color body into pear shape and head into smaller pear shape. Cut point of head shape for open mouth and make indentations where eyes and ears will go with blunt end of orange stick. Flatten bottom of body and head slightly. Model legs into cone shapes, then flatten tops and bend narrow ends into "paws". Make "toes" with knife. Model ears into tiny shell shapes, tail and nose into balls. Flatten two tiny balls and cut out with a large round decorating tube for eye circles.

Put all pieces together, tipping panda's head for a playful attitude, spreading back legs wide and keeping front legs close together. Then pipe a white icing dot on each eye ring and add dark marzipan pupils. Glaze completed figure.

PINK ELEPHANT. Always a happy touch and one of the simplest figures to do. Cut just five pieces from your roll of marzipan dough, the largest for the body and legs, taking about ¾ of the whole amount. Then you'll just need a medium size piece for head, two small equal-size pieces for ears and a tiny bit for the tail.

Keep the original cylinder shape for the body and bend into a half doughnut as shown. Then cut both ends and spread apart for "legs". Bend the front tips of the front "legs" into feet and mark in "toes" with point of orange stick.

Model head portion into elephant head shape shown on page 270 and make two indentations for eyes. Put creases in trunk using orange stick again. Then make a v-shaped cut with knife on underside of trunk and pull open a little for mouth. Flatten ball shapes for elephant ears and work into wide curved petals with your fingers. Roll bit of dough into string for tail. Put all the pieces together, pipe icing dots for eyes, and glaze.

MISCHIEVOUS MONKEY. Rollicking symbol of fun, he'll bring a smile to each small party-goer's face. Cut your dough into eight pieces: a large one for body, smaller for tummy, a small one for head, another same size for face. Cut two medium pieces for arms and legs, a small piece for ears and a tiny piece for mouth. Now, color dough and divide again

276

as needed for figure.

Model body portion into egg shape. Roll tummy portion into ball, then press into flat oval and make an indentation with the blunt end of orange stick for "belly button". Model head into pear shape, flatten bottom of tapered part and press shallow depression into top. Fit face ball into depression and secure with egg white. Model head and face together for a long flattened oval, then make indentations for eyes. Roll out small ball reserved for ears and cut into two circles with point of knife. Using both hands, model both ears at once into shell shapes, thin where they join face, thick on outer edges. Roll a tiny bit of dough flat and cut with large round tube for mouth. Now roll out long, thin cylinders for arms and legs. Keep arm portion in one piece, cut leg portion in two pieces. Press ends of arm portion flat, mark with knife for "fingers". Press one end of each leg portion flat, mark for "toes". Assemble all pieces, curving arm piece over tapered top of body and attaching head on top of it. Pipe two dots of white icing for eyes, press tiny bits of marzipan on them for pupils. Attach mouth, push orange stick in center for "open" look. Glaze.

FRIENDLY LION. Sure to be greeted with a roar of approval. To make him, cut your cylinder into 9 pieces—largest for body, two slightly smaller for front and back legs, next smallest for head, and another about the same size for mane. About half of the mane amount for tail, a small ball for cheeks, two tiny bits for ears. Color as needed, divide again and you're ready to model.

Model body portion into long pear shape, lifting front section slightly. Roll two cylinders for legs, back legs longer than front. Use technique on page 271 to narrow centers of cylinders and curve into U-shapes. Flatten ends of both and cut for "toes". Roll mane portion into thick cylinder, then taper ends and curve into C-shape. Roll head portion into ball, make indentations for eyes. Model small portion of dough into a thick, short roll with narrow center, curve for cheeks. Roll bits into two small balls, use orange stick to make groove for ears. Roll a small cylinder, thicker at one end, for tail. Flatten thick end and point it sharply, then use point of orange stick to mark deep grooves for brush.

Assemble all pieces. Lay body across legs, pushing back legs up into curve, pushing front legs together. Attach cheeks, punch holes for muzzle. Pipe icing dot for eyes, icing point for tongue. Glaze.

ACTUAL SIZE, 2½" TALL

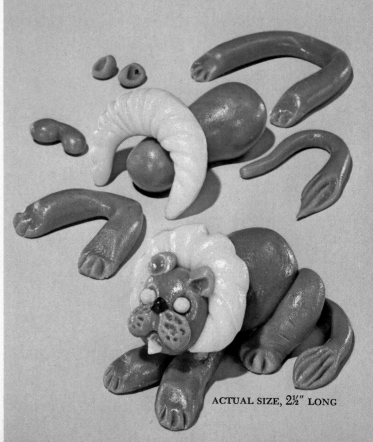

ACTUAL SIZE, 2¼" LONG

277

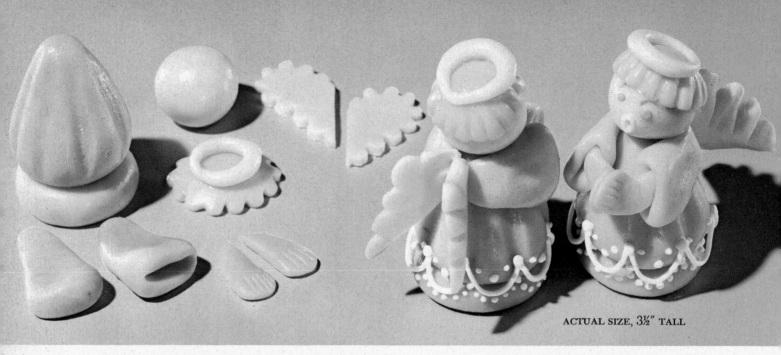

LITTLE ANGELS. Cut 11 pieces from basic cylinder. Divide, knead in color, divide again. Shape body portion into cone, make vertical grooves for folds of robe. Next, flatten base into thick disc to hold body. Shape two cones for sleeves, flatten and cut groove into wide ends where "hands" will go. Roll out hair and wing portions. For wings, cut scal-loped heart shape, cut in half. For hair, cut scal-loped circle. Roll ball for head, roll string for halo. Model little triangles for hands and notch for fin-gers. Press out tiny circle for mouth with decorating tube. While assembling, cut grooves into hair, and press hole in mouth. Pipe tube 3 dots and string to trim robe, pipe dots for eyes. Glaze.

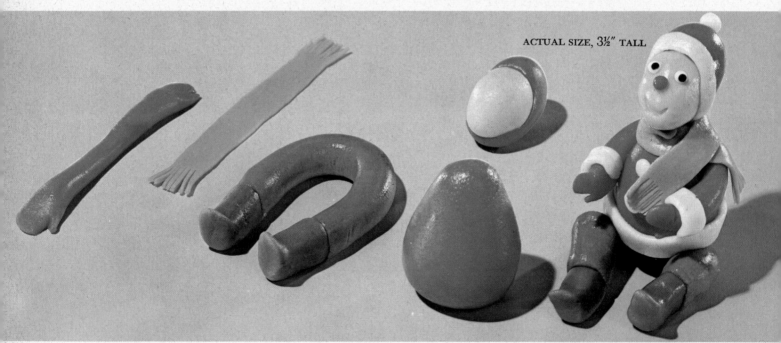

WINTER PLAYMATE. Takes 15 pieces. Begin with 5 or 6 ounces of dough and divide. Model body into cone. Shape hat portion into egg shape and press shallow depression into top. Roll ball for head, se-cure in hat depression with egg white and model into single piece. Cut smiley mouth, make indenta-tions for eyes. Roll long, thick cylinder for legs, curve into U-shape. Roll short cylinders for boots, attach to legs, bend up tips. Roll narrow tube flat for scarf, cut fringe. Roll cylinder for arms, flatten and round ends, cut notch for "mittens". Roll tiny balls for nose, pompon and buttons. Flatten but-tons. Roll cylinder flat, cut into bands for fur trims. Assemble, attaching curved arm piece between body and head. Add icing eyes, marzipan pupils. Paint as explained on page 269 and glaze.

278

CHRISTMAS—AND THE ANGELS SING!

Your adorable marzipan angels add such a charming touch to this pretty Christmas cake. Pure holiday pleasure that serves 14. To decorate, ice a 10″ round, 4″ high cake and divide into 16ths. Then edge top and bottom with Mirror Borders as directed on page 99, using tube 16 for all zigzag, scallops and fleur de lis and tube 17 for puff garlands. Make pattern for cake top, using technique on page 95 to achieve an 8-scallop design, about 5″ in diameter. Outline with zigzag, doing inner scallops to echo borders. Pipe tiny rosettes at all points and top with contrast stars. Top with angels.

TEDDY BEAR CAKE. What toddler wouldn't love it? Ice a cake 8″ square, 4″ high a spring green and use damp sponge to pat top for grassy effect. Edge bottom of cake with tube 18 shells, ring top with upright shells (do larger ones with tube 20, smaller with tube 18). Add dots with tube 3. Scatter tube 225 drop flowers, made ahead, on top, place marzipan teddy bears. Add leaves with tube 65. Serves 12.

BABY CHICK CAKE. Edge iced 10″ x 4″ round cake with rich fleur de lis. Use tube 20 for long shells, 18 for short. Turn top center shells upside down, drape tube 16 stringwork from points, top with tube 18 rosettes. Add more rosettes between bottom fleur de lis. Finish top with tube 18 shells. Pipe tube 3 string back and forth to form "nest", fill with jelly beans, ring with marzipan chicks. Serves 14.

CHAPTER TWENTY ONE
Molds Make Decorative Shapes

Molds in many shapes and sizes offer a tremendous assortment of attractive decorating ideas. Colorful candies, ice creams and, of course, cakes all take on a special flair when shaped in a decorative way. And more important, molded trims can be made in advance to save time on decorating day.

Pictured at right are three cakes all cleverly trimmed with molded shapes. The first, a sweet heart-studded cake, is perfect for Valentine's Day, Mother's Day or Sweetest Day. The trims are jelly candies made in heart molds. With the 9″ x 4″ petalled cake and heart cupcake iced and assembled, and the jelly candies made according to directions on page 282, a few simple borders are all that need be added. Use tube 96 for the petalled cake top and base borders, and tube 16 for the heart cupcake base. Then pipe tube 4 dots, position jelly hearts with icing and the cake's ready for admirers.

The second cake pictured is decked with roses, leaves and pairs of bells all molded of fondant. Here, the roses, when positioned with icing, make a garland that's as pretty as one piped with a decorating tube! To decorate, mold the fondant shapes following directions on page 282. Then ice a 10″ x 4″ square and a 6″ x 3″ round cake and frame the square with circular motion borders using tube 22 for the base and tube 18 for the top. For the round cake, edge the base with tube 18 shells and the top with tube 16 circular motion borders. Now position fondant trims with icing, add tube 16 scrollwork and you've a cake for a birthday party, shower surprise or anniversary tribute.

The third cake, especially fashioned for a children's party, displays a parade of circus chocolates. The menagerie is all shaped of candy to truly delight any youngster. Once again, when the cake is frosted and the candy shapes made, a few simple trims are all one needs to make this cake a sweet success! To make candy shapes follow directions on pages 282 and 283 for molding light and dark chocolate and chocolate coatings. Then ice a 10″ x 4″ round cake and decorate with tube 19 base garlands, tube 3 string and "i" motion and tube 18 top border. Position animals with icing and top cake with a bunch of plastic balloons.

Candy Molds Shape Sweet Trims

Candy molds offer a variety of petite and tempting shapes for molding creamy fondants, velvety chocolates and chewy jellies. They're all sweets just like you'd buy in a fine candy shop so whether served alone or as trims on a cake, they're perfect for parties, holidays and all sorts of special occasions.

FONDANT CANDIES

Use the basic recipe for making fondant found in Chapter Two, page 42 and follow the step by step procedure for mixing and kneading ingredients. With your fondant properly prepared, you're ready to shape it into candies. First heat some of the fondant mixture to 100° F, or until just warm and pourable. Then pour heated fondant into a decorating bag fitted with tube 6 and fill candy molds that have been sprinkled with powdered sugar. After filling molds, tap lightly to assure fondant settling into all mold indentations. Note: before molding fondant candies, you may flavor and color to taste using vanilla for white candies, caramel for light brown candies, raspberry or strawberry for pink candies, lemon for yellow candies and pistachio or mint for green candies.

Allow fondant-filled molds to stand for 45 to 60 minutes to harden into candies. When completely cool, invert molds to release the candies.

JELLY CANDIES

Soft and chewy sugar sprinkled jelly candies can be made in a variety of ways. Here are two recipes, one made with flavored gelatin and one made with agar-agar (a gelatinous substance that may be purchased or ordered from a drug store). Both produce candies that are attractive as well as delicious.

GELATIN RECIPE

2 three-ounce packages flavored gelatin
1 cup water

Boil the water in a saucepan, remove from heat and add gelatin. To dissolve gelatin completely water may have to be reheated, but do not boil. When dissolved, pour into a pitcher with a narrow spout. Oil molds, then wipe out excess oil with a paper towel. Fill molds and refrigerate for about six hours or until firm. To unmold, invert mold on tray dusted with powdered or granulated sugar, sprinkle with more sugar.

AGAR-AGAR RECIPE

1½ tablespoons granulated agar-agar or
    1 tablespoon powdered agar-agar
1½ cups cold water
1½ cups granulated sugar
2 tablespoons plus 2 teaspoons hot water
6 tablespoons light corn syrup
½ teaspoon food coloring
2 teaspoons flavoring (use ¼ teaspoon
    peppermint flavoring)

Combine agar-agar and cold water in a one-quart saucepan and let stand for 30 minutes if granulated, 15 minutes if powdered, stirring constantly. Bring this mixture to a boil, again stirring constantly. As mxture is coming to a boil, combine hot water, sugar and syrup in a two-quart saucepan. Pour boiling agar-agar over this mixture and cook rapidly. Stir occasionally when mixture foams. When it reaches between 220 and 222 F., remove from heat. Add food coloring and flavoring. Stir mixture to blend color and flavor, then pour into double parchment or plastic decorating bag fitted with tube 6. Fill molds, let stand in cool place about four hours and lightly pinch ends of loosened candies to unmold. Place candies on tray dusted with powdered or granulated sugar and sprinkle with more sugar.

TEMPERING CHOCOLATE FOR CANDY

To make light or dark chocolate candies, the chocolate must first be tempered. To do this, heat water to about 175 degrees in the bottom of a 1½ quart double boiler. When correct temperature, remove from heat and place cut up chocolate (one cup at a time), in the top half of double boiler to melt. Stir chocolate every ten minutes until melted and at a temperature of 110 degrees F. Remove melted chocolate from heat and cool until almost stiff. Then it's ready to make candy.

LIGHT MILK CHOCOLATE CANDY

To make candies, reheat tempered light milk chocolate to between 86 and 88 degrees. Pour heated chocolate into a decorating bag fitted with tube 6 and squeeze into clean, dry molds. Tap molds lightly after filling so chocolate fills all mold indentations. Refrigerate chocolate for 20 to 30 minutes or until hard and invert to unmold candies. If necessary, remove any excess chocolate from edges with a small knife.

DARK CHOCOLATE CANDY

For semi-sweet candies, reheat tempered dark chocolate to between 90 and 92 degrees F. Pour heated chocolate into decorating bag fitted with tube 6 and squeeze into clean, dry molds. Tap molds lightly after filling so chocolate settles into all mold indentations. Refrigerate for 45 to 60 minutes or until hard and invert to unmold candies. Remove any excess chocolate from edges of candies with a small knife.

PASTEL CHOCOLATE CANDY

Pastel chocolate coatings are chocolate substitutes that need not be tempered. Pastel colored coatings may be purchased or ordered from most commercial candy stores. To make candies, melt small quantities of coatings in the top of a double boiler. Bring water to a boil, remove from heat and let stand about 30 minutes. Stir melted coating to blend and when it has a liquid look, pour into a decorating bag fitted with tube 6 and squeeze into clean, dry molds. Refrigerate for about 20 minutes or until hard and invert to unmold candies.

A PARADE OF CHOCOLATE ELEPHANTS. Stand-up, stand-out treats! To shape elephants, secure mold halves together with clamps, then invert mold and push into styrofoam or nest in crumpled foil so it remains stable as base openings are filled.

Temper chocolate and reheat, or melt pastel coating. When chocolate or coating is of pouring consistency, place in decorating bag fitted with tube 12 and squeeze into inverted mold. Fill the front feet first, tipping the mold from time to time to make sure chocolate flows into trunk. When mold is full, tap it several times so air bubbles rise and chocolate settles into all crevices. Refill mold, then refrigerate for 2 to 3 hours or until firm. Remove clamps and release, one side at a time. Decorate elephants with rolled marzipan blankets, headpieces and boots— all trimmed with royal icing. Or add any other colorful trims you like!

Special Shapes
Add Interest to Cakes

A special shape adds such interest to a cake that usually very little extra trim need be added. Whether molded for a particular event—bells for a wedding shower, panda bears for a children's party—or just cleverly fashioned to add flair to a dinner dessert, shaped cakes are always sure to win praise.

SCULPTURED CAKE glazed for a party buffet is stunning without lavish trims. Pound cake is perfect for a round mold displaying interesting shapes like this one. When baked and unmolded, the cake is brushed with a warm apricot glaze and placed on an attractive plate. Just before serving, pipe frills of whipped cream with tube 2D and garnish with maraschino cherries.

A PAIR OF BELLS, one of cake and one of ice cream, are prettied with petunias for a spring shower or luncheon. To decorate, pipe petunias with tube 102 on a 1⅝″ lily nail following directions on page 120. Bake cake in bell-shaped mold, cool, then pour on pink fondant. Refer to directions on page 282 for heating fondant to pouring consistency. When icing has set, position cake on pretty plate and attach petunias with icing. To finish, trim flowers with tube 67 leaves, pipe a whipped cream base border with tube 2D and an icing bow with tube 104. To make the cake's refreshing companion, pack bell mold with ice cream following molding directions on page 286, then decorate to match the cake.

ADORABLE PANDAS are shaped of cake in metal bear-shaped molds. After cakes are baked and cooled, outline eyes, noses and grooves with tube 2. To decorate, cover cakes completely with stars, starting with white areas, then doing brown areas. Use tube 14 stars for the bodies, and tube 13 stars for the faces. "Paint" eyes, noses and bottom of paws with softened icing.

ROOSTER CAKE. Bake in rooster-shaped pan and use tube 16 to pipe icing stars for legs, feet and base. Then, still using tube 16, pipe head and beak. To pipe the bright rooster tail, start at base of cake and use tube 70 to squeeze out long icing "feathers" in alternating colors. As you pipe, overlap feathers, slanting tube upward slightly. For body fill two decorating bags, one fitted with tube 67 and one with tube 70 with two different icing colors each. Then working from the bottom up, pipe overlapping feathers starting with tube 67 at the base, then tube 70 for the body and finishing with tube 67 again. Now pipe tube 104 rooster "comb", add tube 16 icing stars under beak and pipe tube 4 eye, glazing with corn syrup.

Frosty Ice Cream Molds

Molded ice cream makes attractive desserts or accompaniments for decorated cakes. And since there are so many different molds to choose from, you can create ice cream sculptures for holidays and parties the year round!

Metal molds work best for shaping ice cream, but plastic molds can be used as well. To shape, fill mold halves with softened ice cream, clamp together and freeze for about five hours or until very hard. To unmold, pat with warm, damp cloth and remove clamps, releasing one mold half at a time. Decorate as you wish, working quickly so ice cream won't melt. Refreeze until serving time.

PINEAPPLE MOLD is made of pineapple ice cream, trimmed with leaves of meringue that have been piped on florist wires with tube 2A and baked. The fluffy base of whipped cream is piped with tube 2D and topped with maraschino cherries.

286

LAMB, BELL AND LOVEBIRDS, at left, all shaped of ice cream are perfect treats for Easter, a wedding shower or an anniversary. Follow ice cream molding procedure and use vanilla and pistachio for lamb and lovebirds and strawberry for bell. While molds are freezing, make the trims of buttercream. Pipe the daisies with tubes 103 and 104, the roses with tube 104 and the wild roses with tube 104. To decorate the lamb, place mold on a nest of tinted coconut, pipe tube 104 neck ribbon and tube 2 eyes and mouth, then position flowers with icing and refreeze. To decorate bell pipe whipped cream base with tube 4D and starred garlands with tube 16. Attach roses with icing, pipe tube 67 leaves and refreeze. To decorate lovebirds, pipe whipped cream at base with tube 4D, tube 2 piping gel eyes. Attach wild roses with icing adding tube 67 leaves. Again refreeze mold.

THANKSGIVING TURKEYS shaped of chocolate ice cream are made in plastic egg molds. Each egg half is packed with ice cream, frozen, unmolded and refrozen while icing trims are piped. Use a pattern for tails and wings. Cover patterns with clear wrap and trace with tube 3 and color flow icings. Long orange wing and tail curves are piped first, then red, then yellow. While these are drying, pipe heads and breasts. Cover plastic egg molds with clear wrap, taping at back if necessary. Figure pipe breast and head on wider end of mold with tube 9 by letting icing build up just below curve of egg as an upward motion is made while easing pressure. Stop pressure, then let icing build up slightly for head and pull out point for beak. Flatten breast with damp finger and cut off lower half. When dry, pipe on tube 2 eyes, beak and comb.

To assemble, remove ice cream turkey bodies from freezer one at a time. Make a slight cut in wider end and push in icing breast and head, propping with a toothpick. Carefully slide tail on and prop with toothpick pieces. Position wings next, propping against tail and anchoring with tiny toothpick pieces. Refreeze assembled turkey until serving time.

ICE CREAM FRUITS AND FLOWERS, so perfectly shaped, are refreshing in summery lemon, peach, strawberry and vanilla flavors. To make, follow basic ice cream molding procedure given on page 286, and pack decorative two-piece molds to sculpt shapes like the roses, lilies, grapes and pumpkins pictured. When frozen hard, about 5 hours or more, unmold and arrange shapes on an attractive serving stand. Quickly pipe tube 122 leaves and tube 2 stamens with tinted stabilized whipped cream and refreeze until serving time.

Molding Buffet Foods

Many molds offer distinctive ways to display foods other than sweets. Shapes of rich paté or creamy butter are just as decorative as the molds we've shown thus far, and they make impressive table centerpieces and servings for holidays, parties, buffets and other special occasions. Like all the previously mentioned molds, these can be made in advance of serving so that when the special time arrives shapes of paté or butter can be quickly placed on the table for all to admire!

MOLDING PATÉ

The swan is such a rich-looking mold, it definitely deserves rich-tasting contents and what better choice than paté.

To shape, simply fill swan mold halves with your favorite paté recipe, clamp mold securely together and freeze for a few minutes or until firm. Then unmold by releasing clamps and removing one mold half at a time. Return swans to refrigerator until serving time. For a gourmet touch, display the molded swans on a bed of leafy lettuce.

MOLDING BUTTER

Perfect accompaniments to a specially prepared dinner are individual portions of butter molded as miniature pineapples or fruit baskets.

To shape, just pack mold halves with softened butter, clamp mold securely together and freeze for a few minutes or until firm. Then release clamps and remove mold halves. Place butter shapes on individual plates and return to refrigerator.

SHAPING FLOWERS OF BUTTER

Blossoms of butter on a bed of tender bibb lettuce is a fresh and appealing touch for a luncheon or special dinner. You can shape them in the morning or the day before serving, then arrange them on lettuce right out of the freezer.

To shape roses and calla lilies you'll need a pound or more of fresh butter, a pair of butter paddles and two large bowls of ice water. Place bowls on a bed of ice and keep paddles immersed in cold water when not in use. For butter rose, wash butter in ice water, kneading gently until it has the feel of wax. Pinch off a small piece about the size of a walnut, drop on grooved side of one paddle, using other paddle in a circular motion to roll butter into a ball. Reverse paddles, roll ball smooth and flatten into a circle about two inches in diameter. Cut in half, lift quickly and carefully off paddle and drop into ice water until flower is ready to assemble. Repeat this same procedure for more half circles, making some slightly larger for outer petals. Press end of one piece to form a rough cone shape to use for rose base. Curve one small half circle around base for center bud, then press out two or three half circles around bud overlapping as shown. Repeat with larger half circles for outer buds to give the look of an opening flower.

For butter calla lily, make butter circles exactly as for rose but about 2½" in diameter and do not cut in half. Shape long cone center for stamen with paddles, then curve a circle for cornucopia shape around "stamen" overlapping at point to elongate.

For butter drop flowers, whip chilled firm butter in an electric beater until consistency of whipped cream. Place in decorating bag fitted with a drop flower tube. Press out butter flower as any drop flower and store in freezer until serving time.

CHAPTER TWENTY-TWO

Figure Piping
Three Dimensional Decorating

Piping dimensional figures in icing has always been thought of as an art reserved for the most advanced and accomplished of decorators. Quite to the contrary, sufficient practice of the basic techniques explained in this chapter puts figure piping well within reach of any decorator.

Two Basic Methods

Fill-in and pressure formation are two basic and distinctively different methods of figure piping.

The fill-in method is accomplished by first drawing an outline of a subject and then filling in the defined space with icing to create a figure.

Pressure formation, the second method, is precisely what its name implies. By applying varying amounts of pressure on the decorating cone, a formation of almost any size and shape can be piped. Both of these figure piping methods are equally important in creating imaginative shapes.

ICING FOR FIGURE PIPING

In order to achieve the most satisfactory results in figure piping, the icing must be of the proper consistency. Here is an excellent recipe.

WILTON PIPING ICING

3 cups granulated sugar
⅔ cup water
¼ teaspoon cream of tartar

4 tablespoons meringue powder
⅔ cup lukewarm water
1¼ cups sifted powdered sugar

Cook the first three ingredients above to 234° F. and set aside. Then beat meringue with lukewarm water until it peaks. Add powdered sugar slowly, then beat meringue and powdered sugar at medium speed until blended. Now pour the cooked mixture into meringue mixture and continue beating at medium speed until peaks form. (Note: It is necessary to use a commercial heavy-duty mixer.)

For a large stand-up figure, four or more inches high, add an additional cup of sifted powdered sugar.

Fill-in Figure Piping

The fill-in method of figure piping offers three avenues of approach—stick figure, pattern sketch and free hand. It's good to practice them all, because one may adapt to a particular decorating situation more easily than another. For example, a more intricate figure may require a pattern sketch, while a simple figure can be piped free hand. Stick figure fill-in piping is especially good for action figures.

Stick Figure Method

This variation of the fill-in method of figure piping is especially good for action figures, because it de-

fines a particular body position with simple stick-figure lines. These lines are piped over with icing and then features are added to complete the figure.

The figure piping possibilities within this method are practically endless because any pose, no matter how intricate, can be reduced to simple line drawings. For example, look at a certain pose you wish to pipe and determine the positions of the head, body, arms and legs; transfer these positions into lines on a piece of paper. With the stick figure now defined, pipe over the lines with a small tube and depending on the size of the figure, pipe over the lines with a large tube to complete the shape. Add features and other details and the figure is finished.

Try the jump rope figure shown below, to practice this method. Draw a stick figure like the one shown at the lower left, tape clear wrap over the lines and pipe over the line drawing with tube 2. Then with tube 7, start just above the leg lines and apply a heavy pressure to squeeze out body shape, easing off pressure as you taper to head. Touch tube to sides and base of body and use a steady, even pressure to squeeze out arms and legs. Now touch the same tube to top of body and use even pressure to fill in head area. Use a light pressure and tube 7 to pipe shoes, tube 1 to pipe hands. For hands, pipe an icing ball for palm first, then pull

out fingers one by one. When piping fingers, squeeze and move tube out and then over to give hands the appearance of holding something. To complete, add ruffles with tube 101, string hair, eyes, nose and mouth with tube 1.

Now decorate a jump rope cake, like the one pictured on the opposite page. Make lots of dainty drop flowers in advance with tubes 217 and 225, referring to flower-making directions in Chapter Nine. Set flowers aside to dry, then ice a 10″ x 4″ round cake and position on a foil-covered board. Edge cake base with tube 17 garlands and frame garlands with tube 15 zigzag. Then, in between each garland pipe tube 2 stems, attach drop flowers with icing and trim with tube 65 leaves. Next, use tube 2 to pipe three jump-rope stick figures on the cake top. Fill in bodies with tube 7, ruffles with tube 101 and hair and facial features with tube 1 just as you did for the previous practice jump rope figure. To complete figures, pipe tube 2 string for jump ropes. Now edge cake top with tube 17 garlands and drape with a double row of tube 2 string-work. Attach a drop flower between each garland with icing and decorate with pairs of tube 65 leaves. Surround your cake with a lacy chain fence and your jump-for-joy figure-piped cake is ready for party time! Serves 14.

FILL IN A STICK FIGURE CLOWN

Just like the jump rope figure on the previous page, this jolly clown is piped from a stick figure. Using the stick figure above as a guide, pipe a tube 3 ring of icing for a head along with outstretched arms, fingers and legs. Then, starting just above leg lines, use tube 9 and a heavy pressure to squeeze out body. Ease off pressure as you approach head so body is tapered. Now tuck same tube into sides and base of body and use a steady, even pressure to squeeze and fill in arms and legs. Fill in head area next, then use tube 4 to fill in hands and feet. For hands, pipe a ball shape for palm first, then one by one pull fingers up and out. For trims, add ruffles around wrists, ankles and collar with tube 101s, buttons with tube 4. Use tube 4 again to pull out points at sides of head for hair, then add eyes and mouth with tube 2, nose with tube 4.

CLOWNS AROUND ON A BIRTHDAY CAKE turn a children's party into a circus. It's easy to pipe because you use the stick figure method. Ice an 8″ x 4″ square cake and place on a foil-covered board. Figure pipe clowns on the cake top, using a toothpick to trace the stick figure lines so the clowns will be uniformly spaced. Pipe over stick figure lines with tube 3, then fill in lines and add features using the same tubes as for the clown shown above. Edge cake base with tube 10 beading, then trace scallops on all four cake sides with a toothpick and cover wtih tube 8 beading. Add pretty piping gel bows as garland trims with tube 2. Present this jolly clown cake as an unforgettable party time treat. Serves 12.

Using a Sketch to Pipe a Figure

This second type of fill-in figure piping is perfect for all kinds of clever cake decorations; and it's relatively quick and easy to do, because you have an exact sketch to work from. You can trace cartoon favorites, storybook characters, coloring book figures—or sketch anything you like and then fill it in with icing for a delightful decoration.

Again, as with any figure piping method, correct icing is of most importance. For this method of fill-in figure piping, it's best to use royal icing. However, if you wish, you may use buttercream icing to fill in a sketch, and then freeze the figure before transferring it to a cake. Another important point to remember: when using a sketch to pipe a figure, never attempt anything too large. Figures between two and four inches high work the best. Any bigger and there's too much area to fill in.

After you have drawn or traced the figure you wish to pipe, tape wax paper over it and fill it in with colorful icings. Practice by filling in figures like the ones shown below.

TEDDY BEAR. Tape the sketch to cardboard, then tape wax paper or plastic wrap over it. Fill in the body and head with tube 12 and a heavy pressure. Next, using a lighter pressure and tube 6, fill in arms, legs and ears. Use tube 10 to fill in balloon

shapes and add strings with tube 2. To complete, pipe pink nose with tube 10 and a light pressure, then add nose detail and piping gel eyes with tube 1.

YELLOW DUCK. Once again tape wax paper over sketch, and fill in face and body first with tube 12 and heavy pressure. Fill in hat area with tube 6, then overpipe blue strings with tube 3, green strings with tube 2. Use tube 6 to fill in wings and feet and to pipe bill, then add piping gel eyes with tube 1.

FAIRY GODMOTHER. Fill in face with tube 6, then pipe blue overlapping lines with tube 5 for the robe. Fill in green dress area with tube 2 string-lines keeping them close together. Add fur trim to robe with tube 6 by filling in first and then overpiping with a circular motion. Use tube 6 again to pipe the fairy's crown, adding string hair with tube 2. Pipe the hands with tube 1 and fill in the magic wand with tube 3 before adding the fingers. Pipe the crown jewels with tube 3, eyes and mouth with tube 1.

When all three figures are thoroughly dry, carefully peel them off the wax paper and attach to cake tops with icing. Add the fairy's wand rays and strings for the Teddy Bear's balloons with tube 1 right on the cake.

293

Fill-in Figure Piping Free Hand

The third and last method of fill-in figure piping is probably the most fun for any decorator because it allows the imagination to play an important part in the creation of a figure. Select the appropriate size tubes for the figure to be piped, describe a basic shape free hand and then add details until you achieve the exact effect you had in mind. Practice and experimentation are important factors in per-

fecting skill at this type of fill-in figure piping, since there are no stick figures or sketches to follow.

For practice, try piping the figures on this and the following pages to get an idea of the variety of decorations this method of figure piping offers. Start with simple shapes—then proceed to more complex ones.

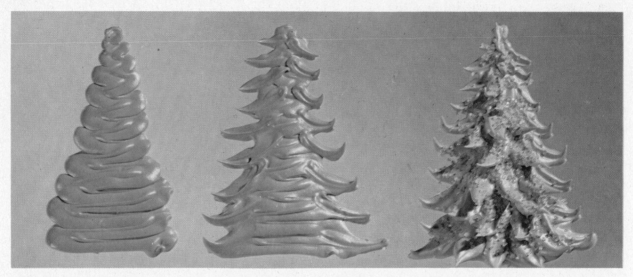

A MERRY CHRISTMAS TREE. Use tube 6 and a side to side motion as you increase pressure and move tube downward to describe a triangular shape. Then tuck tube into triangle at several points along each side and squeeze to pull out peaks for tree branches. Do the same for the front of the triangle until the

entire original shape is covered. Decorate tree with edible glitter for a sparkling holiday effect or use tube 3 to pipe on assorted color icing ornaments. Any way you trim it, this tree is a festive figure piping for Christmastime.

HOLIDAY WREATH. Use tube 6 to pipe out a ring of icing, then with tube 65 cover this ring with tiny leaves. Just touch tube to icing ring and squeeze to pull out leaf points, overlapping them as you move around. Decorate wreath with tube 2 holly berries and tie up top with tube 2 icing bow.

BABY'S RATTLE. Use tube 8 and heavy and medium pressure to squeeze out round balls for rattles. Then connect balls with a strong line of icing using tube 2 and trim this rattle handle with a dainty pink tube 2 bow. A perfect figure to pipe on baby shower and birthday cakes, and one's that quick and easy too.

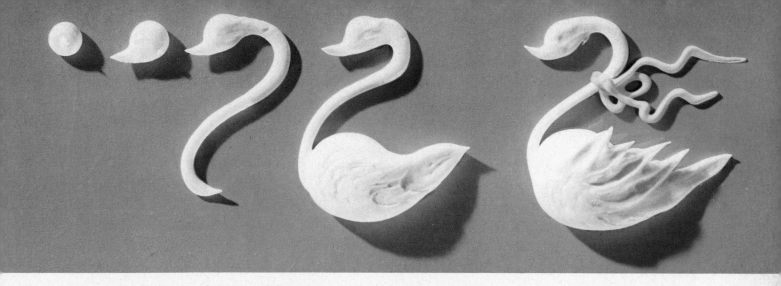

FIGURE PIPE A GRACEFUL SWAN

A lovely decoration to grace party, shower and wedding cakes, and one that's figure piped in four simple steps.

1. Using tube 6 squeeze out an icing dot for head, then ease off pressure as you move tube away to pull out bill.

2. Now touch tube to back of head and in one continuous motion, squeeze to pull out neck as you move tube in a question mark-like motion.

3. With the same tube, begin at the lower end of the neck and use maximum pressure to squeeze and build up icing for the body. As icing mounds up, lift tube slightly, then ease off pressure as you move tube downward tapering off to tail. Stop pressure at tail, but continue to move tube to bring tail to a point as shown.

4. For wing, tuck tube into body and squeeze with a steady pressure as you move tube away at a 45 degree angle, easing off pressure as you go. Repeat this procedure a few times to give icing wing a feathery effect. Now for a finishing touch, trim the swan's slender neck with a tube 2 bow.

Nest of eggs is a colorful trim for Eastertime cakes. To pipe, use tube 6 to squeeze out a ring of icing. Then with tube 2 pipe lots of short icing strings, overlapping and covering ring, to effect the grassy nest. Use assorted icing colors and tube 6 again to fill the nest with eggs.

Chirping chicks are a perfect accompaniment to the nest of eggs. Use tube 4 to squeeze out dot for head, then with the same tube use a heavier pressure to pipe body shape, easing pressure as you taper to tail. Tuck tube into body to pull out wing, add legs, bill and eye with tube 2.

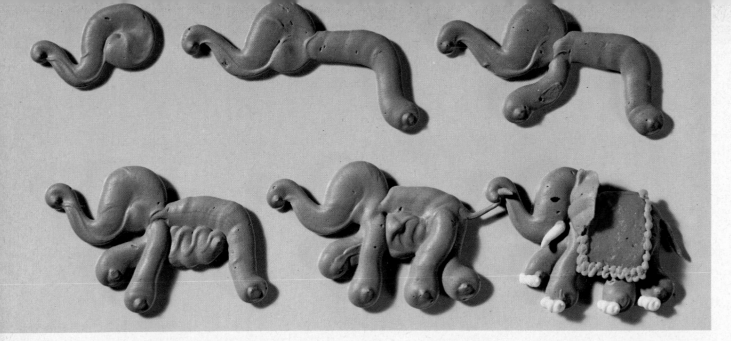

ELEPHANTS. Using tube 10, apply a steady, even pressure to pipe trunk, then curve down, up and around in a circle for head. Next, start at the base of the head and pipe a heavy line for the body and back leg. Stop pressure, move to front of body and pipe two more heavy lines for legs. Fill in stomach area by moving tube up and down to form wavy lines. Using a lighter pressure, pipe square shape for back blanket, smoothing with a knife. To finish, pipe tube 3 blanket trim, tube 4 tusk and toenails, tube 2 tail and tube 127 ear. Connect elephant tails and trunks for a circus parade.

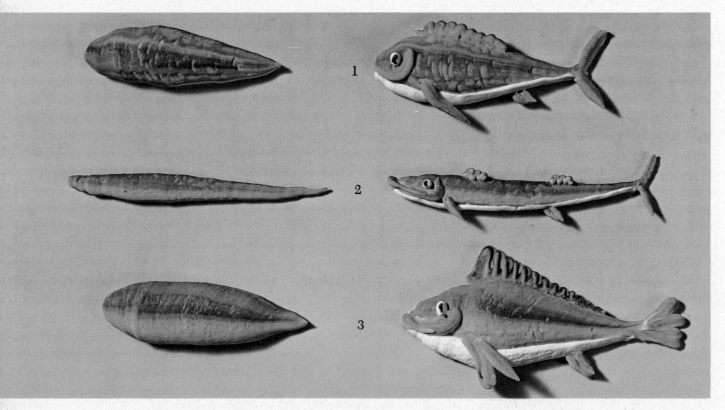

FISH IN VARIETY. Fun to pipe and easy too. For each of the fish shown, brush-stripe a decorating bag and start with nose to squeeze and apply a heavy pressure for body, easing off as you taper to tail.

1. Use tube 10 for fish body then add tube 3 white stripe under body. With the same tube, pipe mouth, fins, wavy line and eye. add pupil with tube 2.

2. Use tube 4 for slender body, tube 1 for white body stripe, fins and wavy lines, and tube 2 for double-line mouth and eye. Add pupil with tube 1.

3. For third fish, use tube 10 for body, tube 4 for body stripe, fins, tapering wavy lines and mouth. To complete, pipe tube 2 eye and tube 1 pupil.

FIGURE PIPE A STORK carrying a precious bundle. Use tube 5 to squeeze out a ball-shaped head, then add bill and eye with tube 3. For neck, tuck tube 5 into back of head and apply a steady even pressure as you squeeze and curve tube out and down. Stop pressure, touch tube to base of neck, then apply a heavy pressure as you build up body tapering it off into a tear shape. Tuck tube into side of body at different points to pull out tail feathers, then pipe two bulbs at body base for leg tops. Pipe straight back leg first with tube 3, increasing pressure at knee joint and at foot to add on toes. Pipe front crossed leg in the same manner. With tube 5 pipe the stork's bundle. Start with a heavy pressure to squeeze out diaper base, then ease off pressure as you move to be up to touch stork's bill. Pipe baby's arms, legs and head with tube 3.

DECORATE A CAKE TO WELCOME BABY. Ice a two-layer 9″ x 7″ oval cake and figure pipe a stork on the cake top. With tube 65 and an up and down motion pipe grass-like decoration under stork and leaves. Use tube 3 to pipe stems and cattails. Ring cake base with tube 16 shells, then drape tube 103 ribbon garland around cake top and base. Pipe tube 8 bead trim and rattles, tube 2 bows. Serves 12.

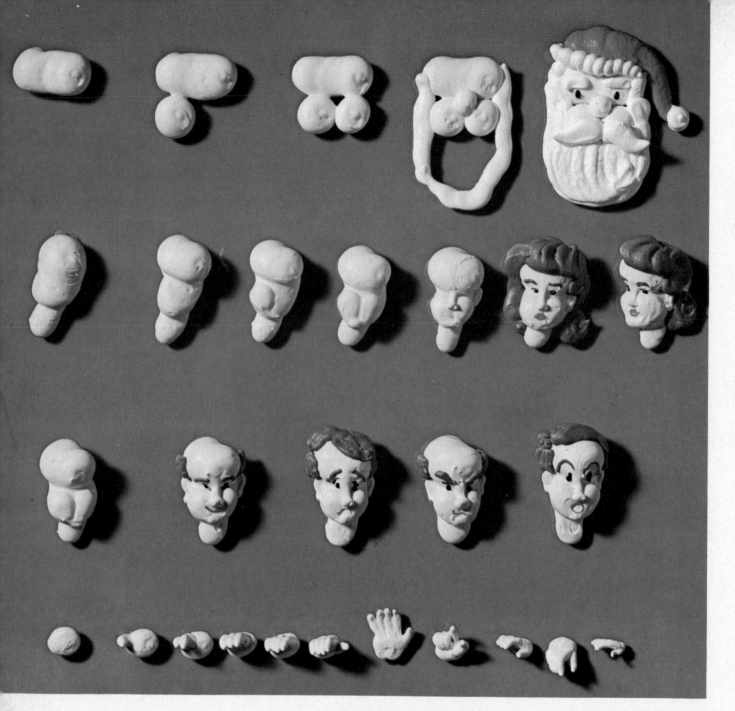

FIGURE PIPING FACES

Piping faces takes practice but once the basic shape is mastered size, hair and features can be altered.

FOR THE SANTA FACE above, use tube 7 and an even heavy pressure to squeeze out a bar-shaped forehead and ball-shaped cheeks and nose. Use tube 3 to outline beard, then fill in with same tube using an up and down motion, starting from the center and working out. Add tube 3 eyebrows, moustache and sausage-shaped hat with ball tassel and cuff trim.

FACE SHAPES FOR THE MAN AND WOMAN are piped the same. Start with tube 7 and squeeze out a short, thick vertical line for neck. Stop pressure, touch tube to top of neck and using a steady, even pressure move tube up, down and up again to form an egg-shaped base. Pipe a short, thick bar across base to make forehead, then insert tip of tube into sides of base to squeeze and build up cheeks. Now touch tube to center base of forehead and apply a gentle pressure to pull down nose. Add features with tube 2, hair with tube 4.

HANDS. Try larger hands first by piping a ball with tube 7 and then inserting tube into ball and applying a gentle pressure to pull out fingers. Attempt several positions using your own hand as a model. Then pipe smaller ones with tube 2.

FIGURE PIPE A WITCH

An icing witch perched on her broom makes a sensational Halloween decoration for cakes. To pipe, fit a decorating bag with tube 4 and fill with slightly thinned icing. Squeeze, apply a heavy pressure, then ease off as you move tube in a curve to form a hooked nose. To pipe chin, start at the wide base end of the nose, apply heavy pressure and move tube around in a comma-like stroke, easing off pressure as you circle around and back up to starting point. For the forehead, start above the nose and in one continuous motion, bring tube down to meet chin. Pipe a vertical row of tear shapes for hair.

Use tube 6 to pipe the witch's body. Start at the base of the chin and apply a heavy even pressure to pipe the thick slanted torso. Ease off pressure as you approach waist, then squeeze out a thick line in the opposite direction for thigh. Now with a lighter pressure, squeeze out calf and witch's shoe. Tuck tube behind knee and again with a light pressure squeeze out back leg and shoe. Tuck tube into side of torso and squeeze to pipe inside arm, then pipe long broomstick and add front arm. Pipe short strings for broom straw and long wavy strings to complete witch's skirt. For the witch's hat, pipe a triangular outline with tube 4 and fill from base to point. Add several long slanted lines for the hat brim and the Halloween witch is complete!

Upright or Pressure Controlled Piping

This method of figure piping is precisely what its name implies. By applying varying degrees of pressure on the decorating cone as it's moved along, figures of almost any size and shape can be piped. Again, as with other methods of figure piping, the icing recipe given at the beginning of this chapter is the vital ingredient in achieving satisfactory results. With this correct consistency icing you can figure pipe shapes of all kinds, using the pressure controlled method, including upright figures like the bird in flight and dove pictured below.

Bird in flight is an attractive figure for special cakes. Use tube 4 to squeeze out a curved line for the outer edge of the wing, then following this curve pipe three more lines making each smaller than the last. Now touch tube to the base of the wing and squeeze out a straight line for a tail. Add three more tail lines, again making each slightly shorter than the last. With the wings and tail formed, practice pressure control for piping the bird's upright body. Hold tube at a 45 degree angle to practice surface and apply maximum pressure. As body builds up, move tube forward and out to shape breast. Now ease off pressure, squeeze out a small string of icing and bring it around in a circular motion to shape head. Touch tube to head and gently squeeze out peak for bill. Now figure pipe the bird's body starting about half way back on the tail. When the body is piped, add inner wing. Touch tube to the side of the body and squeeze out a small curve of icing. Continue working up and adding longer curves until the entire wing is formed.

The dove is another graceful upright figure to adorn cakes for weddings, engagements and anniversaries. To shape, start with tail and using tube 4 and a steady, even pressure move tube up and back to squeeze out a line. Tube should be almost perpendicular to decorating surface as you squeeze. Add another line in the same manner to each side of the first as shown in the upper left hand corner. Then pipe two more lines to complete tail. Now, just as you did to pipe the bird in flight, hold tube at a 45 degree angle about half way back on the tail. Use maximum pressure to build up body base, then move tube forward and up as you ease off pressure. Squeeze out a small string of icing and bring tube around in a circular motion to form head. As string is brought around to touch body, ease off pressure, then pull out slightly to form beak. To add wings, tuck tube into sides of body, squeeze heavily, move back and out, then overpipe.

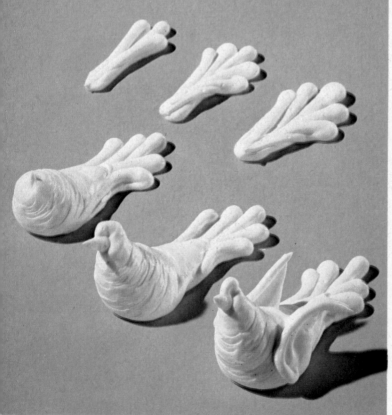

300

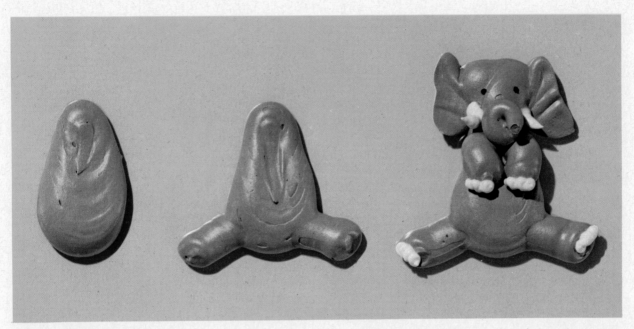

ELEPHANT. To figure pipe a cute sit-up figure like this, use tube 10 and maximum pressure to squeeze out a pear-shaped body. Start at the base and work up, gradually easing pressure as you reach top. To add legs, tuck tube into sides of body base, squeeze and pull out with a steady even pressure. Do the same for the front legs by tucking tube into top of body and then squeezing and pulling down on tube. To pipe the elephant's head, start above the body at left, apply maximum pressure and move tube up and to the right to form wide forehead. Continue squeezing as you move tube back down to head's starting point, then circle up and around to pipe the trunk. Start at the top sides of the head and use tube 127 to pipe the elephant's ears. To finish, pipe tube 4 tusks and toenails and tube 2 eyes. Pipe a row of these playful figures around the sides or top of a cake and delight the youngsters.

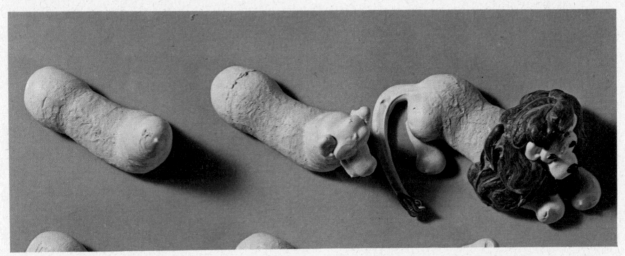

LION. Another frolicsome figure that's ready to proudly pose on a party cake top. To pipe, use tube 7 and a maximum pressure to squeeze out an elongated body, starting at the back and working forward. To form head, tuck tube into body top and apply a steady even pressure as you move up and then down. Use a lighter pressure to pipe circles on face for protruding eye area; then tuck tube into center of face, apply a steady pressure and squeeze out snout. Tuck tube 4 into sides of head to squeeze out ears; then tuck tube 7 into body base to squeeze out two front legs. Use the same tube for back leg only as you apply a steady pressure and squeeze, bring tube up and out slightly for rounded haunch, then move tube down and out for leg. Pipe overlapping layers of icing with tube 4 for lion's curly mane, and add a few tufts of icing "curls" at tip of tail. To finish pipe nose and eyes with tube 2.

FIGURE PIPE A CARNIVAL CLOWN

Pose several cute clowns like the one below around a cake and instantly you've a party atmosphere. To practice this figure, use a styrofoam block as a prop and think of it as the side of a cake as you work.

Holding tube 10 almost perpendicular to your work surface, use maximum pressure to squeeze out the clown's body. Ease tube upward as icing builds up and rests against styrofoam backing. As you reach the top of the styrofoam, stop pressure. Now, tuck tube into sides of the body base and use maximum pressure again to squeeze out legs. Pull one leg out forward, bending it only slightly at the knee. Squeeze to pull the other leg out, but bend sharply at the knee moving the tube back towards the styrofoam in a v-shape motion. Tuck tube into top sides of body to squeeze out arms, piping one right on the side of the styrofoam block and the other up and over the top in a resting pose.

To pipe head, touch tube 4 to top of body and squeeze with a heavy pressure as you move tube up and down to form face. Increase pressure as you move tube to puff out cheeks, then pipe on nose and peaked hat. Pipe the hands and feet next with tube 4, then add the buttons and all the ruffled trim with the same tube. Use a circular motion for the ruffles on the wrists, ankles and neck; and an up and down motion for the ruffles piped on at the waist. Add piping gel eyes and smile with tube 3 and the clown's complete.

When you've successfully piped a clown in this position, try some other poses using the same tubes. Always pipe the body first; then the legs, arms, head and features. For practice, pipe one clown's body and legs the same as the one on this page, but this time pipe both arms up and over the styrofoam. Try another clown sitting sideways with both legs piped in the same direction and arms outstretched. Now try piping a clown's body face down on top of the styrofoam. Drape one leg over the styrofoam, pipe the other on top. When you can pipe several poses, you're ready to decorate a whimsical cake like the one on the facing page.

302

CLOWN CAPERS

Fun to figure pipe and set a circus party theme. To make, bake and ice a 12″ x 4″ square cake and a 6″ x 3″ round cake and position on a foil-covered board as shown. Edge both cake bases with tube 16 rosette borders; then following the directions on the opposite page, figure pipe several frolicsome clowns in assorted poses, propping them on the cake top and sides just as you did with the practice styrofoam prop. Use tube 8 for the clown bodies and tube 4 for the faces, hands, feet, features and other colorful trims. The cuter the poses you pipe, the more fun for everyone! Serves 35.

303

A Portfolio of Figure Piped Cakes

Now that you've become acquainted with the two basic types of figure piping, and have practiced a variety of figures incorporating these methods, it's important to see what decorative touches they can give to party, holiday and other occasion cakes.

In this portfolio are instructions for piping lots of new and fun figures along with clever cakes that display them. Each figure-piped cake is sure to be one you'll want to add to your collection of decorating ideas.

A COLORFUL INDIAN CHIEF with a feathery headdress, sure to please any western fan. To pipe, use tube 7 and a heavy pressure to squeeze out a short bar-shaped forehead. Below forehead use a steady even pressure to pull tube down and pipe two pear shapes for cheeks and chin. Next tuck tube under center of forehead and gently squeeze as you move down to pipe a narrow nose. For the headdress start above the forehead at center and with tube 5 apply a heavy pressure to pipe thick "feather" lines.

Work from the center out on both sides so feathers fan the face. Use tube 2 to pipe feather tips, eyebrows and vertical figure eight braids. To complete, add tube 5 headband over forehead and tube 1 band trim, eyes, mouth, and cheek "war paint".

AN ICE CREAM CONE TEEPEE, perfect partner to the figure piped Indian. Using a wafer ice cream cone as a base, pipe heavy tube 10 lines from bottom to top covering the entire cone. Smooth lines from base to tip with one stroke; then add another line around bottom of cone curving up at end to effect teepee "door". Add zigzag line decorations with tube 4 to complete.

304

TEEPEE CAKE perfect for a little boy's birthday party. Ice an 8″ x 3″ round cake and pipe rims around base with tubes 10 and 5. Smooth inner ring of icing with a knife and decorate with tube 2 zigzag. Follow instructions on opposite page to top cake with teepee and figure pipe Indian Chiefs on cake sides. To complete, ice several toothpicks and push into teepee top. Serves 10.

1. Figure pipe a halloween scene starting with a cornstalk. Use tube 3 to pipe a triangular outline, then fill in using an up and down motion. For stalk top, pipe tube 67 stems pulling them up and over for a sweeping effect.

2. Pipe a plump pumpkin next using tube 7. Start by making two quotation-like marks that touch at top and bottom. Fill in space between with two more quote-like curves that again touch at top and bottom to leave an open center. Fill this center opening with one straight oval-shaped line, then add stems with tube 4.

3. For a scary ghost, use tube 10 to pipe a ball shape for head. Add a wavy line for body, tapering off at end as you ease pressure. Tuck tube into body to pull out arms; add eyes and mouth with tube 2.

4. The witch's face is piped similarly to the Indian chief on page 304. Use tube 7 to pipe a bar-shaped forehead, then add two pear-shapes below for the cheeks and chin. Start with a heavy pressure for cheeks, then ease off quickly as you move tube down for a pointed chin. Add comma-like curves for eyebrows and tube 1 eyes. Next, tuck tube between cheeks and squeeze to pull out and down for hooked nose. Hollow out the mouth with a knife, then outline and add fang-like teeth with tube 1. To finish use tube 4 to pull out hair.

5. For witch's hands, pipe a bar-shaped base with tube 4, then jiggle tube 2 as you pipe fingers.

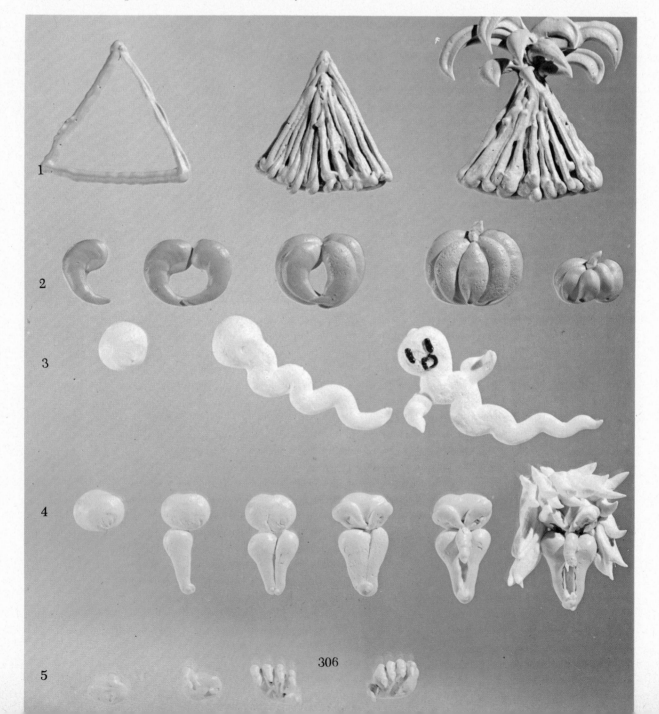

306

FIGURE PIPE A BEWITCHING CAKE

Ice an 8″ x 4″ round cake, then trace and fill in a triangular shape with contrasting icing on the cake top. Next use tube 67 to squeeze out ribbed strokes of icing for witch's arms and body. Figure pipe witch's face and hands along with ghosts and pumpkin following directions given on opposite page. Add pumpkin eyes and teeth with tube 1, leafy trims with tube 67. With top complete, use tube 10 to ring base with icing, smoothing with a knife. Then, once more referring to directions on opposite page, pipe cornstalks around cake sides, framing with smaller pumpkins and tube 67 leaves. Serves 10.

A HARVEST OF FIGURE PIPING FOR FALL starts with a cornucopia. Using a cupcake as a base, pipe a heavy curved line for a tail with tube 22. Then, with the same tube, use a circular motion and a heavy pressure to overpipe tail and cover cupcake, extending beyond top to make a circular opening. Fill this opening with fruits and vegetables.

A BUNCH OF GRAPES. Use tube 4 to pipe a tear drop-shaped base; then starting at the base and working up pipe overlapping beads of icing using the same motion necessary for piping shells.

EAR OF CORN. Use tube 2 to pipe a heavy line for a base; then, starting at the base, cover with vertical rows of beads, making them larger as you approach the top. Add stalks with tubes 1 and 65.

CARROTS. Pipe tube 2 stalks adding short wiggles of icing for leafy carrot tops. Using the same tube, pull out several thick strings for carrots.

THANKSGIVING TURKEY. Use tube 4 and a steady even pressure to fan out short lines of icing for feathers. Then, starting at the base of this feather span, apply a heavy pressure as you move tube up to squeeze out a pear-shaped body. Use tube 2 to add feather tips, head, wings, legs and face.

A GLOWING CORNUCOPIA CAKE

Make this decorative dessert for after Thanksgiving dinner. Ice an 8″ x 3″ round cake; then use a cupcake to pipe a cornucopia and fill with figure piped fruits and vegetables as illustrated on opposite page. Re-fer to same directions to figure pipe turkeys around cake base; then add pumpkins as illustrated on page 306. Trim cake top and sides with tube 67 leaves and present your harvest of fall decorations. Serves 10.

309

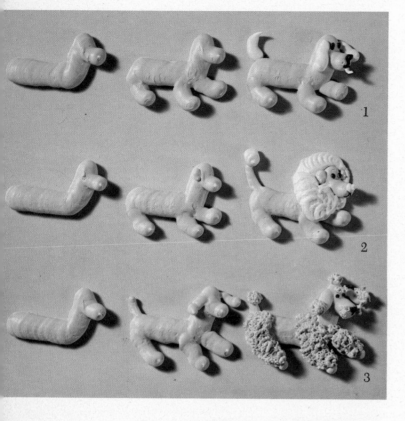

FIGURE PIPE PLAYFUL TOY ANIMALS

Most of the animals are piped with the same tubes; it's the trims that vary. Three animals at left have the same body, head and legs but different features.

1. A frisky pup is the first choice to pipe. Use tube 7 and maximum pressure to squeeze out a long body. Tuck tube into front of body and squeeze to pull for head; then down and out for nose. Tuck tube into body base next and squeeze to pull out legs. Add puppy's ears and tail with tube 4; eyes, nose and tongue with tube 3.

2. For the friendly lion, pipe the same body and head shape with tube 10, adding legs as before. Then pipe ears, eyes and nose with tubes 2 and 3; curly mane and tail trim with tube 4.

3. The perky poodle again has the same body, head and legs as the dog and lion. To pipe the ears, tuck tube 7 into sides of head and squeeze. Pipe nose, ears, eyebrows, tail and leg trims with tube 1: jiggle tube as you squeeze to give the icing a curly, fluffy effect. To finish, add eyes, ball feet and head tassel with the same tube.

4. To pipe a bunny rabbit, use tube 7 and start at the tail to apply a heavy pressure pulling out an oval-shaped body. Relax pressure as you taper off at neck; then tuck tube into body to squeeze and pull out legs. To pipe head, tuck tube between front legs and squeeze as you move tube up and back slightly. With head formed, tuck tube into back and use a steady pressure to pull out ears. Pipe tail, eyes and nose with tube 2.

5. For the chicken, again use tube 7 and start at the tail to apply a heavy pressure as you move forward and then up. Pipe curls of icing with tube 3 for tail, wing and head comb. Add beak and eyes.

6. Figure pipe a bouncy bear with tube 10. Start at the base and apply a heavy pressure as you move tube up and ease off pressure at neck. Tuck tube into top of body and squeeze to pull out head and nose. Then tuck tube into sides of head to pipe ears, and into sides and base of body to pipe legs. To finish pipe eyes, nose and mouth with tube 2.

7. Rattles and diaper pins make cute trims! Use tube 10 to pipe round ball for rattle, add handle with tube 4. Pipe pin with tube 4.

DECORATE A TOY ANIMAL CAKE FOR BABY like the one on the opposite page. Ice an 8″ x 4″ cake and edge base with tube 1D. Use a candle as a prop and the directions above to pipe a bear and elephant on the cake top. Then pipe rattles, pins and more animals around the cake. Serves 10.

PIPE A PROUD LION

1. START WITH A CUPCAKE BASE and prop with a mound of icing. Touch tube 10 to bottom of cupcake and, applying a heavy even pressure, squeeze out icing to build up a thick body shape. As icing mounds, move tube away from cupcake and stop pressure when body is completely formed.

2. To FINISH PIPING CUPCAKE LION, tuck tube into rear of body and use a steady even pressure to squeeze and blow up hip area. Continue squeezing as you move tube down and out to form hind leg, jiggling slightly to effect paw. Now tuck tube into back of body once again, and steadily squeeze to pull out a tail, increasing pressure as you approach tip. For front legs, touch tube to top of cupcake and apply a heavy pressure, jiggling as before for paws. Use tube 7 and a circular motion to pipe tufts of icing on tail and layers of icing for mane.

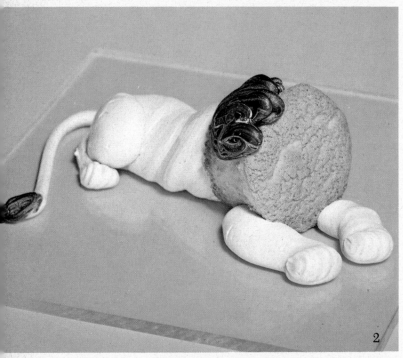

3. CONTINUE PIPING SWIRLS OF ICING for a mane until entire cupcake is covered except for facial area. Then just as for many animal faces previously piped, use tube 7 to squeeze out a bar-shaped forehead. Tuck the same tube into center of forehead and squeeze out two circular shapes to elevate eye area, then increase pressure as you move tube down and out to shape jaw. Tuck tube into center of face and squeeze to pull out snout, then add eyes and nose with tube 1, "c" motion ears with tube 7. Completed, this cupcake lion is one cake decoration that's sure to generate a roaring good time!

4. PRACTICE FIGURE PIPING LION HEADS (shown in picture 1) to use as trims for the top or sides of a cake. Use tube 7 and a circular motion to squeeze out a swirled ring of icing for a mane, then pipe a bar-shaped line of icing across the top of the mane to effect a forehead. Tuck the same tube into the base of the forehead and apply a steady pressure to squeeze out a nose, then tuck the tube into both sides of the head and using a "c" motion pipe the ears. Next tuck the tube into the base of the head and once more applying a steady pressure, squeeze to pull out a jaw; then pipe the eyes, nose, mouth outline and teeth all with tube 1.

DECORATE A LION CAKE like the one pictured below for a children's party. Frost a 10″ x 3″ round cake and ring the base with tubes 10 and 7, smoothing the icing with a knife. Top the cake with a cup-cake lion using the same tubes and procedures as described above. Figure pipe several roaring lion faces on the cake sides and set out the proud decorations for all to see. Serves 14.

FIGURE PIPE A WESTERN SCENE

1. BUCKING BRONCO, the perfect start for a round-up of figure fun. Use tube 10 and a maximum pressure to squeeze out the bronco's hot-dog-shaped body; then tuck tube into top of body to pipe hind leg. Use a gentle pressure to build up thigh, then curve downward for leg applying additional pressure to finish off at hoof. Again, use a gentle pressure to pipe front legs, adding knees and hooves with slight pressure increases. To pipe other hind leg, tuck tube into body and squeeze to build up hip area, then ease off pressure to complete leg. For neck, tuck tube into body between front legs and apply heavy pressure as you move tube in a downward curve.

Now tuck tube into base of neck, squeeze and move tube to right as you gradually release pressure tapering to nose. With tube 5 add white trim under body, on head and on legs. Use tube 3 to pipe swirls of icing for mane and tail. To complete head, pipe tube 3 ears, circular areas for eyes, curves for nose and mouth; then add pupils, nostrils and lips with tube 2.

2. COWBOY. To pipe use tube 7 and a heavy pressure to squeeze out leg, starting from waist and working down. Curve tube up slightly as you pipe to form knee area. Again with tube 7 and a heavy pressure start at waist and move tube upward to squeeze out body. Tuck tube into top of body and use a light pressure to pull out arms, piping one over head and the other down over body. Next pipe neck scarf, then tuck tube into icing above this and squeeze to pull up neck.

Form the head as others piped previously, by first squeezing out a bar-shaped forehead and then adding two comma-like curves below for cheek and chin area. Use tube 10 to pipe a pointed bulb for hat, then add the brim with tube 127 holding the wide end of the tube down and the narrow end straight up. After piping the brim add hair with tube 2, face with tube 1. Use tube 2 to pipe hands, ear and high-heeled boot; then pipe chaps with tube 124. With the narrow end of the tube pointed out, start at the waist and apply a steady even pressure as you move tube down. Trim chaps with tube 3 beading and the cowboy is ready to ride.

3. CORRAL GATE. Use tube 7 to pipe the gate and fence, adding the longhorn skeleton head and face with tubes 4 and 2. Note: You may want to use a toothpick outline to keep the gate and fenceposts evenly spaced. To pipe cactus use tube 199 and start at the base and work up, adding branches last.

To decorate, ice an 8″ x 3″ round cake and pipe a ring of icing around the base with tube 10. Follow the directions on the opposite page to figure pipe a bucking bronco and cowboy on the cake top. Pipe the cowboy the same as before, except that this time he will be piped over the horse. With these two figures complete, add saddle with tube 4, reins with tube 2. Now following the same procedure again as outlined on the opposite page, figure pipe a corral gate and cactus around the cake sides. You may want to outline the gate and fenceposts first with a toothpick before piping them in icing. Complete, your cake is sure to please any young cowboy. Serves 10.

CHAPTER TWENTY THREE
Decorating in Miniature

Petite treats are especially attractive for party and holiday times. Perfect for children, too, because they're just their size.

All of the decorative miniatures found in this chapter employ the same basic techniques that you've learned in previous chapters. The only difference is that they're done on a much smaller scale.

FILIGREE EASTER EGGS pictured below, are made with tinted royal icing and contain sweet treasures of jelly eggs, a traditional family favorite! To make, coat the outside of plastic egg-shaped sugar mold halves with shortening. Place your fingers in the top half of the mold to prop it, pipe a string of icing with tube 2 all around the outside, about ⅜″ above edge. Now place mold half on flat surface at eye level and cover it with a filigree icing design. Pipe scalloped lines, circles, dots—anything you wish.

Just be sure that all lines, circles or dots are joined so the design is one complete piece. Do bottom half of mold the same as top, except that before piping design, squeeze out a spiral string of icing within flat center of mold to provide a base. Let designs dry at least four hours.

When thoroughly dry, place molds in pre-heated 250 degree oven for about 30 seconds to melt shortening and loosen filigree design. Immediately remove from oven. Carefully turn molds over so design rests in your hand then gently push it free with your thumb. Let loosened filigree designs dry a bit longer to harden. To join halves, pipe lines of icing at back part of bottom filigree half, secure top half and prop open with cotton balls. Dry at least four more hours, then add ribbon bow and carefully fill with candy.

316

Decorating directions
on page 318

BUNNY CUPCAKES, (shown on the previous page), are so quick and easy to make, you can serve them as after-school surprises as well as Eastertime treats!

Just bake cupcakes and ice them, along with standard size marshmallows, into round shapes using pastel-tinted icings. Secure marshmallows to cupcakes with toothpicks for bunnies' "heads," then use tube 2 to pipe whiskers and piping gel nose and eyes. Use tube 10 to pipe on paws and tail; then cut bunny ears out of paper, tape to toothpicks and push into marshmallow heads.

Arrange bunnies on an attractive cake stand and watch the children hop to the table as quick as bunnies themselves.

PETITE PROCESSIONAL shows off the bridal party colors in delicate cake and icing. To make, bake cakes in small dome-shaped cupcake pans, invert pans to unmold cakes, cool, then push in plastic doll picks and decorate away!

Pipe tiny tube 217 drop flowers and set aside to dry. Ice cake "skirts" and cover with tube 2 cornelli lace icing designs. Edge the skirt hems with tube 101s ruffles and tube 2 stringwork, then pipe tube 14 stars for the dolls' dress bodice and sleeves. Attach made-ahead drop flowers to dolls' hair and hands with icing, trimming with tube 65s leaves. For the bride, fashion a veil from fine net and attach to a tiny "pearl" crown.

Present your processional at a pre-wedding party or shower to the delight of the bride and her bridesmaids and offer the decorative doll cakes as tiny take-home favors.

As stated before, decorative miniature cakes are perfect for children's parties, and these doll cakes are certainly no exception. Just "dress them" in icing for a party theme, your favorite little girl will love you for it!

318

THE PRETTIEST ENGAGEMENT TEA

Sparked with a dainty display of romance, an engagement tea spells out love with hearts and flowers and the initials of the bride and groom.

To MAKE COOKIES, cut out and bake alphabet sugar cookie shapes to represent the initials of the soon-to-be newlyweds. Use heart-shaped petite cutters to make romantic sugar cookies; then decorate them all with tube 2 string outlines and tube 225 drop flowers, trimming flowers with tube 65 leaves.

To MAKE MINTS, refer to fondant recipe on page 42 and, flavoring it as you wish, use a mint patty funnel to press out candies. To decorate, use thinned royal icing and tube 2 to pipe pairs of hearts and green floral stems, trimming with tube 225 drop flowers and tube 65 leaves. If you find you have no time to make your own mints, buy packaged mints and decorate them the same way.

To MAKE DAINTY SUGAR CUBES, refer to sugar molding recipe and procedure on pages 225 and 226. Use tiny heart and flower-shaped sugar molds to fashion pink and yellow tinted sweets. For a finishing touch, garnish each sugar mold with a tube 225 drop flower.

With your petite sweets colorfully decorated, set them out on the prettiest of serving pieces and call in the guests of honor for a grand celebration.

JOLLY LITTLE HOLIDAY CAKES

Family festivities are just that much more merry and bright with cute little Christmas cakes like these! Children especially love Santa and snowmen, and when the sweets are just the right size for them they are more popular than ever!

THE SANTAS AND ELVES, four little cakes and four cheery little faces. They're so easy to make, the smallest elves around the house will want to help. Just bake a quartet of cakes in 5″ square pans, ice lightly in white buttercream and let icing set to crust slightly. Trace patterns for Mr. and Mrs. Claus and two spritely elfin workers on greaseproof paper.

Place patterns on cake tops and punch lines with a toothpick to transfer faces onto cakes. Outline patterns with tube 2, then fill in with tube 16 stars in assorted icing colors. Cover the remaining cake tops and sides with more tube 16 stars, then border each cake base with tube 16 shells. Pipe ripe red holly berries to trim Mr. and Mrs. Claus with tube 5 and serve the jolly treats! Four cakes serve 16.

CHUBBY CUPCAKE SANTAS, on the opposite page, are clever confections for the night before Christmas. To decorate, push toothpicks into marshmallows and dip into thinned royal icing to serve as cupcake trims. Use standard size marshmallows for Santas' faces, marshmallow halves for the hats, and miniature marshmallows for hat tassels. When marshmallows are dry, bake and ice cupcakes into a round shape. Pipe on belts with tube 44, buckles with tube 3. Next, touch tube 2A towards top back of cupcake and squeeze to pipe arms out and around to front of body; then use tube 3 to figure pipe mittens and add Santa-suit buttons. Secure marshmallow faces, hats and tassels with toothpicks; then pipe fluffy white beards, hair and fur trims with tube 14, using a circular motion for feathery effect. Add eyes, noses and mouths all with tube 3; then serve the Santas with milk or hot cocoa to celebrate the coming of St. Nick!

MR. SNOWMAN AND FAMILY, another holiday taste treat that is made with cupcakes and marshmallows. To assemble, fasten large and small cupcake bodies with wooden skewers, then ice into round shapes smoothing each over with a damp brush. Now toothpick marshmallow "heads" into place, icing and brushing to smooth as before.

To decorate Mrs. Snowman, pipe bonnet strings with tube 44, bonnet bow with tube 101. Ornament bonnet with tube 225 drop flowers that were made in advance, attaching them with icing. Crown snowmen with plastic top hats, then pipe bands and scarves with tube 44. For all snow-family members, pipe eyes, buttons and mittens with tube 4. (Note: Ice Mr. Snowman's mitten over plastic cane to secure in place.) For the final touches, pipe mouths with tube 2, lashes and brows with tube 1 and attach candy corn noses with icing. Arrange the frosty trio on a tray for a miniature treat that brings huge enjoyment to the whole family.

321

FANCY FLORAL CUPCAKES

Ordinary cupcakes turn into dazzling desserts when topped with dramatic flowers of smooth buttercream icing! Perfect for so many occasions, because you can bake the cupcakes in advance and then swirl on the colorful decorations a few hours before serving time. For a shower, cover the cupcakes with the bride's favorite flower—for a party, pipe an assortment of blooms. Any way you trim these tiny treats they're sure to win lots of praise.

To decorate cupcakes like the ones pictured below, ice standard size cupcakes and edge with tube 14 shell and zigzag borders. Drape tube 68 leaves over the borders and you're ready to shape the fancy florals. The cupcake itself serves as the flower nail turntable and on it you can pipe a flower of almost any variety! Refer to flower-making directions in Chapter Nine to pipe the giant carnation and bright daisies with tube 124. Pipe the blushing roses, wild roses and daffodils with tube 127, the chrysanthymums with tube 79.

Arrange your colorful cupcakes around a tiered cake stand and instantly a summertime picnic has a dainty finish that's a feast for the eyes!

Deliciously decorative, these little French cakes look elegant on a tea tray or buffet table. Made of lusciously light sponge cake, petit fours can be filled with a variety of flavorings which give them taste as well as eye appeal. The most popular fillings are moist, fresh fruit jams, but melt-in-your-mouth buttercream is equally favored.

Bake the cake in a shallow sheet cake pan, or cookie sheet. Fill, then chill or freeze and cut into circles, squares or diamonds. Ice with thinned buttercream to contain crumbs and give a base for the fondant. To coat these tiny shapes of cake, use the fondant recipe and pouring procedures given in Chapter Three, pages 42 and 43. When the fondant-covered cakes are ready, decorate with icing flowers as dainty as the cakes themselves. Refer to flower-making directions in Chapter Nine and use tube 102 to pipe daisies and rosebuds, trimming flowers with tube 65 leaves. In addition to floral trims, you can decorate petit fours with tube 2 icing bows as we did, or with candied fruit. Any way you dress them up, they're tiny treats that always make a very big impression for any occasion.

Party Cake Serving Chart

The number of servings a particular size and shape party cake will yield is vital knowledge for any decorator; therefore throughout this encyclopedia we have included that information along with each and every decorated cake. However, since there are so many possibilities for the size and shape of a party cake, we have added this serving chart as a convenient reference guide.

Unlike towering tiered cakes which are conservatively cut to serve large groups of people at weddings, anniversaries and other sizable celebrations, party cakes are generously cut into family-sized dessert portions to serve more intimate gatherings. (Note: for the chart indicating the servings for different size tiered cakes, refer to Chapter Nineteen, page 241.)

The following serving chart is based on the larger family-sized portions as they pertain to a variety of popular party cakes. Figure all of the party cakes illustrated below to be two layers, each averaging 1½" to 2" high. The suggested servings will vary according to personal tastes, but at least they provide a reliable approximation of the number of people you can expect to serve with a given size cake. The chart indicating the amounts of batter for making these cake sizes can be found on the opposite page.

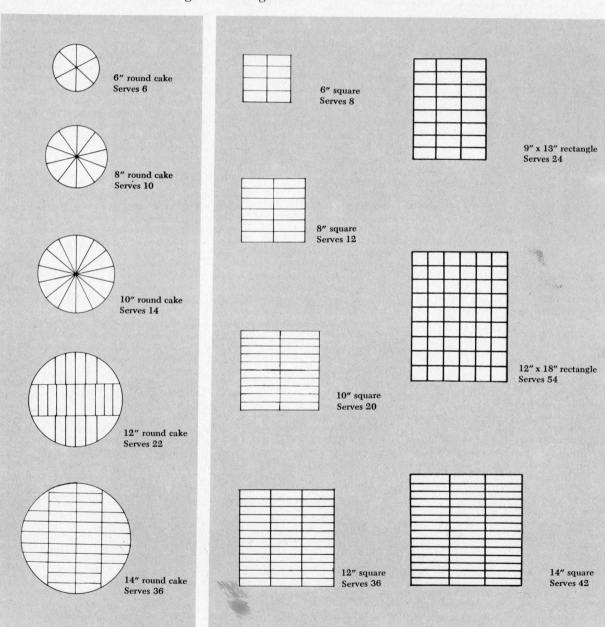

6" round cake
Serves 6

8" round cake
Serves 10

10" round cake
Serves 14

12" round cake
Serves 22

14" round cake
Serves 36

6" square
Serves 8

8" square
Serves 12

10" square
Serves 20

12" square
Serves 36

9" x 13" rectangle
Serves 24

12" x 18" rectangle
Serves 54

14" square
Serves 42

One Cake-Mix Cakes

All of the specially shaped cakes illustrated below take one standard cake mix or six cups of batter. Because of their unusual shapes, it's difficult to estimate exactly the number of servings from cakes of this type. However, since they are all one-mix cakes, you can figure each to serve about 12 people. Number of servings will vary according to individual tastes, but you can use the following suggested cake cuttings as a guide. You'll note that we've indicated the most logical cuttings for each cake; therefore, the star cake only shows a serving of 10. Alter these suggestions any way you wish.

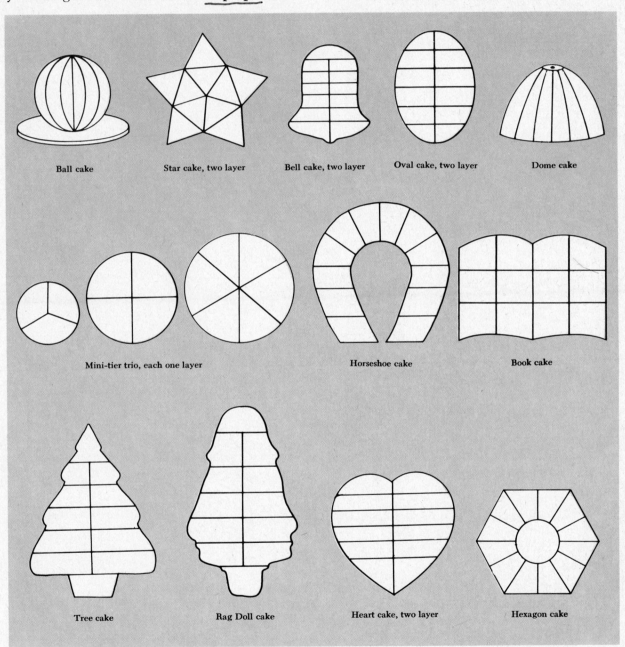

Ball cake

Star cake, two layer

Bell cake, two layer

Oval cake, two layer

Dome cake

Mini-tier trio, each one layer

Horseshoe cake

Book cake

Tree cake

Rag Doll cake

Heart cake, two layer

Hexagon cake

Amounts of Cake Batter for Commonly Used Cake Pans—2″ Layers

6″ round	2¼ cups*	6″ square	3 cups	9″ x 13″ rectangle ...... 8½ cups
8″ round	4½ cups	8″ square	5 cups	12″ x 18″ rectangle ..... 16 cups
10″ round	6½ cups	10″ square	8 cups	
12″ round	9 cups	12″ square	11½ cups	*For a 6″ layer, 1½″ high, use 1½
14″ round	12 cups	14″ square	15½ cups	cups of batter.

INDEX